Race, Republicans,
& the Return of the
Party of Lincoln

THE POLITICS OF RACE AND ETHNICITY

Series Editors Rodney E. Hero, University of Notre Dame
Katherine Tate, University of California, Irvine

Politics of Race and Ethnicity is premised on the view that understanding race and ethnicity is integral to a fuller, more complete understanding of the American political system. The goal is to provide the scholarly community at all levels with accessible texts that will introduce them to, and stimulate their thinking on, fundamental questions in this field. We are interested in books that creatively examine the meaning of American democracy for racial and ethnic groups and, conversely, what racial and ethnic groups mean and have meant for American democracy.

The Urban Voter: Group Conflict and Mayoral Voting Behavior in American Cities
Karen M. Kaufmann

Democracy's Promise: Immigrants and American Civil Institutions
Janelle S. Wong

Mark One or More: Civil Rights in Multiracial America
Kim M. Williams

Race, Republicans, and the Return of the Party of Lincoln
Tasha S. Philpot

Race, Republicans, & the Return of the Party of Lincoln

Tasha S. Philpot

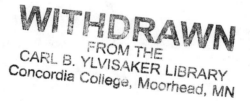
The University of Michigan Press *Ann Arbor*

Copyright © by the University of Michigan 2007
All rights reserved
Published in the United States of America by
The University of Michigan Press
Manufactured in the United States of America
⊚ Printed on acid-free paper

2010   2009   2008   2007   4   3   2   1

A CIP catalog record for this book is available from the British Library.

Library of Congress Cataloging-in-Publication Data

Philpot, Tasha S.
Race, Republicans, and the return of the party of Lincoln /
Tasha S. Philpot.
p.   cm. — (The politics of race and ethnicity)
Includes bibliographical references and index.
ISBN-13: 978-0-472-09967-2 (cloth : alk. paper)
ISBN-10: 0-472-09967-1 (cloth : alk. paper)
ISBN-13: 978-0-472-06967-5 (pbk. : alk. paper)
ISBN-10: 0-472-06967-5 (pbk. : alk. paper)
1. Republican Party (U.S. : 1854–)—Public opinion.
2. Republican National Convention (37th : 2000 : Philadelphia, Pa.)
3. United States—Race relations—Political aspects.
4. African Americans—Politics and government.   I. Title.

JK2356.P47   2007
324.2734089—dc22   2006020162

To my mother, Marcia Philpot

Acknowledgments

I OWE A GREAT DEBT to many people without whom this book would never have been completed. First, I thank my dissertation committee. To Hanes Walton Jr.—mentor, exemplar, and father figure—thank you for sharing with me your endless knowledge of black politics and political parties. Second, I thank Michael Traugott for providing me with guidance, mentorship, and a healthy dose of humor. I also thank Nicholas Valentino and Vincent Hutchings. Working for and collaborating with them proved to be one of the most rewarding learning experiences of my graduate school tenure at the University of Michigan.

I am also grateful to many other scholars who aided in my intellectual growth. First, I thank Janet Boles, my undergraduate adviser at Marquette University, who encouraged me to pursue a career in academia. Second, I thank Nancy Burns and Donald Kinder for allowing me to participate in the National Election Study Fellows workshop and for providing me with funding to complete my dissertation research, which eventually evolved into this book. Finally, I thank Arthur Lupia for taking me under his wing. I only wish he had joined the faculty at Michigan earlier in my graduate career.

This book benefited greatly from financial support from the Howard Marsh Endowment, the University of Michigan's Department of Political Science, the National Election Study, the Gerald R. Ford Fellowship, the University of Michigan's Horace G. Rackham Graduate School, the Frank C. Erwin Jr. Endowment, and the University of Texas at Austin's Office for the Vice President for Research. I also thank Dara Faris, Jim Kelly, Ernest McGowen, Curt Nichols, and Bryan Tillman for their research assistance. In addition, I thank Jim Reische at the University of Michigan Press for his patience with and enthusiasm for this project from beginning to end as well as the anonymous reviewers for providing me with constructive feedback for improving on the original version of this book. Parts of an earlier version of chapter 1 were published in *Political Behavior;* excerpts from "A Party of a Different Color? Race, Campaign Communication, and Party Politics," *Political Behavior* 26 (3): 249–70, are reprinted in this book with kind permission of Springer Science and Business Media.

I am extremely grateful for the support and friendship of a number of colleagues. I particularly thank Ryan Hudson, Amaney Jamal, Harwood McClerking, Brian McKenzie, Joan Sitomer, and Marek Steedman (aka the Dissertation Group); Sean Ehrlich; Gena Brooks Flynn; Mike Hanmer; Corrine McConnaughy; Irfan Nooruddin; Ismail White; and Rochelle Woods for helping me push this project along. I am also indebted to Gary Freeman, Terri Givens, Ted Gordon, David Leal, Bob Luskin, and Daron Shaw at the University of Texas at Austin and Karen Kaufmann from the University of Maryland for helping smooth out that bumpy transition from graduate student to assistant professor. Finally, I also thank some of my friends outside of the academy—Halima Henderson, Bridget McCurtis, and Ann Milo—for their encouragement and support over the years.

I owe the greatest debt of gratitude to my mother, Marcia Philpot. For as long as I can remember, she reinforced the importance of achieving excellence in all that I pursued and of using my success to give back. Although times were not always good, my mother always made sure my needs were met. Her sacrifices paved the way for me to succeed. Thank you for standing behind me and giving me a push when it was needed.

Finally, I thank my partner in life, Eric Leon McDaniel, whose love brings me endless happiness.

Contents

Introduction

Inclusion or Illusion?

I wanna tell you, ladies and gentlemen, that there's not
enough troops in the army to force the southern people
to break down segregation and admit the nigger race
into our theaters, into our swimming pools, into our
homes, and into our churches.

—J. Strom Thurmond, 1948

The history of the Republican Party and the NAACP
has not been one of regular partnership. But our nation
is harmed when we let our differences separate us and
divide us. So, while some in my party have avoided the
NAACP, and while some in the NAACP have avoided
my party, I am proud to be here today.

—George W. Bush, July 10, 2000

I want to say this about my state: when Strom Thurmond ran for President, we voted for him. We're proud
of it. And if the rest of the country had followed our
lead, we wouldn't have had all these problems over all
these years, either.

—Senator Trent Lott, December 5, 2002

DURING THE 2000 ELECTORAL CYCLE, observers of the political
landscape witnessed the emergence of a "new" Republican Party.
Characterized by the catchphrase "compassionate conservatism," the
Republican Party reached out to minority voters in ways it had not in
recent history. Without making any substantial changes to its platform,
the GOP presented itself as a more diverse party that welcomed African
Americans and other minority groups into its tent.

For example, George W. Bush became the first Republican presidential candidate in twelve years to address the National Association
for the Advancement of Colored People (NAACP) at its national convention in Baltimore. During his speech, Bush declared that he was

there because he believed "there is much [the NAACP and the Republican Party] can do together to advance racial harmony and economic opportunity." He admitted that for the Republican Party, "there's no escaping the reality that the Party of Lincoln has not always carried the mantle of Lincoln." Nevertheless, Bush argued that by "recognizing our past and confronting the future with a common vision," the GOP and the NAACP could "find common ground" (Bush 2000).

This theme of reclaiming the "mantle of Lincoln" and opening up the Republican Party to minority voters would continue throughout the months leading up to Election Day. Perhaps the best example of the Republican Party's minority outreach occurred during the 2000 Republican National Convention. As Denton (2002) notes, "The Republican convention presented a friendlier, more inclusive, and moderate convention than in 1992 and 1996. Republicans made direct appeals to those of Democratic leanings" (8–9). In addition to its 85 black convention delegates (a 63 percent increase from the 1996 convention), the 2000 Republican convention in Philadelphia featured prime-time appearances by Condoleezza Rice, George W. Bush's former national security adviser and Secretary of State during his second term; and retired general Colin Powell, former chair of the Joint Chiefs of Staff and secretary of state (Bositis 2000, 2). In fact, during the convention, Powell challenged the Republican Party to bridge racial divides and reclaim the "mantle of Lincoln" by overcoming blacks' "cynicism and mistrust" toward the Republican Party and reaching out to the African American community (Powell 2000).

Newspaper coverage of the 2000 Republican convention suggested that the GOP's diversity effort was part of its "search of a new package for its core philosophy." Republican Party chair Jim Nicholson was quoted as saying that the 2000 convention in Philadelphia was "a different kind of convention, for a different kind of party" (Von Drehle 2000). During the convention, the Republican Party tried to distance itself from its "battered old image" as "a bunch of mean moralizers" while portraying itself as being "a new, happy and inclusive Republican Party that wants to keep the good times rolling" (Dionne 2000).

Two years later, during a 100th birthday celebration for longtime senator J. Strom Thurmond (R-SC), Republican senator Trent Lott publicly remarked that the country would have been better off if Thurmond had been elected president in 1948. Lott's comment referred to the Dixiecrat revolt of 1948, led by Thurmond, in which many southern Democrats rebelled against the Democratic Party as a result of President Harry S. Truman's extension of civil rights to African Americans. Thurmond's candidacy marked the South's commitment to segregation and white supremacy in spite of the party's changing attitudes toward civil rights. Observers thought that Lott believed that the United States would have been better off if Jim Crow had remained intact.

Lott's remarks eventually incited a media frenzy. He was forced to publicly apologize several times, and ultimately decided to resign as Senate majority leader. Not surprisingly, Lott faced great criticism from the Democratic Party and civil rights leaders. Perhaps more surprising was the political heat Lott took from his own party. Republicans might have forgiven Lott's comments had they not occurred on the heels of the George W. Bush–led Republican campaign to paint itself as the party of racial harmony.

In light of this political chain of events, *Time* reporter Andrew Sullivan wrote an article on "Why Lott's a Menace to His Party." Sullivan claimed that Lott "undermine[d] the inclusive spirit that Bush ha[d] tried to build." Sullivan assumed, however, that the "compassionate conservative" strategy had succeeded in reshaping perceptions of the Republican Party. It is quite possible that even after the Republican Party's attempt to appear more inclusive, voters had not changed their perceptions of the party. After all, the party did not change its position on racial issues such as affirmative action or reparations for slavery.

This book seeks to provide a means of assessing which image of the Republican Party—the Party of Lincoln or the Party of Trent Lott— pervaded. The injection of race into political discourse is nothing new, of course, and is never more evident than during election cycles. History is saturated with examples of racially framed issues in campaign advertising, including the 1988 Willie Horton ad and the 1990 Jesse Helms "hands" ad. But while Lott's remarks were consistent with positions taken by previous Republican elites, the example of the Republican Party using racial images to signify inclusion deviates from its previous playing of the "race card."[1]

More broadly, this book develops a theoretical framework for

---

1. This is not to say that race-baiting has been purged from the arsenal of campaign tactics. Rather, in addition to the "hands" and Willie Horton ads, the electorate faces a sea of ads that give a new, multicultural face to many of the Republican Party's long-standing policies.

understanding what is needed to change party images in voters' minds. No current theories help to explain how citizens update their perceptions of political parties in light of changes in the parties' projected images. Scholars have noted shifts in partisan alignments when the parties adopt drastically different positions on political issues. But a difference exists between changes in political parties marked by critical realignment on public policies and the much smaller changes parties make from election to election. How, then, do voters respond to these marginal changes? Can a party reshape its image without making substantial changes to its platform? If so, are there limits to this strategy's effectiveness?

This book focuses on answering these questions. I identify some of the constraints that bind political parties when they attempt to expand their electoral bases. Specifically, I examine what happens to an individual's image of a political party when that party repackages its core without making changes to the core itself. I argue that a party will succeed in reshaping its image when voters perceive the new image as different from the old. In other words, when people recognize that a party has changed in some way, they will adjust their perceptions of the party to correspond with the party's projected image. This sounds simple enough; however, parties face several obstacles when proving to the electorate that they have changed.

First, parties must battle their histories. Neither party has entrenched positions on some issues—generally those that are new or less salient, such as stem cell research. Shaping and reshaping party images on these issues should be relatively easy. In contrast, on some issues—such as race, defense, and abortion—the parties have taken clear and long-standing positions. Parties will find it more difficult to reshape their images on such issues. The more history surrounding an issue a party must overcome, the harder it is to reshape its image on that issue.

Second, change means different things to different people. For some people, change means altering the party's policy positions; for others, simple cosmetic changes are enough to signal change. When making superficial changes to its image with respect to a particular issue, a party can expect to succeed only among those for whom the party's actual issue position is less salient.

Finally, when attempting to reshape their images, parties must contest countervailing information found simultaneously in the political environment. Such information can come from political opponents, the media, or, in the case of Trent Lott, other party members. By highlighting aspects of the party that have not changed or by contradicting the party's projected image, these other information sources can convince citizens that the party has not changed. The greater the presence of competing information, the more difficulty political parties will encounter in altering their images in voters' minds.

In what follows, I empirically test this central proposition. To do so, I focus primarily on the use of racial imagery at the 2000 Republican National Convention, which provides a unique opportunity to explore the current political landscape in areas previously uncharted. First, as I will demonstrate, the theme of inclusiveness that characterized the convention program deviates from previous party activities, making the convention a reasonably timely example of a party attempting to reshape its image. Second, examining the convention allows us to observe how parties try to reshape their images with respect to race and to what extent these efforts succeed. Race is one of those issues on which the parties have developed distinct and enduring reputations. Thus, if we can identify conditions under which a party succeeds in changing the racial component of a party image, we may apply these findings to other less salient issues. With the exception of Spence and Walton (1999), the political science literature has failed to examine African American convention participation. This study provides the first systematic examination of convention attendees beyond delegates and candidates. Finally, this book is one of the only studies to examine a political convention as a form of political communication.

The double entendre in the introduction's title forecasts what is yet to come. The obvious reference is to the analysis of the theme of inclusion presented at the 2000 Republican National Convention. I ask the question, "Inclusion or Illusion?" to gauge voters' evaluations of the GOP's outreach activities. Campaign rhetoric can but does not always substitute for real policy changes when political parties attempt to reshape individuals' perceptions. For certain individuals, the presence of African Americans at the 2000 Republican National Convention signaled a more inclusive Republican Party. For others, the presence of blacks represented a mere illusion that masked the conservative position of the Republican Party on racial issues.

The more obscure reference relates to the broader theme of this book. Here, the question "Inclusion or Illusion?" ascertains whether citizens revise their party images when presented with new information about political parties. Do people include all or even some of this new information, or do they dismiss the information as nothing more than an illusion? I argue that citizens update their perceptions of political parties to correspond with the parties' projected images. I challenge the notion that short-term political strategies aimed at disrupting existing electoral coalitions simply do not work (Cowden and McDermott 2000; Green, Palmquist, and Schickler 2002). While I do not dispute the fact that such approaches do not create major shifts in partisan identifications, I contend that these activities allow political parties to pick up voters at the margins. In light of recent presidential elections in which every vote made a difference, understanding where, when, and how parties can expect modest increases in vote share is imminently important.

For that reason, chapter 1 reintroduces the question at hand: Can aesthetic changes unaccompanied by corresponding changes in policy positions alter voters' perceptions of political parties along a particular dimension? This chapter brings together the relevant literatures in political science, psychology, and communication studies to establish the importance of this question and develops a general theoretical framework for answering it. I argue that a party's ability to change its image with respect to a particular issue domain depends on its history on that issue, the presence of competing information, and individuals' standards for what it means to be a changed party. In this chapter, I also explain how the general framework applies to the test case, the use of racial images at the 2000 Republican National Convention.

Chapter 2 establishes the historical context for understanding the contemporary role of race in American party politics. Specifically, this chapter describes how the two major parties have dealt with African Americans and issues of race over the years. This chapter illustrates the magnitude of the obstacle faced when the two parties try to reshape their images with respect to race, given their existing reputations on this issue.

With the historical foundation thus established, chapter 3 examines how party activities have resonated in the minds of the American public. I employ survey data collected over the past fifty years by the American National Election Study as well as data obtained from focus groups and qualitative interviews. Chapter 3 provides a baseline assessment of party images. The findings from these analyses demonstrate that people have clear pictures of the parties that correspond and move with their positions on race. Currently, individuals overwhelmingly perceive the Democratic Party as more racially liberal than the Republican Party.

In chapter 4, I include a discussion of the news media's role in facilitating the response to the 2000 Republican National Convention. I include a chapter on the media because most people obtain information about political events through the media rather than through first-hand experience. Using data drawn from three nationally circulated newspapers (the *Los Angeles Times*, the *New York Times*, and the *Washington Post*) and thirteen African American newspapers, I examine how the media framed the convention. This chapter seeks primarily to determine the level and scope of countervailing information in the campaign environment at the time of the convention. The content analysis reveals that substantial variance occurred in the coverage of the convention and that individuals had the opportunity to encounter information that competed with the Republican Party's new projected image.

Using both survey and experimental data, chapter 5 explores whether the Republican Party's racial appeals affected individuals' perceptions of the party. First, I use secondary analysis of the Gallup Organization's Post–GOP Convention Poll to show that those who watched the convention were more likely to believe that the Republican Party did a good job reaching out to minorities. Further, the results indicate that the effect of convention watching depended largely on the viewer's race.

While the results of the polling data provide insight into how the Republicans' use of racial appeals resonated with the general electorate, the polling results by themselves do not answer the research question sufficiently because they cannot isolate the causal relationship between convention exposure and perceptions of the Republican Party. To establish causality, the research design used in this book incorporates several experiments. This method is ideal for testing the argument that competing information found in the campaign environment undermined the Republican Party's attempt to appear more inclusive. Consequently, I use an experiment in chapter 5 to demonstrate that subtle variation in the media's conveyance of convention events significantly affected the effectiveness of the GOP's strategy. Again, these effects were moderated by the race of the perceiver.

Chapter 6 further explores the effect of countervailing information by examining what happens when the party's activities contradict its new projected image. In particular, chapter 6 examines how much of the headway gained as a result of the convention was undone by the dispute over the 2000 election results. First, I examine how the print news media discussed the Republican Party from Election Day until Al Gore conceded the election. I find that most of the coverage focused on the Florida recount. In addition, the media devoted a fraction of this coverage to discussing the recount in conjunction with the impact on minority groups and how the Republican Party's actions undermined the spirit of "compassionate conservatism." Using the 2002 American National Election Study, I find a link between the media coverage and public opinion. That is, I find that believing that George W. Bush was unfairly elected president in 2000 negatively correlated with perceptions of the Republican Party's ability to represent minority groups.

While the preceding chapters discuss the impediments encountered in the process of party image change, chapter 7 discusses a strategy for overcoming these obstacles. Specifically, I consider how repeated attempts to reshape citizens' party images can minimize the presence of countervailing information and increase the strategy's success. To do so, I revisit the compassionate conservative strategy by examining the 2004 Republican National Convention. Although on a smaller scale, the 2004 electoral cycle was once again marked by the Republican Party's concerted effort to reach out to minority groups. Analyses of experimental data reveal that the recurring effort at the 2004 convention allowed the Republican Party to make inroads among African Americans, a group unaffected by the 2000 Republican National Convention.

Although this book focuses primarily on the Republican Party, the approach used to examine party image change applies to political parties in general, as chapter 8 illustrates. I test the boundaries of the theoretical framework developed in chapter 1 by applying it to the Democratic Party. Specifically, I explore the party's limitations if it tried to reshape its image with respect to race. The results reveal that the Democratic Party would have to overcome the same obstacles when trying to prove to the electorate that it was more racially conservative that the Republican Party had to overcome in trying to appear more racially liberal.

Finally, chapter 9 concludes the discussion of the politics and process of party image change by summarizing the findings and discussing their implications. In this chapter, I speculate about the future of race and party politics. As the U.S. electorate continues to grow and change in racial/ethnic composition, I contemplate how political parties will respond. I also theorize about how this project's framework can be applied to the study of other issues and groups in U.S. politics. Chapter 9 closes with a discussion of potential avenues for future research.

1 Toward a Theory of Party Image Change

WHILE THE IMPORTANCE and study of party identification has been duly noted, the study of party images—individuals' perceptions or stereotypes of political parties—has received significantly less attention. Based on the extant literature, we know the contents of party image (Matthews and Prothro 1964; Trilling 1976; Sanders 1988) and the impact of party image on candidate evaluation (Rahn 1993). Less explored are the conditions under which individuals' party images can be altered. Studies (e.g., B. Campbell 1977; Carmines and Stimson 1989) have observed changes in party behavior and attempted to link them to similar changes in partisan alignment. Scholars, however, have not examined changes in party image at the individual level. More specifically, scholars have not incorporated party activities into models of party image change. As a result, we do not know which party strategies alter party images and what circumstances moderate the strategies' impact. This chapter seeks to develop a theoretical framework for understanding when party images can be reshaped. In particular, I answer the question of whether aesthetic changes unaccompanied by corresponding changes in policy positions can alter voters' perceptions of political parties along a particular dimension. I argue that a party will succeed in reshaping its image when voters perceive the new image as different from the old.

Party Images

Each of the two major parties[1] is associated with political symbols—policies, candidates, and constituencies—that give meaning to these

---

1. The discussion of political parties in this project is limited to the behavior of the national organizations.

organizations for members of the U.S. electorate.[2] Sears (2001) explains, "When presented to us, these political symbols rivet our attention and evoke strong emotion. These emotions are dominated by a simple good-bad, like-dislike evaluative dimension" (15). Since affective evaluations of the parties are a function of their symbolic components, political parties manipulate the symbols with which they are connected to gain favorable evaluations and ultimately electoral victory. Parties seek to manipulate not only which symbols get associated with their party but also the meaning individuals assign to these symbols.

The totality of the political symbols one associates with a political party is known as a *party image*. Party images form because at some point, political parties become synonymous with certain policy positions and groups in society. Petrocik (1996) suggests that

> parties have sociologically distinctive constituencies and the linkage between a party's issue agenda and the social characteristics of its supporters is quite strong, even in the United States. It is a completely recursive linkage: groups support a party because it attempts to use government to alter or protect a social or economic status quo which harms or benefits them; the party promotes such policies because it draws supporters, activists, and candidates from the groups. Issue handling reputations emerge from this history, which, by the dynamics of political conflict, is regularly tested and reinforced. (828)

These reputations develop into an individual's party image (the "voter's picture of the party") and guide subsequent evaluations of a party (Matthews and Prothro 1964). Party image is not the same as party identification. While the two concepts are related, party image differs in that "two people may identify with the same party but have very different mental pictures of it and evaluate these pictures in different ways" (Matthews and Prothro 1964, 82). Trilling (1976) argues that "an individual's party image not surprisingly is likely to be related to his party identification, but his party image will consist less of purely psychological, affective components and more of substantive compo-

---

2. Borrowing Sears's (2001) definition, a political symbol is "any affectively charged element in a political attitude object" (15). The political attitude object in this study is a political party.

nents" (2).[3] Milne and MacKenzie (1955) describe party images as "symbols; the party is often supported because it is believed to stand for something dear to the elector. It matters little that the 'something' may be an issue no longer of topical importance; the attachment to the symbol, and the party, persists" (130). Symbols in this case denote not simply mascots and insignias but also candidates, issue positions, and historical events that exemplify a political party.

Each element can be categorized as either policy oriented or devoid of policy. For example, an individual can associate the Republican Party with issue positions such as opposition to affirmative action, opposition to big government, or support for capital punishment. Individuals can also link the Republican Party with more symbolic icons such as the GOP elephant, Ronald Reagan, Trent Lott, and George W. Bush. Likewise, the Democratic Party can be represented by the Democratic donkey, the Kennedys, or Jesse Jackson. Issue positions associated with the Democratic Party could include support for affirmative action or support for social spending. Thus, party image consists of all the substantive components a person associates with a given political party.

Moreover, party image incorporates the interpretation individuals assign to these components. According to Elder and Cobb (1983),

> While a symbol references some aspect of reality external to the individual, precisely what is referenced is often unclear and varies from one person to another. When a person responds to a symbol, he is responding not simply to external reality but to his conception or interpretation of that reality. Thus, the meaning he gives to the symbol will be based on information and ideas he has stored away in his mind. To understand how symbols acquire meaning, we must inquire into the kinds of cognitive meanings that a person has available to assign to a symbol. (40–41)

In this sense, two individuals' party images can contain the same symbols but ultimately differ by the meaning these symbols signify. For example, two individuals can associate Trent Lott with the Republican

---

3. The key difference between party image and party identification is that party image is the foundation on which party identification is built. Essentially, party image provides the basis for liking one party over another. As mentioned earlier, people can have different party images but the same party identification. Party image is how people perceive the party, and party identification is the evaluative outcome of what individuals perceive.

Party but can reach different conclusions about where the Republican Party stands on race depending on whether they view Lott as racially conservative. Thus, party images are subjective and can vary across individuals. Regardless of interpretation, the symbols and the meaning assigned to them by an individual can potentially be used in evaluations of party activity. Consequently, evaluations of a party depend not only on what exists in an individual's party image but also on what is noticeably absent and how the individual makes sense of all this information.

Citizens develop their partisan images (also referred to as partisan stereotypes) through socialization and through (direct and indirect) encounters and experiences with party members (Rahn 1993). Information used to form party images can come from the parties themselves or from competing sources of political information such as the media or other political organizations. The information is filtered through the individual's political predispositions. Interactions with political parties shape not only the political symbols people associate with a given party but also the interpretation people lend to those symbols. Further, an individual's experiential knowledge also guides the affective weight he or she places on those political symbols. The affective valence and the salience of these symbols and the interpretation individuals assign to the symbols (i.e., the frames individuals use to make sense of the symbols) then guide party preferences.

Understanding party images is important because of the role these images play in the political process. Party images shape how individuals perceive political parties and can affect not only how people vote but also whether they choose to engage in the political process at all. As a result, party images can affect who wins and loses elections, which ultimately affects which interests are represented in the political arena.

It is no wonder, then, that political elites often attempt to reshape party images when seeking electoral success. After all, they must keep up with the changing face of the political landscape. First, the nature of political competition changes from election to election. Second, the electorate experiences demographic changes. Finally, issues rise and fall in importance. Thus, political parties must adapt to their changing environment. This includes altering the way different groups in the electorate perceive the political parties.

When attempting to reshape a party's image, however, political elites face a dilemma—they must attract new voters while maintaining their current support base. One way a political party might reshape its image is by adopting new issue positions. But as scholars note, doing so will likely upset current constituents and confuse potential voters. The alternative is to reshape the party's image in a more cosmetic way. Specifically, a party can use different representational images to convey to voters that the parties have changed without making any substantive changes to the party's platform. But does this strategy work?

Altering Party Images

While the party image literature does not currently address the question of what incites modifications in individuals' party images, we can glean some insight from research on party evaluations in political science and research on stereotypes in social psychology. If we consider a party image a form of stereotype, then social psychology research suggests that party images may be updated in the face of inconsistent information. Partisan stereotypes as well as stereotypes in general can be thought of as a schematic structure. A *schema* is a "a cognitive structure that organizes prior information and experience around a central value or idea, and guides the interpretation of new information and experience" (Zaller 1992, 37). Thus, schemata allow us to interpret what is ambiguous, uncertain, or unknown by applying it to a standing, known framework that exists in our heads. Schemata can be used in making inferences about events, other people, and ourselves. For example, when we encounter new people, we use either ascribed (e.g., age, race, sex) or achieved (e.g., experience or training) characteristics about that person to activate a set of role-based expectations about that person (Fiske and Taylor 1984). Fiske and Taylor (1984) assert that "one way to think about stereotypes is as a particular type of role schema that organizes one's prior knowledge and expectations about other people who fall into certain socially defined categories" (160). Political party stereotypes, then, would be "those cognitive structures that contain citizens' knowledge, beliefs, and expectancies about the two major political parties" (Rahn 1993, 474).

Accordingly, when an individual has associated an event, issue, or person with a particular stereotype, he or she then ascribes the stereotypic content to that situation, regardless of how much or how little the situation may actually resemble the stereotype (Fiske and Taylor 1984, 160). "The main principle of schematic memory is that the usual case overrides details of the specific instance" (Fiske and Taylor 1984, 162). For example, when individuals have identified a candidate as a

Democrat, in the absence of additional information they will attribute all the features of what they imagine a Democrat to be to that candidate, regardless of whether that candidate is a moderate or ideologically at the extreme left.

When an individual receives new information, updating the stereotype depends on whether the newly presented information conflicts with existing knowledge. If the information presented in the stimulus is consistent with individuals' existing schematic information, they will encode that information and store it in their memory with the rest of the relevant considerations. Fiske and Taylor (1984) explain that "inconsistent behavior requires explanation, which takes time when the information is encountered—that is, at encoding. If people can attribute inconsistent behavior to situational causes, they can forget the behavior and presumably maintain their schema-based impression" (164).

This process of absorbing consistent information more readily than inconsistent information has a reinforcing effect on stereotypes in general (Fiske and Taylor 1984) as well as on partisan stereotypes in particular (Rahn 1993). Partisan stereotypes or images consequently are not easily altered because party images "are not created de novo" (Rapoport 1997, 188) each time voters receive new information about the parties as they would during a campaign. Current party images constitute the starting point from which new evaluations begin (Rapoport 1997, 188). Hence, when individuals encounter inconsistent information, they must weigh that information against all previously received information. In a sense, prior beliefs have an anchoring effect on how people encode new information.

This is not to say that party images or stereotypes cannot be altered. Rahn (1993) examined under what conditions people abandoned their use of party stereotypes when evaluating a candidate. Using an experimental design, Rahn tested to see whether people would incorporate policy information into their candidate evaluations when the policy information associated with a candidate was incongruent with the candidate's party affiliation. Rahn's results show that voters "neglect policy information in reaching evaluation; they use the label rather than policy attributes in drawing inferences; and they are perceptually less responsive to inconsistent information" (492). Furthermore, she found that even when voters faced extreme inconsistency, people still relied on their partisan stereotypes to make candidate evaluations. But at the same time, she admits that her results are not absolute. For example, Rahn speculates that voters may abandon their partisan stereotypes when the inconsistency is even more extreme or involves an issue that is particularly salient to the voter (487).[4] In other words, stereotypes should break down when people can substitute an equally salient alternative means of categorization (Fiske and Taylor 1984; Hamilton and Sherman 1994).

If we consider party image a form of party evaluation, then the literature suggests that party images shift only when the parties switch positions in salient issue domains. The structure and dynamics of party evaluation have long been debated, with the debate centering on the question of whether party preference (usually measured by party identification) was fixed or malleable. Early studies (e.g., Downs 1957) modeled party preference as a function of an individual's issue positions relative to those of a party's position. This model assumed that voters updated their party preferences when they perceived changes in the platforms of a party or experienced changes in personal policy positions. In the Downsian sense, party evaluation was a continuous process. In contrast, party identification as conceptualized by A. Campbell et al. (1960) posited a view of party preference that was rooted in early childhood socialization and experienced very little alteration in later years. This perspective viewed party identification as a lot less malleable and more stable over time. In other words, party preference had very little to do with the evaluation of a party's activities but rather resulted from a psychological attachment to a party inherited from one's parents.

Subsequent studies have found that party preference lies somewhere between the two extremes. For example, Fiorina (1981) contends that while party identification is updated by changes in political factors, it is still ingrained in past policy preferences. Similarly, Jackson (1975) argues that "voting decisions are largely motivated by evaluations of where the parties are located on different issues relative to the persons' stated positions and to a much lesser extent by party identifications unless people are indifferent between the parties on issues" (183). Jackson contends that party preferences are "motivated by individuals' desires to have public policy reflect their own judgments about what

---

4. For additional evidence on the abandoning of partisan stereotypes in connection with issue saliency, see Ansolabehere and Iyengar 1994.

policies should be followed and by the policies each party and its candidates advocate. Parties are important, but only if they constitute policy oriented, politically motivated organizations reflecting the distribution of positions among voters and competing for the support of the electorate" (183–84).

These and other studies show that party preferences are "more than the result of a set of early socializing experiences, possibly reinforced by subsequent social and political activity" (Franklin and Jackson 1983, 968). Rather, support for a political party depends on that party's ability to maintain some congruence between its platform and an individual's issue positions. In this sense, Franklin and Jackson (1983) argue that "although previous partisan attachment acts to restrain change, it is like a sea anchor, which retards drift rather than arrests it entirely. If the tides of policy evaluation are strong enough, conversions can and will take place" (969). And in fact, scholars have found that shifts in partisanship among political elites (Clark et al. 1991; Adams 1997) and among the mass electorate (Carmines and Stimson 1989) occur when parties adopt salient issues that create key distinctions between them and individuals attempt to realign themselves with the parties' positions on this issue.

To summarize, the social psychology and political science literatures suggest that party images will be updated when voters face inconsistent information and attempt to realign the new version of the party with the old. Updating party images, however, will be contingent on the perceived level of inconsistency. More specifically, altering party images is a two-step process. First, the party must project an image of itself that is inconsistent with its existing image. Second, the change must be large enough to meet an individual's threshold for what constitutes real change.

Meeting the Threshold

To spread the word that they have changed in some way, political parties will usually launch a campaign during the course of an election cycle. As Iyengar (1997) contends, "In the television era, campaigns typically consist of a series of choreographed events—conventions and debates being the most notable—at which the candidates present themselves to the media and the public in a format that sometimes resembles a mass entertainment spectacle" (143). According to Kinder's (1998) definition, campaigns are "deliberate, self-conscious efforts on the part of elites to influence citizens. Campaigns expend various resources—money, organization, technique and expertise, words, symbols, and arguments—in an attempt to influence what citizens think, what they think about, and ultimately, what they do" (817).

As they strive to shape public opinion and behavior during the course of a campaign, elites construct frames, which are "rhetorical weapons created and sharpened by political elites to advance their interests and ideas" (Kinder 1998, 822). Framing is the process by which elites define and construct political issues or events (Iyengar and Kinder 1987; Nelson, Clawson, and Oxley 1997). Through framing, elites try to shape the meaning or interpretation people assign to events, candidates, and issues. Frames allow elites to influence what information people deem applicable to their evaluations. In other words, frames used within the context of a campaign remind prospective supporters of the relevance of "pre-existing political attitudes and perceptions" (Bartels 1997, 10).

Essentially, elites create frames in an attempt to invoke specific feelings, opinions, and ideas that potentially translate into mobilization and/or support while displacing sentiments that might work to the detriment of the elites' goals. The assumption is that if certain emotions or beliefs can be brought to mind, the outcome of an evaluation can ultimately be altered. As Kinder (1998) explains, frames "spotlight some considerations and neglect others, thereby altering the mix of ingredients that citizens consider as they form their opinions on politics" (822). Frames also "lead a double life" by serving as "cognitive structures that help individual citizens make sense of the issues that animate political life. They provide order and meaning; they make the world beyond direct experience seem natural" (Kinder and Sanders 1996, 164). In this sense, framing "is both a process and an effect in which a common stock of key words, phrases, images, sources, and themes highlight and promote specific facts, interpretations and judgments, making them more salient" (Tucker 1998, 143).

Altering party images is no more than reframing citizens' pictures of a political party. Existing party images are the initial set of emotions, symbols, and beliefs people use to describe a party. When reshaping party images, political elites seek to reconstruct these frames. During a campaign, parties will project a frame or an image of themselves and hope that individuals will adopt the same framing of the party.

Much like partisan stereotypes, the frames people possess come primarily from elite debate. "[P]ublic opinion depends not only on the circumstances and sentiments of individual citizens—their interests, feelings toward social groups, and their political principles—but also on the ongoing debate among elites" (Kinder and Sanders 1996, 163). Nevertheless, individuals can reject the frames they dislike, rework the frames they adopt, or create their own frames (Kinder and Sanders 1996, 165). As Neuman, Just, and Crigler (1992) argue, "People think for themselves, and media and official versions of problems and events make up only part of their schema for public issues" (112). This point is crucial, because it speaks to individual agency in controlling just what information will apply to any political scenario.

Thus, the key to altering party images is knowing when and why individuals will reject the newly framed version of the party. It is not enough for elites to project a new image; citizens must be willing to accept the new picture of the party. For each party and each issue domain, individuals will set the lower boundary for determining what signifies change when called on to revise their party images. The party's projected image will be incorporated into people's partisan stereotypes when it meets or exceeds the height of the bar for determining what constitutes a new party. This can prove to be somewhat difficult, however. Because the height of the threshold varies across individuals, meeting the threshold is like trying to hit a moving target. Moreover, the political arena includes alternative sources of information that affect whether people believe that parties have met expectations.

Figure 1 depicts the process of changing a party image. The reshaping process begins with the party projecting a new image along some dimension or dimensions. The first hurdle to overcome is the party's existing image. Each political party has long-standing reputations for handling certain issues. On other issues—usually newer or less salient issues—the party may have less known positions or no positions at all. A party will have an easier time reshaping its image on these issues because individuals will require less convincing that the party has changed. Here, the bar is set low because little information is available to contradict the new image of the party. When trying to modify its image in issue domains in which its reputation is more entrenched, however, parties face an uphill battle. Parties have more difficulty convincing the electorate that they have suddenly changed when they have

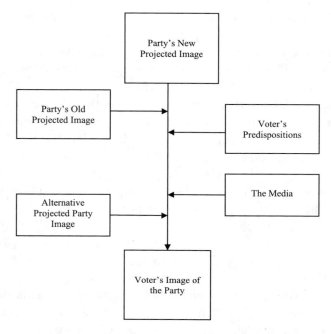

Fig. 1.   Hypothesized process of party image change

spent decades building an image in a particular domain than in starting from scratch to build a reputation with respect to another issue area.

The second impediment to party image change is transcending the predispositions of voters. As is evident from prior work on campaign effects, susceptibility to elite discourse is not universal (Berelson, Lazarsfeld, and McPhee 1954; A. Campbell et al. 1960; Iyengar and Kinder 1987; Krosnick and Brannon 1993). Individuals' willingness to adopt the frames they receive from elites (including candidates, party strategists, and the media) depends largely on individuals' predispositions and attentiveness to the message (Zaller 1992). Adopting Zaller's (1992) definition, predispositions encompass the "variety of interests, values, and experiences that may greatly affect their willingness to accept—or alternatively, their resolve to resist—persuasive influences" (22). This definition implies that while predispositions may manifest themselves as some attitudinal dimension (e.g., egalitarianism, party identification, racial prejudice), predispositions are made of information gathered through direct and indirect encounters with the political and social world that give meaning to the predisposition. In other words, an individual's preference for one party over another is not simply guided by some hollow liking for that party. Rather, an individual's preference for one party over another is based on the political symbols that give meaning to the party for that individual.

Predispositions affect the process of party image change by determining what information becomes encoded into party images. Predispositions predict whether individuals will accept the cosmetic changes made by a party or demand changes to the party's platform before altering existing party images. As noted earlier, individuals can have the same party image but have different party identification. Conversely, people can have the same party identification but have drastically different partisan stereotypes. It is quite possible to be a strong partisan because of a party's position on one issue but to place little value on the party's position in other issue domains. Therefore, when a party tries to reshape its image along a particular dimension in which it has a well-established position, the party will make the most headway among those individuals who place relatively little importance on that issue. Under these circumstances, the threshold for change will be lower, regardless of party identification. Party identification may explain some but not all responses to a party's attempt to reshape its image.

Finally, the success of a campaign is affected by what other information is available to the campaign's targeted audience. The success or failure of a campaign can hinge on whether the information is one-sided or if competing frames exist. For example, Zaller (1992) argues that "the most important source of resistance to dominant campaigns . . . is countervailing information carried within the overall stream of political information" (253). He finds that when "people are exposed to two competing sets of electoral information, they are generally able to choose among them on the basis of their partisanship and values. . . . But when individuals are exposed to a one-sided communication flow . . . their capacity for critical resistance appears quite limited" (253). Thus, the presence of conflicting information can prohibit political parties from meeting the threshold for change. With respect to reshaping partisan stereotypes, two important sources of information include the media and alternative projections of the party's image.

Because political information is usually filtered through the media, they play an important role in the process of party image change. In attempting to reach a large audience, political parties must rely on the media. But the media do not passively participate in the political process. They have the ability to present as much or as little of a party's campaign message as they choose. The media also have the capacity to put their own spin on the message a party is attempting to convey to voters. When a party projects a new image, the media can decide not to highlight the change or can remind voters that the new image does not differ substantially from the old. In this case, parties will find it hard to meet the threshold of change in voters' minds.

In addition, to convince citizens that a party has changed, it must project a consistent image. Political campaigns are undermined when party members engage in activities that otherwise contradict the new image of the party. The incongruity confuses voters. Because the party bears the burden of proof of change, voters are more likely to keep their existing images than to modify them.

Racial Symbolism

The remaining chapters will empirically test the proposed process of party image change. While party images can have many components, I focus only on the part of a party image that relates to race. One of the most (if not the most) persistent cleavages between the two major parties has been race. As Carmines and Stimson (1986) put it,

> Race has deep symbolic meaning in American political history and has touched a raw nerve in the body politic. It has also been an issue on which the parties have taken relatively clear and distinct stands, at least since the mid-1960s. Finally, the issue has had a long political life cycle. It has been a recurring theme in American politics as long as there has been an American politics and conflict over race has been especially intense since the New Deal. (903)

In fact, scholars have posited race as the underlying determinant of partisan division (B. Campbell 1977; Carmines and Stimson 1989; Huckfeldt and Kohfeld 1989; Frymer 1999; Valentino and Sears 2005). Because of the highly salient cleavages surrounding race, the subject provides an interesting backdrop for the examination of how elites can use symbolic images to reshape party images. Moreover, if we can identify conditions under which a party succeeds in changing the racial component of its image and the meaning assigned to that component, we may also apply this information to other less salient issues.

If claims about the role of race in party politics are correct, citizens support political parties in large part (although not necessarily exclusively) based on perceptions of the parties' racial symbolism or reputation with respect to race. *Racial symbolism*, as it is used in this study, is the interpretation an individual assigns to a political party's activities based on all of the racial, political, and social symbols that have come to be associated with that party. It is the frame individuals use to give meaning to a party's race-related activities. Racial symbolism is the product of the symbols in a party's image, the racial valence of those symbols, and the weight of each symbol. To be included in an individual's perception of the racial symbolism of a political party, a political symbol must receive a racial valence. It must also have an affective tag (whether the individual likes or dislikes the symbol) and a weight (importance). Thus, as figure 2 illustrates, the interpretation of a party's race related activities depends on the political symbols associated with the party, whether these symbols are racialized, the affective evaluation of the symbol, and that symbol's importance to the individual.

For example, if the political symbol in figure 2 were Jesse Jackson, for him to be included in an individual's perception of the racial symbolism associated with the Democratic Party, the individual would first have to recognize Jackson as a racialized figure. Second, the individual would have to place some importance on Jackson. If Jackson was not salient to the individual, Jackson would not factor into the individual's calculus. Finally, the individual must have an affective evaluation of Jackson—that is, view him as either a positive or negative figure. If all three conditions are met, Jackson could then be used to evaluate the Democratic Party's racial symbolism. As an important, positive, racialized symbol, Jackson would yield a positive racial symbolism associated with the Democratic Party. The opposite would be true if he were a negative figure.

As a subsection of one's party image, racial symbolism can then be used to make subsequent evaluations of a party. Provided that a political party's race-related activities are salient to people, they can make more global evaluations of a party based solely on the party's racial symbolism. For example, when asked whether they like a political party, people can recall the racial symbolism of the party and answer based on this information rather than draw on a totality of information about the party stored in their memories. If a political party is perceived to have a positive racial symbolism and an individual values this

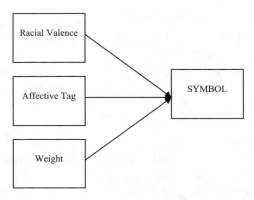

Fig. 2.   Racial symbols

criterion, then the individual will give the party a positive affective evaluation. Similarly, if an individual is racially conservative and associates a political party with a negative racial symbolism, that individual will have a positive affective evaluation of the party.

When attempting to revise their racial symbolism without altering their policy positions, the two major parties have to find representational images that convey change. For the Republican Party, this means using images that convey racial liberalism. Likewise, the Democratic Party must link itself with images that evoke racial conservatism. More specifically, the Republican Party must update its image from the one described earlier to the Big Tent, which incorporates icons such as Colin Powell, Condoleezza Rice, and the Rock into the party ranks while maintaining the same policy orientation. The Democratic Party now reverts back to the party of Strom Thurmond and George Wallace while keeping its liberal position on affirmative action and social spending.

Is increasing the presence of African Americans or racial conservatives enough to alter the racial symbolism associated with a political party? According to Sears (1993), a "group represents an attitude object like any other and therefore evokes affective responses in the same manner. Groups may behave like other political symbols, mainly evoking symbolic predispositions (as in patriotism or nationalism or class solidarity)" (127)—or, in this case, as in racial conservatism or racial liberalism.

What about the other images associated with the party's racial symbolism? The ability to overshadow the other political images associated with a party's racial symbolism depends on the importance of the other symbols. When the (unchanged) policy-oriented symbols are more important, images will not be enough.

Improving Party Evaluations by Altering Party Images

The underlying assumption behind the theory of party image change is that altering party images should lead to electoral gain. In other words, if the parties reshape their images, these changes should lead to a subsequent improvement in individuals' affective evaluations of the parties. Affective evaluations of the parties are a function of the affective evaluations of their symbolic components. As Sears (1993) explains, "[M]ost attitude objects contain multiple symbols. In the symbolic politics view, each such symbol should evoke the specific evaluation associated with it, with overall evaluation of the full attitude object being some simple function of those individual evaluations" (125). For example, if the negative racial symbolism associated with the GOP resulted in negative evaluations of the party, replacing this racial symbolism with a new framing of the party should improve overall affective evaluations.

The challenge to this proposition is that political elites must make the racial symbolism of the party applicable to more general evaluations. People possess multiple bits of information that may affect their understanding of a given concept. For example, thinking about the Republican Party may bring to an individual's mind a host of considerations, including specific candidates associated with the party, the party's ideology, or particular policies and issues owned by the party. This point is critical because, as Zaller (1992) notes, "[I]ndividuals do not typically possess 'just one opinion' toward issues [or in this case parties], but multiple potential opinions" (38). The considerations used to form an opinion or make an evaluation are cued or signaled by an individual's environment. How might this process work?

The human mind, at least in terms of information processing, can be divided into two components: the long-term memory and the working memory. The long-term memory can be described as "a library of information whose main property is the more or less permanent storage of vast amounts of data" (Lodge et al. 1991, 1358). Similarly, long-term memory has been conceptualized as a "knowledge store" that contains "a network of constructs including information about social objects and their attributes (OA); goals, values, and motivations (GVM); and affective or emotional states (AS)" (Price and Tewksbury 1997, 24). These networks of constructs, analogous to schemata, hold together potentially associated bits of information. The knowledge store contains the full range of stereotypic considerations associated with any given concept.

An individual does not draw on all of this information when making a judgment, however. In instances where people need to make an assessment, only the information in working memory is used. Working or active memory is "where information is consciously attended to and actively processed" (Lodge et al. 1991, 1359). At any given moment, only a fraction of the knowledge store moves into the working memory. Further, the constructs that become activated tend to be the most accessible, defined by recency or frequency of use. The more a construct has been repeatedly or recently used, the more accessible or salient that construct is.

Activation occurs when an actor receives a stimulus from an external source—in this case, a campaign message. The individual's activated schemata guide the way the information presented in the campaign message is encoded. The activated schemata then provide a framework for interpreting the meaning of the campaign message and will influence what information from the campaign message the perceiver stores (Cohen 1981, 50). When an individual tries to retrieve the previously stored information about the campaign message, the relevant schemata will be reactivated to fill in what is unknown or forgotten about the stimulus (Cohen 1981, 50). After information has been activated—that is, transferred from the long-term to the working memory—actors must conduct their evaluation, whether voting or answering a survey question, by "averaging across accessible considerations" (Zaller 1992, 49).[5]

During the course of a campaign, political elites attempt to activate particular constructs to be transferred into working memory. The goal

5. This model of information retrieval is consistent with both memory-based and impression-driven or online processing. The memory-based model assumes that the evaluation is based on some mix of pro and con evidence, while the online model assumes the existence of a "judgment tally" that is updated as new information is introduced. Either way, when presented with a stimulus, some form of existing knowledge must be retrieved. Furthermore, evidence suggests that "people sometimes rely on their memory of likes and dislikes to inform an opinion, while at other times they can simply retrieve their on-line judgments" (Lodge, McGraw, and Stroh 1989, 401).

of the stimulus is to define what considerations are applicable to the situation. "A construct is deemed applicable, and is likely to be activated, when its key features correspond to the salient features of the stimulus" (Price and Tewksbury 1997, 31). Referring back to the Republican Party's racial symbolism, by displaying the party's racial diversity and invoking the name of Abraham Lincoln, the campaign message should prime people to link thoughts of racial inclusiveness with the Republican Party. As Price and Tewksbury (1997) note, however, success in priming particular considerations for activation for evaluation depends on the overlap between the existing stored constructs (and their accessibility) and the information presented in the stimulus. If the stimulus presents individuals with an undefined concept or a consideration that does not currently exist in their long-term memories, they may add a new construct that can be used in future evaluations.

The weighting process is a function not just of how much information is balanced against the new information but also of how salient the prior constructs are. When certain constructs are repeatedly activated, they become chronically salient. If this occurs, the chronically accessible considerations tend to be activated when making relevant decisions, regardless of the intentional or unintentional priming of other constructs by environmental stimuli. For example, when making presidential evaluations, Iyengar and Kinder (1987) found that differences in the susceptibility to certain primes occurred among individuals along partisan lines. Specifically, they found that "priming is strengthened among Democrats for problems that are prominent on the agenda of the Democratic Party, among Republicans for problems that are prominent on the agenda of the Republican Party" (96). The authors conclude that priming effects are reduced among individuals who are predisposed to reject the prime.

In sum, the same campaign that catalyzes the process of party image change with respect to a particular issue domain can also prime the use of that section of party image in affective evaluations of the party. Because of the recency and salience of the construct, it should be front and center in voters' working memories, ready for use in their political decision making. Reshaping party images along a particular dimension, however, does not necessarily guarantee a subsequent improvement in overall evaluations of the parties and their candidates. Citizens have some autonomy in the priming process and can substitute another aspect of party image that is more salient to their daily lives. In this case, individuals will revise their party image but not apply the new framing of the party to more macro evaluations of the party.

From Theory to Practice

Testing the central proposition that aesthetic changes unaccompanied by corresponding changes in policy positions alter voters' perceptions of political parties when voters perceive the new image as different from the old requires identifying an instance when such a strategy was employed. As discussed in the introduction, the 2000 Republican National Convention offers an excellent test case. The Republican convention can be thought of as a campaign. Beginning in the early 1950s, a series of reforms shifted the selection of presidential nominees from the conventions to state-level primaries and caucuses. As a result, the convention has become less a "deliberative body" and more an "extended, four-day infomercial" (Karabell 1998, 7). During conventions, the parties present the unifying themes of that election cycle.

The 2000 Republican National Convention was no exception. The slogan integrated throughout the convention program, "Renewing America's Purpose. Together," characterized the goals of the Republican Party for the 2000 election cycle. These objectives included making the party more attractive to minority voters:

> We offer not only a new agenda, but also a new approach—a vision of a welcoming society in which all have a place. To all Americans, particularly immigrants and minorities, we send a clear message: this is the party of freedom and progress, and it is your home. ("Republican Platform 2000")

To achieve this goal, the convention featured notable minority Republican leaders and supporters. In the next chapter, I will demonstrate that the party did not alter its position on racial issues such as affirmative action. How, then, did the use of racial images resonate among those exposed to the convention? Applying the theorized process of party image change, I argue that the impact of the convention is a function of the Republican Party's historical reputation for handling race, how much of this history citizens find relevant, the media's willingness to convey the party's message undistorted, and party members' ability to commit to the theme and avoid engaging in activities that would contradict its new projected image.

First, to have an impact, the display of diversity had to have been inconsistent with voters' existing pictures of the party. This was indeed the case. Six months prior to the convention, 79.0 percent of blacks and 49.2 percent of whites believed that the Democratic Party better represented the interests of blacks. In contrast, only 12.3 percent of whites and 4.2 percent of blacks believed that the Republican Party better represented African Americans. Moreover, 72.5 percent of blacks and 48.6 percent of whites believed that the Democratic Party was better able to improve race relations, while 18.9 percent of whites and 6.5 percent of blacks believed the Republican Party would do a better job.[6] These figures indicate that shortly before the convention, the Republican Party was not perceived as racially liberal, at least relative to the Democratic Party. Given the contradictory nature of the 2000 Republican National Convention, I hypothesize that exposure to the convention will improve perceptions of the GOP's racial symbolism.

Second, when attempting to reshape party images, we also know that a balancing act takes place between what individuals already know and the new information being presented. The stronger the existing information, the harder it will be to incorporate new information. In the case of the 2000 Republican National Convention, I expect African Americans to be the most resistant to the use of diverse racial images to signal change since African Americans place a higher premium on the parties' policy positions. National survey data provide support for this claim.

Table 1 presents summary statistics from the 1996 American National Election Study and shows that prior to the 2000 election cycle, African Americans were more likely than whites to believe that racial issues such as social spending and government aid to blacks were extremely important. African Americans were also more likely than whites to see a difference between themselves and the Republican Party on the same issues. Because of the importance blacks place on racial issues and the relative distance from the GOP on these issues, exposure to the 2000 Republican National Convention will have less of an impact on blacks.

---

6. These figures were estimated using the CBS News Monthly Poll #1, February 2000, obtained from the Inter-University Consortium for Political and Social Research (available at www.icpsr.umich.edu).

TABLE 1.   Importance of and Placement on Racial Issues, by Race (in percentages)

	Importance of Racial Issues	
	Social Spending	Government Aid to Blacks
African Americans	36	53
Whites	25	18

	Placement on Racial Issues Relative to the Republican Party			
	Social Spending		Government Aid to Blacks	
	No Difference	More Liberal	No Difference	More Liberal
African Americans	23	75	17	62
Whites	40	50	28	25

Source: 1996 American National Election Study.

Third, regardless of the individual's race, the impact of convention exposure will be moderated by alternative projections of the party. When people are exposed to versions of the convention in which the party's racial outreach is not highlighted or when the race strategy is discussed in conjunction with other aspects of the party that have not changed, the magnitude of the effect of convention exposure will be minimized. Likewise, framing the Republican Party as illegitimately winning the presidency will have negative consequences for people's perceptions of the GOP's racial symbolism, undermining any headway made during the convention. Conversely, the Republican Party will have more success in reshaping its party image when citizens are informed that in 2004, the party repeated the effort initiated during the 2000 election cycle as a sustained commitment to racial diversity.

Conclusion

As political parties seek additional votes at the margins, they make small, superficial changes to their images. Voters' receptivity to these changes depends on a number of political and social factors often outside the party's control. This book primarily delineates some of these elements. In what follows, I will show that for some voters, cosmetic changes are enough to change perceptions of political parties. For others, however, the issue-relevant elements of a party image are more important. For this second set of voters, their image of a party will change only if the party changes its policies—aesthetic modifications will not be enough.

2 Party Politics and the Racial Divide

I recognize the Republican party as the sheet anchor of the colored man's political hopes and the ark of his safety.
—Frederick Douglass, August 15, 1888

George Bush doesn't care about black people.
—Kanye West, September 2, 2005

WHEN ASSESSING THE malleability of party images, it is essential to examine how crystallized the party's reputation is along particular dimensions. Further, it is equally important to recognize how the party built that reputation to assess the feasibility of counteracting it. The presumption is that political parties consciously engage in activities that contribute to the formation of the public's perceptions of the parties. Yet the parties' actions are often taken for granted.

Research on party identification indicates that although party identification remains quite stable over time (A. Campbell et al 1960; Converse 1964; Converse and Markus 1979), it does experience short-term deviations at both the individual (e.g., Allsop and Weisberg 1988) and aggregate (MacKuen, Erikson, and Stimson 1989) levels. If only for a short period of time, voters may find something appealing about a party that they had not in previous elections, causing them to upset their current partisan loyalties. Although such deviations have been explained in terms of emerging candidates (Rapoport 1997), issues (Carmines and Stimson 1989), or national political and economic circumstances (MacKuen, Erikson, and Stimson 1989), this body of work has neglected to look at the activities of the parties themselves. One might ask (borrowing a phrase from Aldrich 1995), Why parties? Or more specifically, why would it be important to look at political parties in explaining short-term deviations in partisan alignments?

One of the many functions of political parties is to gain and/or maintain electoral success. In so doing, political parties seek to strengthen existing partisan loyalties while attracting new supporters. This means making themselves more attractive to groups that formerly found the parties uninviting. Therefore, it is imperative to identify what parties have done to induce changes in the way they have been perceived.

With respect to race, the two major parties' reputations have not remained constant over time. The perceived ability to handle race has shifted so much so that the party that was once racially conservative is now the more racially liberal party, and vice versa. For example, Frederick Douglass believed that the Republican Party was the political party more amenable to the African American quest for political incorporation, seeing it as the "party of freedom and progress" (Platt 1989). Judging by support for the Republican Party during the first eighty years of its existence, most blacks believed the same. How, then, did we get to the point where rapper Kanye West exclaims to the American public that Republican president George W. Bush does not care about African Americans and where fewer than 10 percent of blacks support Republican presidential candidates in any given election? In particular, what historical events contributed to the massive shift in perceptions of the Republican Party? Moreover, how did the Democratic Party become a more attractive alternative?

This chapter seeks to answer these questions. First, I discuss the historic and contemporary role of political parties in U.S. democracy. Second, I reveal how the two major parties have created a racial divide in U.S. politics. Finally, I use this historical context to provide a backdrop for understanding the potential motivation behind and the impact of the 2000 Republican National Convention.

The American Political Party System: A Brief Overview

The term *party* is derived from "part" and is meant to refer to a subset of "some unified whole" (Lipset and Rokkan 1967, 3). Within the context of western politics, "party" represents "division, conflict, [and] opposition within a body politic" (Lipset and Rokkan 1967, 3). Eldersveld (1964) defines a party as "a structural system seeking to translate or convert (or be converted by) social and economic interests into political power directly" (6). He argues that parties consist "of a set of socio-economic interests groping for political recognition, articulation, and control" (6). To this definition, Ware (1995) adds that power is usually sought by attempting to occupy positions in government (5).

While parties may carry with them a negative connotation, citizens and scholars alike render parties a necessary evil. In a representative democracy, in which the people do not have direct control over governmental affairs, institutions must link citizens to government and provide a means of holding rulers accountable to the governed. Ranney (1962) argues that "the popular control over government which is the essence of democracy can best be established by the popular choice between and control over alternate responsible parties; for only such parties can provide coherent, unified sets of rulers who will assume collective responsibility to the people for the manner in which government is carried on" (12). Schattschneider (1942) contends that political parties have played a major role in the development of democratic government and that "modern democracy is unthinkable save in terms of the parties" (1). In general, those holding democratic principles believe that "the political party is a specialized subsystem of group action indispensable for the working of the political system" (Eldersveld 1964, 18). As Eldersveld (1964) argues, "The public recognizes and accepts the party battle as central to government in a democratic society" (19).

For the most part, U.S. politics functions within a two-party system. While third parties periodically arise and exert power over government and politics, the election of the president has been dominated by the Democratic and Republican Parties (Key 1942, 252).[1] Duverger (1963) argues that "the two-party system seems to correspond to the nature of things, that is to say that political choice usually takes the form of a choice between two alternatives" (215). Stated another way, the two-party system essentially presents the electorate with an either/or choice—between the party in power and a single alternative (see Key 1942; Schattschneider 1942).

The structure and function of American parties have evolved over time. The first two parties, the Federalists and the Jeffersonian Repub-

---

1. While most third or fourth parties rarely receive more than 1 or 2 percent of the vote in a presidential election, examples of more successful attempts can be seen in 1912, 1924, 1948, 1968, 1980, and 1992.

licans, were "organized first and most importantly to solve social choice problems" (Aldrich 1995, 294). Elites created the parties to facilitate the development of U.S. political institutions (Aldrich 1995, 295). The Constitution was adopted under the presidential rule of the Federalist Party (Key 1942). The Republican Party dominated throughout this era until it factionalized during the 1820s (Eldersveld and Walton 2000).

Key (1942) argues that Andrew Jackson's 1828 election marked the beginning of the contemporary party system (266). The expansion of the franchise coupled with an increase in the number of elections under Jacksonian reforms allowed parties to become an ideal vessel for contesting elections during what Ware (1995) calls the party era (the mid-1830s to mid-1890s) (315). With the rise of the present-day Republican Party in 1856, the two major parties vying for political power became the Democrats and the Republicans. From this time until about 1960, the American parties (Jacksonian Democrats, Whigs, and then Republicans) existed as mass parties whose primary function was electoral mobilization (Aldrich 1995, 294). Aldrich (1995) maintains that "the mass party was created for, and was critical to, the extension of democratic practices in nineteenth-century America" (295).

The Populist Party temporarily disturbed the Democratic-Republican dominance of the two-party system. Populist candidates won gubernatorial races in Kansas, North Dakota, and Colorado. In the 1892 presidential election, the Populist candidate won approximately one million popular votes and 22 electoral votes. But by 1896, the Populists no longer posed a viable threat to the two-party system because the Democratic Party in the South had co-opted the Populist Party (Eldersveld and Walton 2000).

The Republican Party dominated presidential politics from 1896 until 1912, "when Roosevelt's Bull Moose Progressive movement split the party and led to two national presidential victories for the Democrats with Woodrow Wilson" (Eldersveld and Walton 2000, 54). Although Roosevelt received only eight Electoral College votes, he won 27.5 percent of the popular vote. Like the Populist movement, however, the Bull Moose Progressive movement was short-lived, and the two-party system was restored in 1920.

Since the 1920s, three viable threats to the two-party system have arisen. First, Robert M. La Follette's Progressives won 17 percent of the popular vote in 1924. Second, George Wallace captured 13 percent of the popular vote in 1968. Third, H. Ross Perot received 19 percent of the popular vote in 1992. However, the two-party system has remained stable since 1932.

Historical changes and technological advances made the mass party form obsolete in the twentieth-century. This gave rise to a third party form, described by Aldrich (1995) as the party in service, which organizes and facilitates the electoral and the governing process for party members (294). This contemporary party form is the "candidate-centered party designed by and meant to serve its office seekers and its new brand of benefit seekers, and it was intended to transform the conditions of party government into a reasonable approximation of that party government in practice" (296). Eldersveld and Walton (2000) contend that this era has been marked by the rise of the use of mass media in campaigns, an increased importance on the role of interest groups, and ideological conflict within party competition. Key (1942) notes, however, that while the names of the parties have changed over the years, the parties' coalitions have remained fairly stable (263).

While parties by necessity adapt to changing political environments, they continuously perform three major functions in American politics. First, parties help to organize the way people think about issues and candidates. Party labels serve as heuristics and allow people to make political decisions with minimal information. Second, parties organize elections. Party primaries, caucuses, and conventions select which candidates will run for which offices. The Democratic and Republican National Committees prioritize campaigns based on viability and then help fund candidates accordingly. Finally, parties help to organize government. Party leadership within government determines committee assignments, procedures, and schedules.

Consequently, political parties' actions can have profound effects on the electorate. For example, Eldersveld (1964) found that "party effort is associated with increased voting turnout, strengthening party identifications and loyalties, and developing attitudes favorable to working for the party operation" (541). He also found that contact with parties led to greater interest in national, domestic, and local affairs (542). Rosenstone and Hansen (1993), who also found that party mobilization efforts significantly affect voter turnout, explained the phenomenon:

Political participation arises from the interaction of citizens and political mobilizers. Few people participate spontaneously in politics. Participation, instead, results when groups, political parties, and activists persuade citizens to take part. . . . In mobilizing citizens for political action, political leaders intend only their own advantage. Seeking only to win elections, pass bills, amend rulings, or influence policies, they target appeals selectively and time them strategically. Nevertheless, in doing so, they extend public involvement in political decision-making. They bring people into politics at crucial times in the process. Their strategic choices impart a distinctive political logic to political participation. (37)

Thus, parties are vehicles for both interest articulation and aggregation (Kitschelt 1989, 47).

In summary, political parties, by definition and conception, provide the vehicle through which societal groups have their policy preferences actualized. In a representative democracy, parties connect voters to elected officials. Although the structure of the U.S. party system has evolved, the parties' goals have remained the same. Parties organize government, organize the way citizens think about government and their elected officials, and facilitate the electoral process both for candidates and for voters. In so doing, political parties maintain electoral coalitions that have remained stable for more than 100 years. At the same time, the parties further exploit divisions already present in American society. In the next section, I discuss one of the more enduring cleavages sustained by political parties in their quest to wield political power.

The Southern Strategy: The Creation of the Racial Divide in Party Politics

Whether explicit or hidden behind code words and symbols, race has played and continues to play a central role in the U.S. party system. Since early in the country's history, foreign observers from Alexis de Tocqueville (1835) to Gunnar Myrdal (1944) have recognized the racial tension that has existed in the American populace. Race remains one of this country's political hot buttons. Because of this enduring racial tension, party elites have included race when determining which strategies to employ, which policies to adopt, and which constituencies to pursue. As a result, race has helped shape the existing party coalitions and has affected how the public perceives political parties.

In attempting to assemble winning electoral coalitions, parties must mobilize their supporters and simultaneously demobilize the supporters of their opponents. This task becomes easier when those constituencies can be placed in opposition to one another. One of the most effective and widely used tactics involves exploiting racial divisions in the American polity by racializing campaign rhetoric.[2] Injecting race into campaign communication has typically been manipulated for two purposes: (1) to attract blacks into a party's coalition or (2) to attract racially conservative whites in the South. Both of the major parties have used each of these tactics at different times (Walton 1975; Frymer 1999).

Early in American history, political parties learned that they could repeatedly exploit the competing interests of blacks and southern whites when seeking public office. First, the politics of the South is marred by racial conflict. As Key (1950) wrote,

In its grand outlines the politics of the South revolves around the position of the Negro. It is at times interpreted as a politics of cotton, as a politics of free trade, as a politics of agrarian poverty, or as a politics of planter and plutocrat. Although such interpretations have a superficial validity, in the last analysis the major peculiarities of southern politics go back to the Negro. Whatever phase of the southern political process one seeks to understand, sooner or later the trail of inquiry leads to the Negro. (5)

Second, with respect to their political behavior, blacks and southerners behave as distinct electoral blocs. In other words, African Americans and the South constitute two groups that have fairly cohesive voting patterns.[3] These two factors led to the development of the "southern strategy."[4]

---

2. While scholars have noted the need to define race and racial politics beyond the black-white paradigm (Marable 1995), race here denotes the divide between African Americans and whites. Race is confined to this narrow definition primarily because the black-white cleavage has remained distinct and persistent throughout the history of U.S. party politics. Its origins and maintenance are well documented, providing a good beginning point from which this type of analysis can be expanded in the future.

3. The origins of the cohesiveness between these two groups can be explained by the identification of a shared history within each group. For example, Key argues that the Civil War and Reconstruction brought unity among the Confederate states. Prior to the war, southern states exercised much more independence. Similarly, scholars such as Dawson (1994), Tate (1993), and McClerking (2001) argue that the political unity among African Americans is derived from exposure to institutions that reinforce the existence of a common history among African Americans.

4. O'Reilly (1995) defines the term *southern strategy* as "regionless code for 'white over black'" (8). This strategy is rooted in the assumption that electoral success depends largely on political elites' ability to frame elections in terms of black and white, pinning African

Yet leading scholars in the field of political science rarely acknowledge race's contribution to the formation and perpetuation of the American party system. For example, Schattschneider (1956) recounts the political histories of the early Democratic and Republican Parties but omits a discussion of race's role in the formation of the modern-day two-party system. He recognizes the importance of the business elite within the ranks of the Republican Party and even acknowledges the tension between the business community and the Solid South. He discusses the Republican Party's difficulties in establishing itself in the South and attributes those problems to the party's business faction. In actuality, the bigger contention was between the existence of African Americans in the Republican Party and the unwillingness of southern whites to coexist in a party with blacks.

Sundquist (1983) discusses the role of race in the realignment of the American party system during the slavery and civil rights movement periods. Sundquist's treatment of race falls short in that he ignores the role of race between these two eras and from the aftermath of the civil rights movement to the present. Similarly, Milkis (1999) "probe[s] the philosophical and historical roots of America's struggle to create democracy on a grand scale" (8) but almost completely ignores African Americans' political struggle. He discusses race only briefly and superficially in a section on slavery and the civil rights movement.

In an examination of the formation of political party systems in the United States, Burnham (1967) highlights the presence of three enduring cleavages. First, he discusses the clash between the South and the Northeast, arguing that "the more Americans of the New England and Southern subcultures came to learn about each others' social values and political goals, the more pronounced their hostility toward each other grew" (283). Second, he discusses the tension between "community" and "society" (283). A cleavage that fell along regional lines, the battle between community and society essentially constituted a conflict between the working class and the business elites. Finally, Burnham acknowledges an ethnic-cultural conflict, but he restricts his discussion to European immigrants. Like others, Burnham does not

---

American interests and the interests of whites in opposition to one another (10). This definition is consistent with that of Aistrup and others who define the southern strategy in terms of a Republican strategy utilized in the past four decades "to transform the Republicans' reputation as the party of Lincoln, Yankees, and carpetbaggers into the party that protects white interests" (1996, 8).

discuss the conflict between blacks and white liberals and racial conservatives primarily in the South.

In sum, with the exception of Key, most seminal works on political parties in the U.S. context ignore or minimize the role of race in the formation of the political system. Scholars who do acknowledge the role of race center their discussions on key historical moments such as slavery, Reconstruction, and the civil rights movement, arguing (incorrectly) that race was not an issue in the eras before, after, and/or between these time periods.

In actuality, the history of what contemporary scholars call the "southern strategy" of electoral politics can be traced back to the founding of the Republican Party in 1854. Walton (1975) describes political parties as

> electoral devices which must appeal to the general electorate for the right to administer the government of the state. Before a political party can gain control of the government, it must, through numerous appeals, form a coalition of voters from as many sectors of the population as possible. (1)

In 1854, the Republican Party had begun seeking new groups to incorporate into its electoral coalition. Because many of the new Republicans were antislavery advocates who had already received black support as part of the Liberty and Free Soldiers Party, "an appeal to the Free Blacks who could vote, was a natural way to enlarge the ranks of the party" (Walton 1975, 4).

During Reconstruction (from about 1868 to 1876), blacks achieved many political successes within the ranks of the Republican Party. For example, during its 1884 convention, the party appointed John R. Lynch, a black state legislator from Mississippi, as the convention's temporary chair (Gurin, Hatchett, and Jackson 1989, 21). Moreover, 13 percent of the 1892 Republican National Convention's delegates were black (Gurin, Hatchett, and Jackson 1989, 21). As Republicans, African Americans "went to the Senate and the House of Representatives, to governors' mansions, courts, state departments of education, and ambassadorial posts, to aldermen, judgeships, and to numerous positions of power throughout the South and the North" (Walton 1972, 87). During this period, Gurin, Hatchett, and Jackson (1989) argue, black political incorporation into the Republican Party reached levels unmatched by either party until the 1960s (21).

The relationship between blacks and the Republican Party began to deteriorate as a result of the Compromise of 1877, which enabled Republican Rutherford B. Hayes to assume the presidency after a dispute between southern Democrats and northern Republicans over contested votes from Louisiana, South Carolina, Florida, and Oregon. In exchange for the withdrawal of federal troops from the South, the Democratic Party conceded the election (Gurin, Hatchett, and Jackson 1989, 21–22).

Walton (1972) argues that the election of 1876 signaled to Republican leaders that the party needed to integrate southern whites into the GOP's ranks (89). Prior to the end of Reconstruction, the South was overwhelmingly Democratic. Without the presence of federal troops overseeing southern political institutions, including elections, the southern states adopted instruments to disenfranchise blacks, thereby depriving the Republican Party of its black constituents and leaving it politically impotent in the region (Key 1950). Consequently, Walton (1972) notes, the Republican Party made a concerted effort in subsequent presidential elections to pursue policies that would attract southern white voters. Many of these policies, however, came at the expense of black Republicans (88). For example, several black Republicans in leadership positions were forced to vacate their posts and were replaced by whites (Walton 1972, 90).

Yet the South remained very resistant to the Republican Party. First, southern whites still regarded it as the party of blacks. Second, Key adds, two-party competition would have diluted the South's electoral strength and thus its dominance of national politics. Key (1950) argues that the South's solidarity was necessary so that "the largest possible bloc could be mobilized to resist any national move toward interference with southern authority to deal with the race question as was desired locally" (8–9). To maintain the status quo, many southern states adopted suffrage restrictions. Although the Fifteenth Amendment to the U.S. Constitution prohibited the denial of franchise on the basis of color, Democrats in the South found ways around the amendment by complicating voting procedures so that people with little to no education found it difficult to cast ballots. Instruments such as the Australian ballot, literacy tests, and multiple box laws disenfranchised between 8 and 18 percent of whites and between 39 and 61 percent of blacks in the South (Kousser 1974, 55). Other tools of disenfranchisement included the poll tax and the white primary. By restricting suffrage, southern Democrats not only controlled opposition from the Populist and Republican Parties but also prohibited blacks from gaining political power.[5]

While the South was resisting building a relationship with the Republican Party, African Americans sustained their relationship with the GOP for a number of reasons. First, many blacks still felt a loyalty toward the party of Lincoln. Second, a small but influential number of black politicians were still drawn to party positions and federal jobs. Most importantly, however, was the fact that blacks really had no place else to go (Sherman 1973, 2). Political independence was ruled out as an option because "not many were willing to follow a course that seemed so uncertain in leadership and unpromising in results" (Sherman 1973, 3). Because of its "white supremacy principles and policies as well as the violent actions and terrorism," the Democratic Party remained an unattractive alternative (Walton 1975, 39). Thus, blacks had no option but to remain loyal to a "political organization that was increasingly uninterested in their welfare and that took their support largely for granted" (Sherman 1973, 3).

But blacks' steadfast allegiance to the Republican Party collided with the pursuit of southern white Republicans and the purging of the Republican Party of blacks. This led to a polarization within the Republican Party ranks between lily-white Republicans and black-and-tan Republican factions (Walton 1975; Gurin, Hatchett, and Jackson 1989). Lily-white Republicanism was an attempt to make the Republican Party more appealing to the South (Key 1950). The term *lily-white* referred not only to the faction's racial composition but also to its philosophy of white supremacy and racial segregation (Walton 1975, 45). Black-and-tans have been described as "satellite black political organizations [attempting] to operate as Republican organs at the local level [to] gain recognition and acceptance by the national Republican party" (Gurin, Hatchett, and Jackson 1989, 24). These organizations fought for African American political equality and unlike lily-white Republicans did not endorse segregation (Walton 1975, 45–46).

For years, these factions competed with each other for Republican Party recognition and patronage, but the black-and-tan factions eventually could no longer survive. "Lack of motivation and a variety of set-

5. For a more in-depth discussion of voting restrictions and their effects, see Kousser 1974; Key 1950.

backs" caused some groups to dissolve (Walton 1975, 139). Black-and-tan Republicans also faced aggressive opposition from lily-white factions. In North Carolina and Alabama, for example, black Republicans were prohibited from attending Republican conventions (Woodward 1951). According to Gurin, Hatchett, and Jackson, a few black-and-tan factions existed in Texas and Louisiana until the 1920s, but most disappeared after Reconstruction, when most blacks were disenfranchised (Gurin, Hatchett, and Jackson 1989, 24). After disenfranchisement, black-and-tans relied on presidential elections and national conventions for state patronage (Walton 1975, 140). President Herbert Hoover and others' sustained support for lily-white Republicanism killed the black-and-tan Republican factions (Walton 1972, 93).

Contrary to the observations of many analysts and scholars, blacks did not move from the Republican Party to the Democratic Party en masse. The shift to the Democratic Party began at the local level, both in the North and in the South. As early as 1876, southern blacks reportedly supported Democratic candidates and independent Democratic movements. Furthermore, between 1890 and 1915, several southern black Democrats were elected to local offices (Walton 1972, 103). In the North, small black Democratic organizations existed as early as 1868 (Walton 1972, 104). Walton (1972) notes, however, that although blacks supported the Democratic Party at the local and even state levels, they generally continued to vote Republican at the national level (105).

The shift toward the Democratic Party at the national level began around 1900. Two movements, the Negro National Democratic League and the Niagara Movement, endorsed Democratic presidential nominee William Jennings Bryan (Walton 1972, 111–12). Groups of northern and southern blacks later organized Democratic clubs to support Woodrow Wilson in the 1912 presidential election (Walton 1972, 112). Nevertheless, "just as Lincoln and the Emancipation Proclamation cemented blacks to the Republican party, so Roosevelt and the New Deal became the forces that finally cemented blacks to the Democratic party" (Walton 1972, 116).

Scholars differ on how well blacks fared under the Roosevelt administration. Bunche (1939) argued that the New Deal fell "far short of meeting adequately the minimal needs of the Negro" (3). While the agencies created to eradicate the effects of the depression only modestly helped blacks, FDR created a "black cabinet"—a group of black policy advisers assembled to aid in the creation of programs aimed at the black community. Roosevelt also issued Executive Order 8802, establishing the Fair Employment Practice Commission and banning government contractors from racial discrimination (Walton 1972, 116). But Weiss (1983) argues that the black cabinet had little policy impact (139). Moreover, FDR refused to commit to racial justice issues. Because of the potential political fallout that would be connected with interfering with states' rights and the "southern way of life," Roosevelt did little in the way of antilynching legislation (Weiss 1983, 119). In fact, the Roosevelt administration failed to enact any civil rights legislation even though more than 150 bills were introduced during Roosevelt's tenure as president (Tate 1993, 51). Nevertheless, Weiss (1983) contends that "meager though the Negro's share may have been, it came in the form of tangible benefits that touched the lives of millions of black Americans" (298).

In any event, the New Deal marked the beginning of the formation of a new electoral coalition for the Democratic Party. Still in the coalition was the Solid South: according to Lamis (1999), "Within the southern one-party system, pro-New Deal and anti-New Deal factions emerged, but both sides were firmly wedded to the Democratic party and what it stood for in racial terms" (399). The New Deal coalition also consisted of whites in larger cities, labor, and African Americans in the North. The incorporation of African Americans proved especially important during the 1944 presidential election, when blacks provided Roosevelt's margin of victory in Pennsylvania, Maryland, Michigan, Missouri, New York, Illinois, and New Jersey (Gurin, Hatchett, and Jackson 1989, 36).

FDR's death raised the question of whether black support for the Democratic Party was candidate-specific or would endure through other administrations. At this point, blacks' alliance with the Democratic Party was economically related rather than characterized by "any new Negro devotion to the Democratic Party" (Bunche 1939, 10). Scholars agree that Truman's commitment to civil rights in conjunction with the legacy of Roosevelt's economic policies kept blacks loyal to the Democratic Party, at least until 1956 (see Walton 1972; Gurin, Hatchett, and Jackson 1989). This phenomenon, coupled with growing dissatisfaction with the Republican Party's pursuit of southern white support, resulted in the African American allegiance to the Democratic Party that typifies contemporary partisan coalitions

(Bunche 1939). Nevertheless, in 1948, African Americans again played a critical role in electing a Democrat to the presidency (Gurin, Hatchett, and Jackson 1989).

For a brief period between 1956 and 1960, blacks defected, although not overwhelmingly, to the Republican Party in support of Eisenhower. The decision to support Eisenhower likely resulted from his enforcement of school desegregation. By 1964, however, blacks returned to the Democratic Party in full force "when it became clear to the nation that the Democrats would support black interests and civil rights more than the Republican party" (Dawson 1994, 106).

This transition upset the Democratic Party's white southern constituents. For example, Aistrup (1996) describes the Dixiecrat revolt led by South Carolina governor Strom Thurmond, who ran for president in 1948. Thurmond had considerable success in four southern states, and according to Aistrup (1996),

> [t]his event was significant for two reasons. First, it was the initial split between Northerners and Southerners within the Democratic party over the issue of race. Second, it was a harbinger of increasing numbers of Southern white voters supporting non-Democratic candidates for president. (6)

Throughout the 1950s, however, southerners found it difficult to disconnect the Republican Party from its image as the party of Lincoln. Republican president Dwight Eisenhower and a Republican-dominated U.S. Supreme Court supported, even if reluctantly, the fight against school segregation. Aistrup (1996) argues, however, that the Republican Party eventually reshaped its image among southern voters by welcoming "segregationist candidates under their party umbrella" (6). Arguably, however, the proverbial straw that broke the camel's back was a southern Democratic president's ardent support for civil rights reforms. Even as he signed the 1964 Civil Rights Act, however, Lyndon Johnson said that the Democratic Party had "just lost the South for a generation" (Walton and Smith 2000, 206).

Nixon sought to exploit the strained relationship between southern whites and the Democratic Party for electoral gain in the 1960 presidential election. Specifically, Nixon "hoped to woo Southern support so ardently that there might once again develop a solid political South—but this time committed as firmly to the Republican party as it once had been to the Democratic Party" (Murphy and Gulliver 1971,

3). In his pursuit, Nixon devoted much of his resources to educating the American public about the Democratic Party's "love for and infatuation with blacks" (O'Reilly 1995, 285). Nixon essentially sought to categorize the Democratic Party as the party of blacks, much as his own party had been labeled a hundred years earlier.

Although Nixon did not win the 1960 presidential election, his strategy inspired a transformation of the Republican Party at the national level. The Republican National Committee began more openly to support segregationist candidates and to promote states' rights and racially conservative policies. By 1964, Barry Goldwater's presidential candidacy solidified the Republican Party's new image as the party of the South (Aistrup 1996). Goldwater did not win, but his candidacy marked the first time in decades that five southern states had voted for a Republican presidential candidate (Bullock and Rozell 1998).

After his defeat in the 1960 presidential election and a subsequent defeat in the 1962 California gubernatorial election, Nixon took a brief hiatus from politics. He reentered the political arena in 1968, winning the Republican Party's presidential nomination (Kalk 2001). Nixon resurrected the southern strategy: scholars agree that the "bargain of Atlanta" sealed the relationship between Nixon and the South (O'Reilly 1995; Aistrup 1996; Kalk 2001). The agreement resulted from a May 31, 1968, meeting among Nixon, Thurmond, and a number of other southern leaders. As Kalk (2001) explains,

> Nixon met with southern state GOP chairmen upon his arrival. The following day, the candidate spoke with Thurmond and [Texas Senator John] Tower. In return for the group's support for the Republican nomination, the former vice president made several specific promises. For one, he pledged to stop the accelerating federal commitment to racial integration by easing pressure on southern school boards and discouraging plans to bus students in order to achieve racial balance. Second, Nixon promised to nominate conservative "strict constructionists" to the Supreme Court. A Nixon administration would regularly consult southern GOP leaders, the candidate further pledged, which gave Senator Thurmond the distinct impression that there would be a "southern veto" over White House policies that affected the section. (82)

Although the third-party candidate, Alabama governor George C. Wallace, minimized Nixon's margin of victory, the Republican won the 1968 presidential election. Nixon received 32 percent of the southern vote and carried five southern states—Florida, North Carolina, Tennessee, Virginia, and South Carolina (Scher 1997).

Once in office, Nixon kept his campaign promises. Although he had no control over the legislation enacted under the Johnson administration or past Supreme Court rulings, he did control the implementation of civil rights legislation and future judicial rulings. Using the Justice Department, Nixon delayed the enforcement of school desegregation and even introduced a "freedom of choice" amendment to the Constitution that would have allowed students to remain in local schools and would have prevented children from being bused to schools outside of their neighborhoods (Kalk 2001, 90).

Nixon's implementation of the southern strategy while in office proved successful; in the 1972 presidential election, Nixon won every southern state by an overwhelming majority, receiving more than 70 percent of the vote in Florida, Alabama, Georgia, Mississippi, and South Carolina and more than 60 percent of the vote in Texas and Louisiana (Kalk 2001). Nixon had accomplished his goal, creating a solid political South aligned with the Republican Party.

But the alliance Nixon created temporarily broke apart during the 1976 presidential election, when the South returned to the Democratic Party as a consequence of the combination of the Watergate scandal and the presence of Jimmy Carter, the first presidential candidate from the Deep South in more than a century (Bullock and Rozell 1998). Carter won all of the southern states except Virginia. At the same time, however, the African American votes garnered by Carter "proved to be the margin of victory in twelve states" (O'Reilly 1995, 336). This balance between southern whites and blacks in both the North and South resulted partly from Carter's refusal to exploit the division between these two groups to the same extent that his predecessors had (O'Reilly 1995).

Carter's balancing act toppled during the 1980 election, when his opponent, Republican nominee Ronald Reagan, resurrected the southern strategy. In a campaign speech at the Neshoba County Fair in Philadelphia, Mississippi, Reagan announced, "I believe in states' rights." As O'Reilly (1995) notes, "The men who murdered Schwerner, Chaney, and Goodman sixteen summers earlier believed in states' rights, too, and there was no mistaking Reagan's intent"

(350).[6] Reagan's campaign speeches also featured stories about "strapping young bucks," a term previously used to describe black males at slave auctions, "who used food stamps to purchase T-bone steaks and booze or cigarettes" (O'Reilly 1995, 351).

Like Nixon and others, Reagan successfully used the southern strategy. Scher (1997) contends that

> Southerners loved the 1980 Republican nominee, conservative Ronald Reagan, former governor of California. The verities he espoused and homilies he gave were dear to the hearts of southern traditionalists: strong families, simple religious fundamentalism, . . . old fashioned patriotism, a powerful military, a hard-line anti-communist foreign policy, conservative economic policies, and maintenance of traditional social institutions and roles. To the new middle-class white southerner and the transplanted white-collar northerner or midwesterner now living in a new southern city or suburb, he promised relief, an end to inflation and budget deficits, and policies geared to help them. For southern blue-collar industrial workers and farmers, he promised an "America first" policy and better times ahead. (108–9)

Reagan's use of such racial code words as *states' rights* and *strapping young bucks* was enough to win back the South. While Carter won 95 percent of the southern black vote, he garnered only 41 percent of the overall vote in the region. In contrast, Reagan won 51 percent of the popular vote and won every state in the Deep South except for Georgia, Carter's home state (Gurin, Hatchett, and Jackson 1989, 51).

But Reagan's southern strategy reached beyond the South. By the 1980s, the entire white working and middle classes had shifted their allegiances to the Republican Party (O'Reilly 1995, 361). Perpetuated by Reagan and later by George H. W. Bush, the modern-day southern strategy extended past the Mason-Dixon Line to appeal to northern voters burdened by having to support "welfare queens" and "street criminals" with their hard-earned tax dollars (O'Reilly 1995). In fact, the Reagan rhetoric surrounding tax issues became as racialized as the

---

6. Michael Schwerner, James Chaney, and Andrew Goodman were civil rights workers who were murdered by the Ku Klux Klan in Philadelphia, Mississippi, during the summer of 1964.

debate over school desegregation and affirmative action (Edsall and Edsall 1991). This strategy sought to exploit racial divisions among working- and middle-class whites who had previously been loyal to the Democratic Party. Among these groups of whites, racial interests displaced economic interests. The Reagan Democrats no longer saw their economic position as a reason to politically coalesce with blacks. Rather, their position put them in direct competition with African Americans (O'Reilly 1995, 365–66). By the end of his two terms in office, Reagan was extremely popular among whites. The majority of blacks, however, believed Reagan was a racist (Carter 1996, 68).

The best illustration of the Reagan race strategy occurred during the campaign of his successor, George H. W. Bush, in his 1988 campaign against Massachusetts governor Michael Dukakis. During this campaign, Republican strategists devised the Willie Horton ad. William J. Horton Jr. was convicted of first-degree murder in 1974. While released as part of the Massachusetts' criminal furlough program in 1987, Horton kidnapped Clifford Barnes and his fiancée, Angela Miller, and assaulted Barnes and raped Miller. The Bush campaign convinced the American electorate that Dukakis bore the blame for Horton's crime rampage (O'Reilly 1995; Kinder and Sanders 1996; Mendelberg 2001). Bush subsequently won the election by a landslide, in part because of this strategy (Kinder and Sanders 1996; Mendelberg 2001).

Ironically, the Republican Party did not completely abandon any hope of getting at least a fraction of the black vote. In fact, after the 1988 presidential election, Lee Atwater, Republican strategist and mastermind behind the Willie Horton ad, stated that "[a]ny Republican who can capture 20 percent of the black vote, while holding the GOP base, won't even have to campaign in 1992: The election will be his" (O'Reilly 1995, 389).

Even before Atwater, Republican strategists had recognized the benefits of breaking up the black bloc vote and thereby cutting into the Democratic Party's margin of victory. In 1977, while serving as chair of the Republican National Committee, Bill Brock hired African American political consulting firm Wright-McNeill and Associates to develop an outreach plan to attract blacks to the Republican Party. The resulting strategy was "to change the party's negative image while leaving its basic philosophy intact" (Robinson 1982, 220). Brock expended substantial resources on recruiting and funding black candidates, helping white candidates become more appealing to minorities and otherwise generally reshaping the party's image (Robinson 1982, 230). As a result, many blacks supported state and local Republican candidates in the 1980 elections. At the national level, however, Reagan's conservative platform discounted him among blacks as a viable alternative to Carter—95 percent of African Americans voted for Carter (Gurin, Hatchett, and Jackson 1989, 51).

After the 1988 presidential election, the Republican Party again attempted to break apart the black voting bloc. Bush appointed Atwater as chair of the Republican National Committee, and in this role, Atwater sought to double the percentage of blacks voting for Bush from 10 to 20 percent by attracting black middle-class voters. Atwater believed that the growing U.S. black middle class was "good for [the Republican Party], the party of the middle class. [The GOP is] looking to attract the baby-boom blacks, the more educated, more open-minded blacks" (O'Reilly 1995, 389). As part of this strategy, Atwater got himself appointed to Howard University's board of trustees, but he was forced to resign when the school's students took over the administration building in protest (O'Reilly 1995). The Howard University example was prophetic—Bush failed to increase his support among black voters, even those who self-identified as conservatives (Bolce, DeMaio, and Muzzio 1993). Nevertheless, these two attempts to attract black voters provided the precedent for a subsequent strategy that will be discussed later.

Bill Clinton was arguably the presidential candidate most skilled at simultaneously pursuing white voters in the Deep South and maintaining the black vote. Clinton visited black churches and other black venues as well as white middle America, where he promised welfare reform and touted himself as a new type of Democrat who was tough on crime. In both the 1992 and 1996 elections, Clinton won six of the twelve southern states while benefiting from more than 80 percent of the black vote (Walton and Smith 2003, 160).

Enacting the Southern Strategy

In pursuing the southern strategy—or any strategy, for that matter—many tactics may be used to attract and maintain constituencies, including proposed legislation, executive and legislative appointments, and executive orders. But parties and their candidates do not always have these tools at their disposal. Moreover, the resulting public debate surrounding the use of these tools may confuse the electorate—multiple and sometimes competing interests are often involved. An easier and more simplistic way to convey messages to the electorate is through a more symbolic form of communication. As Popkin (1994) explains, "To communicate their opinions rapidly, candidates and their strategists search for concrete symbols that serve as information short-cuts, as cognitive placeholders and focal points, to their position on larger abstract problems" (102). Similarly, Elder and Cobb (1983) argue that symbols "represent the focal objects of political attitudes and opinions and serve to define the procedural and substantive concerns of government" (9).

In addition to being efficient, symbolic communication serves another important function. If political elites try to signal change by waffling on policy positions, they will "confuse supporters, divide the party base, and make a candidate look like an unprincipled opportunist—and politicians who flip-flop on issues are among the most popular targets of attack in American politics" (Popkin 1994, 107). The use of symbolic communication enables political actors to avoid such criticism by allowing them to maintain their traditional policy positions and ideologies. At the same time, they can use symbols that convey ideals and information that can signal change without changing their core.

Over the years, political parties, strategists, and candidates have developed creative means of symbolic communication. One of the most prominent methods of communicating is through the personal endorsement. Election after election, candidates and parties seek out recognizable figures to associate with the electoral enterprise. This type of communication takes its form in the presence of a supporting cast of speakers and entertainers at political conventions, at rallies, or on the campaign trail. Through this form of communication, voters can judge political candidates and parties by the company they keep and do not keep. In other words, the images associated with a party convey to citizens information about what the party stands for.

Though often very subtle, this form of communication resonates strongly with the electorate and can have both positive and negative consequences, sometimes unintended. For example, Presidents Grover Cleveland and Theodore Roosevelt caught political heat from white constituents for having dinner with African Americans. In response, "Cleveland denied it and Roosevelt, who invited Booker T. Washington to the White House for dinner, promised never to do it again"

(Walton and Smith 2000, 204). In spite of his apology, Roosevelt was called "the worst enemy of his race of any white man who has ever occupied so high a place in this republic" (Woodward 1951, 465).

Jimmy Carter gained support from black voters by aligning himself with several prominent black leaders, including Atlanta mayor Andrew Young and Martin Luther King Sr. These leaders helped Carter disseminate information to black voters about his commitment to civil rights. For example, Carter relied on black leaders to convey to black voters that if elected governor, he would hang a picture of Martin Luther King Jr. in the Georgia Capitol (Popkin 1994, 160). As Popkin (1994) argues, "This two-step media flow of information mediated by reliable elites provided effective cues to black communities throughout the country" (160).

Ronald Reagan's pursuit of a southern strategy began well before he ran for president in 1980. In 1964, Reagan was a vocal supporter of Senator Barry Goldwater's presidential candidacy (Popkin 1994, 167). As a result, Reagan built a foundation of Republican supporters seeking a more conservative leader who would oppose many of the policies adopted under the New Deal (Popkin 1994, 167). This early association with Goldwater helped legitimize Reagan as a conservative who would protect working Americans from having their tax dollars filtered into government-funded social programs.

Democratic president Bill Clinton provides the most clever and multifaceted example of this strategy. For example,

> Other than appearances in black churches . . . and a spot on Arsenio Hall's television show, where he was cool enough . . . to play sax in shades, Clinton emphasized race as a nonissue from the primaries forward. He kept black advisers in the background, made no promises, accepted the nomination at a Democratic National Convention that had two hundred fewer black delegates than in 1988, and timed his rare appearances at black events so that they would be too late for the evening news or overshadowed by other events. (O'Reilly 1995, 409–10)

To further distance himself from African Americans—at least in the eyes of non–African Americans[7]—Clinton posed for several pho-

---

7. Bill Clinton was one of the most popular presidents among African Americans. Author Toni Morrison, in an essay printed in the *New Yorker,* even referred to him as the first black American president.

tographs with Georgia senator Sam Nunn at the Stone Mountain Correctional facility. The photographs, taken during the height of the 1992 presidential primary season, featured a backdrop of several black convicts. Political analysts posited that this photo op was part of a preemptive strike against any Michael Dukakis/Willie Horton–like attacks (O'Reilly 1995).

Finally, the 2000 presidential candidacy of Al Gore illustrates the importance of striking a balance between pursuing the support of blacks and pursuing the support of southern whites. Like Clinton, Gore courted the black vote by attending African American churches and appearing at other black events. Gore did so, however, at the expense of southern voters. Not only did the George W. Bush camp outspend Gore in terms of television adverting money in the South, the Republican Party's presidential and vice presidential candidates spent more time making personal appearances in southern states (Shaw 2006). Consequently, Gore lost every southern state, including his home state of Tennessee. Failure to court the southern states was one of the factors contributing to his defeat. Another factor—the Republican Party's ability to strike a balance between attracting southern white voters and black voters—will be discussed later in this chapter.

The 2000 Republican National Convention: Rethinking the Southern Strategy

The southern strategy, which proved convenient and easy to employ in the past, has become increasingly difficult to sustain. With the changing times, the expression of racially conservative attitudes has become politically incorrect. As Mendelberg (2001) explains, "White Americans recognize that it is no longer acceptable to seem like a racist, not for elites or for citizens. . . . Most people want to avoid not only the public perception that they are racist, but also thinking of themselves as racist" (7). At one point, political elites modified their strategies and utilized more subtle tactics to exploit the division between blacks and racially conservative whites. By color-coding the victims and villains associated with seemingly nonracial public policies such as welfare (Gilens 1999), taxes (Edsall and Edsall 1991), and crime (Valentino 1999; Mendelberg 2001), political elites have evoked racial attitudes and polarized the electorate.

But, Mendelberg (2001) argues, political elites are constrained. Racial symbols must be disguised to give a prima facie appearance of equality and fairness. If their intent to evoke negative racial stereotypes is made explicit, thereby violating the norm of equality, elites risk alienating voters (8). This is true for the Republican and Democratic Parties, both of which have previously played the race card.

For the modern-day Republican Party, the challenge has been to continue to appeal to racial conservatives without appearing overtly racist by tapping into political supporters' latent fears and resentment without appearing to do so. The GOP has done so by relying on racial code words and images to maintain and increase its white electoral base (Frymer 1999). Campaign strategies such as the 1988 Willie Horton ad appeared to have struck this balance. But while evidence suggests that using implicit racial appeals succeeded in the short run, Democratic and African American leaders uncovered the strategy, possibly costing Republicans part of their more liberal electoral base in the long run. For example, while its conservative stance on race over the past forty years solidified the South into the Republican winning electoral coalition, this conservatism "turned away many in the party's longtime traditional base of support"—that is, moderate and liberal Republicans in the northern states (Speel 1998, 205). As Speel explains, the realignment of the northern states "was caused in large part by disaffection with the increased conservatism and increased role of the South in the Republican party, and possibly less by any great attraction to Democratic policies and presidential candidates. For that reason, many voters in traditionally moderate and liberal Republican areas may be voting regularly for Democratic presidential candidates without feeling any strong attachments to the [Democratic] party" (199). Nevertheless, Speel explains that "by 1992, enough moderate and liberal Republicans were abandoning the party to hand Bush the first defeat for an incumbent Republican president since 1928" (205).

Bill Clinton's success in contrast to the relative unpopularity of his opponents—George H. W. Bush in 1992 and Bob Dole in 1996—left the Republican Party searching for a new strategy. The Republican Party had to attract enough new voters to form a winning coalition without alienating its current constituents. Doing so meant proving to voters that the Republican Party was no longer racially insensitive, even though it still maintained its conservative policy positions. The solution: add a new face to the race card. Instead of trying to evoke negative racial stereotypes, the Republican Party had to appeal to feelings of racial egalitarianism. In other words, the Republican Party had to reframe its activities to portray the party as racially inclusive and diverse. This party was the same on the inside but now had a new face.

An ideal setting for deploying this strategy was the 2000 Republican National Convention. The presence of religious conservatives at the 1992 convention and the Religious Right's alleged influence on that year's platform alienated many moderate and liberal voters. "Coupled with uncompromising speeches by Pat Robertson . . . and by Marilyn Quayle . . . the story line that emerged from the 1992 convention was that the Republicans were angry, small-minded and exclusive" (Cannon, Dubose, and Reid 2003, 158). Although the Republican Party tried to soften its image by featuring Colin Powell and several minority politicians at the 1996 convention, many voters believed that Bob Dole and his party remained too rigid and insensitive.

In 2000, the Republican Party again attempted this strategy, but on a grander scale. Karl Rove, George W. Bush's chief political strategist, "was convinced that Bush's policy prescriptions, particularly on taxes, would do fine with the electorate, even though they were not popular with the press. But this would hold true only as long as voters didn't think of Bush and the Republican Party as harshly conservative" (Cannon, Dubose, and Reid 2003, 157–58). Thus, one of the prominent themes of the 2000 Republican National Convention was the party's inclusiveness and diversity. Although this thread ran throughout the 2000 election cycle, the message of inclusion was loudest during the convention. Republicans had

> a new determination to control things tightly, and a heightened appreciation for the purely symbolic nature of modern political conventions. With the media waiting to pounce on the Republicans for any sign of small-mindedness, intolerance or generally Neanderthal attitudes, the convention speakers had to have perfect pitch. The right demographics would help, too. (159–60)

To illustrate the implementation of this strategy, table 2 presents a comparison of Republican National Conventions since 1988. In general, the presence of African Americans was greatly increased in 2000. For example, the number of black convention delegates increased from 52 in 1996 to 85 in 2000. In addition, the 2000 Republican convention in Philadelphia featured a dramatic increase in the number of black speakers, including important appearances by Condoleezza Rice and Powell (Bositis 2000, 2). Moreover, the number of blacks featured during prime time increased greatly, from 4 in 1996 to 11 in 2000. In fact, more black speakers were featured on the first night of the 2000 convention than had appeared during all four days of the 1996 convention.

To add to the convention spectacle, the lineup featured a number of prominent entertainers, including recording artists Brian McKnight and Harold Melvin's Blue Notes, professional wrestler the Rock, and singer Chaka Kahn. In 2000, the Republican Party used images of African Americans to convey to the public that the party had become diverse and inclusive.

Almost as obvious as who was present at the convention was who was missing. Hidden from convention spectators were the more conservative actors in the Republican Party such as Pat Buchanan, who spoke during the 1996 convention, and former speaker of the house Newt Gingrich.

The Republicans made very few substantive changes to their positions on traditionally racial issues such as affirmative action or social spending but rather preserved their conservative policy platform. An examination of the prevalence of race and racial issues in the Republican platform from 1988 to 2000 shows that, overall, the Republican Party generally devoted between one and four paragraphs to issues such as diversity, racism, minority interests, and capital punishment. The number of paragraphs devoted to each of these issues remained constant over time—for example, two paragraphs on affirmative action in each of the four years. Two paragraphs were devoted to racism in 1988; from 1992 to 2000, however, the GOP devoted only one para-

TABLE 2.   African American Presence at Republican
National Conventions

	1988	1992	1996	2000
Delegates	61	107	52	85
	(2.7%)	(5.0%)	(2.6%)	(4.1%)
Speakers	10	11	10	18
	(9.7%)	(8.7%)	(7.4%)	(26.9%)
Musical entertainment	1	1		6
	(12.5%)	(10.0%)		(50.0%)

Source: Official Reports of the Proceedings of the 34th, 35th, and 36th Republican National Conventions; Republican National Committee; Joint Center for Political and Economic Studies; C-SPAN Archives.

graph to racism in each platform. A slight increase occurred in the number of paragraphs devoted to diversity, but this increase resulted in only four paragraphs devoted to this issue. Finally, the number of paragraphs devoted to capital punishment decreased from three in 1988 to one in 2000.

The Republican platform consistently devoted a relatively large number of paragraphs to crime, education, and welfare. Although the number of crime-related paragraphs decreased slightly after 1996, the Republican platform devoted an average of 16 paragraphs to crime. The Republican Party devoted an average of about 31 paragraphs to education, although this number declined steadily after 1998. Finally, the GOP devoted roughly 9 paragraphs to welfare. The number of paragraphs devoted to welfare peaked in 1996, after President Clinton signed the 1996 welfare reform bill. Even after the welfare system was reformed, the Republican Party devoted 9 paragraphs to welfare.

Table 3 summarizes the GOP's positions on explicitly racial issues from 1988 to 2000. In general, the platforms exhibited a great deal of consistency from year to year. For example, the 1996 Republican platform stated with respect to affirmative action,

> The sole source of equal opportunity for all is equality before the law. Therefore, we oppose discrimination based on sex, race, age, creed, or national origin and will vigorously enforce anti-discrimination statutes. We reject the distortion of those laws to cover sexual preference, and we endorse the Defense of Marriage Act to prevent states from being forced to recognize same-sex unions. Because we believe rights inhere in individuals, not in groups, we will attain our nation's goal of equal rights without quotas or other forms of preferential treatment. We scorn Bill Clinton's notion that any person should be denied a job, promotion, contract or a chance at higher education because of their race or gender. Instead, we endorse the Dole-Canady Equal Opportunity Act to end discrimination by the federal government. We likewise endorse this year's Proposition 209, the California Civil Rights Initiative, to restore to law the original meaning of civil rights. (Republican National Convention 1996)

Four years later, the GOP's affirmative action plank read,

> We believe rights inhere in individuals, not in groups. We will attain our nation's goal of equal opportunity without quotas or

other forms of preferential treatment. It is as simple as this: No one should be denied a job, promotion, contract, or chance at higher education because of their race or gender. Equal access, energetically offered, should guarantee every person a fair shot based on their potential and merit. (Republican National Convention 2000)

While not as elaborate as the 1996 statement, the 2000 platform contained the same basic premise—the Republican Party did not support quotas. Furthermore, the GOP used the language of civil rights to refer to the rights of the majority, not those of minorities, and sought to protect the majority (whites) from job or education discrimination. The same language appeared in 1988 and 1992.

With respect to diversity, the Republican Party platforms from 1988 to 2000 indicated that the party was proud of the American public's diversity and viewed it as a source of strength. The party's sole recommendation with respect to diversity, however, was to encourage institutions of higher learning to incorporate a multicultural approach through their presentations of arts and humanities. In all four years, the Republican Party denounced racism and in 1988 vowed to vigorously pursue cases of illegal discrimination.

The 1988 Republican platform boasted an increase in jobs for members of minority groups under the Reagan-Bush administration. The 1988 platform also pledged to increase minority business ownership, to devote considerable resources to increasing the number of minorities in institutions of higher learning, and to encourage and facilitate the adoption of minority children. Finally, the 1988 Republican platform invited minority participation in the party. In 1992, the only references to minorities involved opposition to including sexual preference under the heading "minority" and the continued support of minority businesses. The support for minority businesses was present in the 1996 platform but absent in the 2000 platform. In 2000, the GOP reextended its invitation to minorities to join the party and increased funding to the National Institutes of Health to further research on diseases that disproportionately affect minority populations.

Quite a bit of consistency also existed across the years in terms of the Republican platform on racialized issues.[8] The discussion of welfare

---

8. Racialized issues are those issues that were race-neutral at conception but that have become racialized through political rhetoric.

TABLE 3. Republican Platform on Racial Issues

	1988	1992	1996	2000
Diversity	• Is proud of diverse heritage of Americans • Supports diversity • Encourages educational institutions to emphasize diversity of Americans through arts and humanities	• Is proud of diverse heritage of Americans	• Is proud of diverse heritage of Americans	• Believes that the diversity of the nation is reflected in 2000 platform • Believes that diversity is a source of strength
Racism	• Denounces persons, organizations, publications, and movements that promote racism • Will vigorously pursue cases of illegal discrimination	• Denounces persons, organizations, publications, and movements that promote racism	• Denounces persons, organizations, publications, and movements that promote racism	• Denounces persons, organizations, publications, and movements that promote racism
Minorities	• Has increased minority jobs under Reagan-Bush administration • Invites minority participation in the party	• Will increase, strengthen and reinvigorate minority business development	• Supports minority small-business owners	• Invites minority participation in the party • Increased NIH budget to further research on diseases that disproportionately affect minority populations

| Affirmative action | • Will increase, strengthen, and reinvigorate minority business development
• Will encourage and facilitate the adoption of minority children
• Will devote resources to increasing the number of minorities in institutions of higher learning | • Opposes housing quotas
• Believes quotas are reverse discrimination | • Opposes housing quotas
• Believes quotas are reverse discrimination | • Opposes housing quotas
• Believes quotas are reverse discrimination | • Opposes housing quotas
• Believes quotas are reverse discrimination |

Source: Republican Party Platforms, 1988–2000.

was quite detailed in the Republican platforms. Overall, the Republican Party supported state and local control of welfare services. The assumptions underlying the Republican Party's position on welfare remained the same from 1988 to 2000. In general, the GOP supported personal responsibility and accountability and believed that the solutions to poverty were education and work. The Republican platforms indicated that the party believed that community and faith-based organizations should play a prominent role in delivering social services. Finally, the Republican platforms advocated two-parent households.

With respect to education, the Republican Party supported school choice. Beginning no later than 1988, the GOP advocated the creation of charter schools and a school voucher system. The Republican Party also continued to believe that the education system should be decentralized, with parents wielding primary control; communities and lower levels of government should "support and stimulate the parental role" (Republican National Convention 1988).

Of the other racialized issues examined, the Republican platforms were most extensive on crime. In general, the Republican platforms called for stiffer penalties for all crimes. The party supported the establishment of a federal death penalty and the use of capital punishment in drug trafficking cases. In all four years, the Republican Party supported tougher penalties for white-collar crimes and crimes against the elderly. In 1988 and 1992, the platforms focused on drug-related crimes and violent crimes in general. In 1996 and 2000, the focus shifted to juvenile crime. In both years, the Republican Party advocated that juveniles accused of felonies be tried as adults. By 2000, the platform increasingly emphasized combating terrorism and international crime.

In summary, from 1988 to 2000, the Republican platforms experienced very little change with respect to racial and racialized issues. First, little change occurred in the number of paragraphs devoted to these issues. Relative to other issues such as defense, racial and racialized issues did not constitute major agenda items for the Republican Party. Other than broad statements about the party's position on diversity, no policy initiatives addressed the GOP's plan to protect minority rights. Second, the Republican Party did not significantly alter its positions on race-related issues. When the platform included statements about the Republican Party's policy positions on racial issues such as affirmative action, the positions were consistent across all four convention years. Further, the additions to the GOP's platform on racial issues in 2000 represented a more detailed explanation of its extant positions. At no point did the Republican Party switch positions on these issues during the years examined. Concurrently, the number of African Americans present at the 2000 Republican National Convention increased. Convention observers questioned whether the increased visibility of African Americans represented a strategy aimed at attracting blacks and other minorities or an attempt to attract liberal/moderate white voters, and little evidence explains the precise motivation. Regardless of motivation for the change, examining the impact of the 2000 convention proves an intriguing task given the GOP's historical reputation and platform.

Conclusion

In the modern-day party system, political parties function primarily to simplify the electoral process for candidates and voters. A chief task in this endeavor is mobilizing voters and building winning coalitions. In performing this function, however, political parties have helped to drive a wedge between African Americans and southern whites, the U.S. electorate's two largest voting blocs. By playing the race card, parties have signaled to voters which party is racially conservative and which is racially liberal. Parties can often send these signals by supporting legislation that conveys this information. More often, however, parties use more symbolic communication. In the past, the use of racially coded images and words has polarized the electorate.

The chapters that follow explore whether racial images can be equally successful when they are not used to tap into negative racial stereotypes and prejudice. Specifically, I examine whether the use of positive racial imagery during the 2000 Republican National Convention reshaped the Republican Party's image with respect to race. In light of their race-related histories, both parties should encounter some difficulty in altering the way people perceive them, especially when it comes to striking a balance between blacks and southern whites.

3 Party Image over Time, Contemporary Party Images, and the Prospects for Change

> Attachments to partisan labels live long beyond events
> that gave them birth.
>
> —V. O. Key Jr., 1949

BASED ON THE HISTORICAL background provided in chapter 2, we know that both the Republican and Democratic Parties have engaged in a range of activities in an attempt to convey to the electorate on which side of the racial divide the parties have stood. From symbolic to legislative strategies, both parties have attempted to attract either African Americans or racially conservative whites. Neither party, however, has permanently stayed on one side of the fence. Teetering back and forth, the Democratic and Republican Parties have adjusted their strategies based on their electoral prospects at any given moment. In light of these historical activities, I now turn to examining how the parties' actions have manifested in people's perceptions.

First, I use the 1948–2002 American National Election Study (ANES) to gauge racial symbolism over time. Since 1952, the ANES has asked a set of open-ended questions designed to assess respondents' perceptions of political parties. I use these responses to ascertain whether individuals believed that a party had positive racial symbolism—that is, that the party was good for blacks and other minorities—or negative racial symbolism. (For a more detailed description of the data and methodology, see the appendix.) To bolster these findings, I also examine perceptions of the two parties on the issue of government aid to blacks and other minorities. This item is the only other question asked in repeated years in which respondents' had to assess the political parties along some racial dimension. Specifically, people were asked to place both parties on a scale from 1 to 7, where 1 was "government should help minorities" and 7 was "minorities should help them-selves." (See the appendix for exact question wording.)

Second, I examine contemporary party images using a series of qual-itative focus groups and interviews. Participants in the qualitative study were asked about the Democratic and Republican Parties in general and then asked specifically about the two parties' ability to handle issues related to race. (See the appendix for details about the qualita-tive study.) Like the open-ended questions asked by the ANES, the qualitative study allowed respondents to articulate in their own words their perceptions of the two parties. Unlike the survey questions, how-ever, the qualitative interviews and focus groups enabled me to follow up and probe responses in greater detail.

When attempting to reshape their images along a particular dimen-sion, parties will have more success when their existing reputation in that area is not particularly well established in the minds of the mem-bers of the electorate. Therefore, this chapter seeks to investigate the obstacles the two major parties must overcome when trying to reshape party images along the dimension of race. Specifically, I answer three questions: (1) Can people recognize differences between the two par-ties, especially when it comes to race? (2) How salient are these dis-tinctions relative to one another? (3) Do party images vary by race? I demonstrate that perceptions of party images move in predictable ways that correspond to historical events.

Party Images over Time

Figure 3 indicates that racial symbolism has not remained constant over time. The movement in racial symbolism, however, seems to match the historical data. For example, during the 1950s, people per-ceived both the Democratic and Republican Parties as racially liberal. Both parties had a positive racial symbolism. Perceptions of the Demo-cratic Party during this period probably reflected a carryover effect from the Roosevelt era, when blacks were first drawn into the New Deal coalition, and from Truman's commitment to a civil rights agenda. Also during this period, citizens witnessed a Republican-led Supreme Court declare school segregation unconstitutional and a (reluctant) Republican president dispatch the U.S. Army to enforce the Court's decision in Arkansas.

Throughout most of the 1960s, a clear distinction existed between the Democrats and the Republicans, with the Democrats perceived as

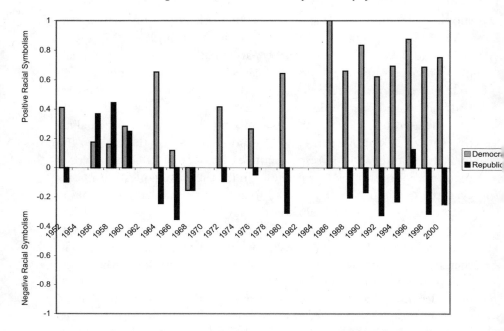

Fig. 3.   Perceived Democratic and Republican Party racial symbolism, 1952–2000. (Data from American National Election Study Cumulative File, 1948–2002).

more liberal on the issue of race. This perception was undoubtedly driven by Kennedy's and later Johnson's support of civil rights legislation and by Goldwater's presidential candidacy, in which he declared the Republican Party the party of racial conservatism. In 1968, however, the perceived racial symbolism of the Democratic Party was negative. Perhaps this was driven by the prominence of southern white Dixiecrats and their support for Alabama governor George Wallace.

During the 1970s and 1980s (with the exception of 1980), the racial symbolism of the two major parties was not marked as much by the Republican Party's racial conservatism as by the Democrats' racial liberalism. This phenomenon quite possibly resulted from cues sent by Democratic leaders. For example, during his tenure in office, Jimmy Carter "appointed a number of blacks to high-level positions in his administration and to the federal courts, supported affirmative action in the form of the *Bakke* case, and reorganized the civil rights enforcement bureaucracy" (Walton and Smith 2000, 207).

By 1988, a clear divergence appeared between the perceptions of racial symbolism in the Republican Party and the Democratic Party. Republicans were clearly perceived as racially conservative and the Democratic Party as racially liberal. Again, looking at signals sent by party leadership, we could reasonably infer that such actions as George H. W. Bush's veto of the 1990 Civil Rights Act drove perceptions of the Republican Party. At the same time, the Democratic Party's reputation for handling racial issues was reinforced by Bill Clinton, who scholars argue "is as free of racist and white supremacist thinking as any white person can be" (Walton and Smith 2000, 210).

I then examined the average placement of the two parties on a racial issue over time. Figure 4 presents the results. The perceptions of the Democratic and Republican Parties on race follow the same pattern. Throughout the thirty-year period, the Democratic Party was perceived to be more liberal than the Republican Party on the issue of government aid to minorities. While neither party, on average, lies at the extreme of the 7-point scale, each year features at least a 1-point difference between the parties. In some years, the size of the difference between the two parties doubled. In 1980, for example, the difference between the Democratic and Republican Parties increased to 1.9 points. This increase makes sense within the historical context. In addition to Carter portraying himself as a racial liberal, Reagan painted the Democratic Party as extremely racially liberal to establish himself as the candidate better able to represent average Americans' needs. Although the placement of the two parties leveled off after 1984, the Democratic Party was perceived as more liberal during the 1990s than it had been during the 1970s.

Figure 5 illustrates the average perceived difference between the two parties by race of the respondent. The figure was created by subtracting the Democratic Party's placement from the Republican Party's placement. Positive values indicate that the Republican Party was more conservative. With the exception of 1994, African Americans recognized a greater distance between the Democratic and Republican Parties on this issue. On average, blacks believed that the Republican Party was more conservative than the Democratic Party on race. Blacks' placement of the Democratic Party on government aid to minorities was almost identical to that of whites. The Republican Party, however, was perceived to be about 2 points more conservative than the Democratic Party, twice the difference perceived by whites. The gap between

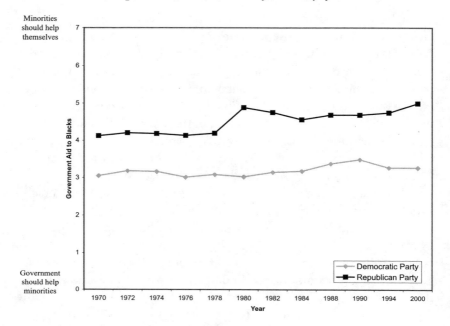

Fig. 4.   Perceived positions of Democratic and Republican Parties on government aid to blacks and other minorities, 1970–2000. (Data from American National Election Study Cumulative File, 1948–2002.)

blacks and whites narrowed in 1980 because whites placed the Republican Party as more conservative. The difference between blacks and whites also decreased throughout the late 1980s and 1990s. During this period, African Americans believed that the Democratic Party was more conservative than had been the case in previous years. At the same time, whites viewed the Republican Party as more conservative. Nevertheless, both blacks and whites placed the Republican Party to the right of the Democratic Party on race.

In sum, the data suggest that a distinction existed between the two parties on the issue of race. Beginning in the 1970s, the Democratic Party was perceived as the more racially liberal party. The gap between the two parties was even more pronounced in the minds of African Americans. In the next section, I further explore some of the reasons why citizens make these distinctions.

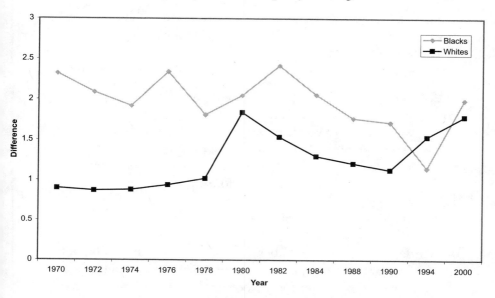

Fig. 5. Perceived difference between Republican and Democratic Parties on government aid to blacks and other minorities by race, 1970–2000. (Data from American National Election Study Cumulative File, 1948–2002.)

Contemporary Party Images

Of course, this analysis is purely speculative. There is no way to determine if individuals indeed based their judgments of the two parties' racial symbolism on historical events. It is possible to determine, however, what information has driven contemporary perceptions and what modern-day party images look like. As Lippmann (1922) argued, "[W]e cannot fully understand the acts of other people, until we know what they think they know, then in order to do justice we have to appraise not only the information which has been at their disposal, but the minds through which they have filtered it (57). Thus, in this section I use qualitative interviews and focus groups to investigate how people describe the two major parties and how these descriptions vary across race and party identification.

First, I examine African American perceptions of the Republican Party. When asked what came to mind when they thought of Republicans, African Americans responded overwhelmingly negatively. For example, several respondents described Republicans as inhumane:

R1: It's all about hav[ing] money and power, not looking at other people around you. It makes me think, How were you raised and what have you been exposed to? Have you gone out to the inner cities? Have you seen all the crap that minorities have to go through? Do you have colleagues that have expressed issues of discrimination? I mean, where do your values stand? And those are questions that I ask that make me think—okay—Republican—it's all about the money and less about the people.

R2: Democrats are more liberal . . . and more humane. Republicans are more tangible—emotions, feelings and all that are not that important for the bottom line of what they're going after—what they want to accomplish.

R3: [The Republicans] would rather have a stealth bomber rocket than help somebody help a school building.

Respondents also described the Republican Party as being "snobbish, fake," "tied to [racist] special interests [like] the Christian Right and the gun lobby . . . intolerant, rich," "the party of racists and bigots— either they're naive about race relations or they're prejudiced—they promote big business over [the interests] of the working class and their families." Thus, African Americans viewed the Republican Party as having negative (or racially conservative) racial symbolism.

These responses seem even more dramatic when compared with the descriptions of Democrats.

R2: [A hypothetical Democratic candidate] is more down to earth—someone who can talk and be comfortable around middle-class people—someone who can identify with people of lower incomes. I think of a Democrat as someone whose success was self-made and not born into. Not liberal but open-minded—and respectful of diversity—can embrace diversity and respect other opinions.

R4: [Democrats are] more accepting of new ideas—I think of Democrats as more interested in the arts and more willing to spend time and money on the arts and also education. I think of the stereotypical Democrat as being interested . . . in the general growth of the human being—and they focus on that more than money.

Most of the black respondents in my sample also better identified with the Democratic Party. As one respondent mused,

> R2: When I think of a Democratic candidate, I think of somebody that I can identify with whether they're black or white or whatever. It's somebody who's grown up in a similar background to mine or they can identify with my background— middle-class background, went to public school.

As suggested earlier, favorable evaluations of the Democratic Party were closely tied to the party's symbols, like its candidates and issue positions, which African Americans interpreted as being positive for blacks. One respondent equated the Democrats with Jesse Jackson, someone she thought would "be looking out for minorities in particular, [who would] stand up for injustice when it comes to unfair treatment especially when it comes to race, discrimination, things like that—more liberal, less conservative on issues like abortion, affirmative action definitely." Another respondent supported Al Gore in particular because "he supports affirmative action policies, particularly in higher education, employment, business contracting. So he's sensitive to those issues which are key to African Americans." Finally, one black female respondent noted,

> R5: There have been some things the Republican Party has done to benefit people [of color]. And I am from Kansas, a Republican state. But I still am a Democrat and I still believe [Al] Gore will do more things for the programs that I'm interested in. I'm interested in health care, community programs that empower our neighborhoods, and I'm definitely concerned about the number of black males in prison, and I'm concerned about the death sentence, and I'm concerned about a lot of things that have to do with the black community—I need to make myself clear—the things that are important to the black community are really important to America. I mean, there's nothing peculiar about wanting health care and education and good housing and not being forced to go to jail for

peculiar reasons just because of your color. I really think the black platform is an American platform.

Given the evaluations of the Republican Party, especially compared to those of the Democratic Party, I was interested to see how African Americans interpreted racialized campaign appeals and the prevalence of African Americans at the Republican convention. As could be expected, most of the reactions were negative. More specifically, the respondents indicated that the appeals seemed disingenuous.

R6: I'm not happy with what's going on. I'm not happy with the charade of the election. I'm not happy with the speeches I see on television. I'm not interested in this glitzy media profile. . . . As a matter of fact, I don't watch television because I'm not interested in the charade. When I saw all those racist displays and all those black people standing behind all those people at the Republican convention, I was sick. I'm not interested in the charade. I'm interested in what is the final result.

R4: I watched parts of the Democratic convention and the Republican convention before. I don't know, I just felt like so much of it was BS, like I couldn't stand watching it. Do you know what I mean? I felt like everything was about getting elected—I'm more interested in the people that come off as really caring, and I think that's what we're trying to get at with the whole Republican candidates—that they don't care as much. And I'd be more interested at this point to go online or read the paper to see what Gore has to say just because there's this intuitive sense that I get about him . . . he's somewhat sincere, and I really don't get that about [George W.] Bush, and I haven't gotten that about a whole lot of Republican candidates.

R3: I'm glad to see that both parties are trying to appear as if they're inclusive, but when the Republican Party does it, it comes across as bullshit. You know [Condoleezza Rice and Colin Powell] are only tokens—it's patronizing—if the Republicans were more inclusive, they would go and do it and not do this staging—go to Harlem, go to Compton—Republicans make it seem that by coming to the NAACP, they make it seem like he's doing us a favor. [Bush is] supposed to do that—that's your job as president. You're suppose to be accountable to all people—that's what you should be doing. Like Chris Rock said, people always want credit for stuff they're supposed to do—he gets no cool points for that.

Some respondents, however, had positive reactions to the Republican strategy. One black male replied that these appeals made him feel like the Republican Party had "finally decided to pay attention to me because my vote may count this election." When I asked if this meant that the respondent would consider voting for a Republican candidate, he replied,

> R7: I always consider voting for the GOP candidate and sometimes do, but not in an election where I am a targeted group—because I am a means to an end, not a person who [the candidate] will listen to after the election is over with. I'm just a way to get in office.

In another respondent's eyes,

> R8: It's actually a sign of progress in a certain way for the Republican Party. I think it's good that [George W. Bush] actually had black people on his team and that they are actually participants—I don't think it's all for show, like some people. But the thing is, it's going to take more than four or five black people to change the ideological slant of the Republican Party unless those guys can find some way to make the Republicans make some real policy changes that are acceptable to African Americans. If not, their show of diversity is just a show without much substance.

These quotes suggest that in the context of a campaign, Republican messages of diversity seem insincere. The last two quotes, however, may indicate that genuine movement on the part of the Republican Party to be more inclusive, without blatantly displaying it as an electoral strategy, may motivate African Americans to at least consider supporting the GOP. But the ability to change African Americans' perceptions of the racial symbolism associated with the Republican Party ultimately hinges on the party's willingness to make substantive rather than just cosmetic changes.

No matter how negatively or favorably the respondents evaluated the Republican Party, all those interviewed supported retired general Colin Powell.

> *R3:* If Colin Powell ran, I would strongly consider voting for him—Colin Powell's opinion on affirmative action is consistent with African Americans', but it's not consistent with the Republican Party—I think he's a good, decent man.
>
> *R6:* [We need] more Republicans like [Colin Powell]. If we had more Republicans that were open to being real human beings, I think [black] people would accept [the Republican Party] a little bit.

But Powell was not the only exception to the general sentiment toward the Republican Party. One respondent noted,

> *R4:* There are so many counterexamples that it's ridiculous. You know I'm looking at the governor of New Jersey . . . Christie Todd Whitman, she's a Republican. But she's done so much good for our state. You know, she's increased the budget of the arts and really worked on education and really gone to the cities that needed help and really tried to make a difference.

Again, this finding seems to suggest that African Americans recognize and will support Republican candidates who seem to exhibit the qualities that blacks value in Democrats. Republican candidates need not convert Democratic ideals in every respect, only on a few critical issues such as affirmative action.

The warm feelings that Powell generates within the African American community[1] raise another interesting possibility for where Republicans could gain support from black voters—if Powell (a black Republican) can make African Americans consider voting for a Republican candidate, so too should other black Republican candidates. Hence, I asked my respondents how they felt about black Republicans and if they would ever vote for a black Republican. One respondent really was not sure how to decipher black Republican candidates:

---

1. The evidence for this positive opinion not only appears in my data but also emerges in opinion polls. For example, in its 2000 National Opinion Poll, the Joint Center for Political and Economic Studies found that 70 percent of the black population gave Colin Powell a favorable rating (Bositis 2000b, 18).

R1: If it's a black Republican candidate, which is unusual, we have
to sit and question it because on one side they're black, so
obviously we should support them. But at the same time
they're Republican. So we're looking at it like, hmm . . .

While most of those interviewed did not rule out the possibility of
voting for a black Republican candidate, all indicated that it would
depend on the individual.

R2: Well we have some black people that really—they're so into
mainstream America, they don't care about blacks that are in
lower classes. They are actually trying to escape from them—
they're trying to run away from that—they don't even want to
associate themselves with that type of lifestyle—the lifestyle of
their cousins or whoever, you know what I'm saying. I don't
think that they're necessarily going to represent you well.
They might full well be Republican—you know there are
black Republicans. That doesn't mean that you're against
black people, but . . . it just depends on how the person grew
up, what values they've constructed through their different
situations that they've gone through in life and what it is that
they want to give back to their community or to society just
in general. And if they are not caring about, if they're more
for money.

Respondents commonly compared Powell—someone they perceived to be a good and decent Republican candidate—to J. C. Watts
and Clarence Thomas, whom the interviewees perceived as unsavory
Republican candidates.

R3: I think you have people like Colin Powell who are good people and whose heart is in the right place who you hope can
make a difference, but I don't think they will. And you have
people like J. C. Watts, who essentially have to go against
everything people stand for to be successful. Maybe he
believes that, but he's not serving the interests of black people. He's really a pawn for the Republicans.

In summary, then, African Americans have not completely dismissed
the Republican Party as a viable option. Changing blacks' perceptions
of the Republican Party's reputation for handling race-related issues,

however, is highly contingent on the party and its candidates addressing those issues important to the African American community. As one respondent stated,

> *R8:* A lot of interests of the Republican Party, blacks are on the other side—unless the Republican candidate can actually make some changes in the ideological platform that are of interest to blacks, they can't represent blacks.

As a result, it is highly unlikely that displaying the blacks in the party (or being a black Republican candidate) is enough to signal to African Americans that the Republican Party will best represent them.

The white respondents' descriptions of both parties provide an interesting contrast to blacks' evaluations of the two parties. When asked about the Republican Party, white respondents converged on the same few issues, including taxes, the military, and social spending. When asked to describe the GOP, one Republican respondent said that members of his party

> *R9:* think of the government more as a business, and they are more for the army, more military than the Democrats are. It seems like the Republicans have a stronger economy than the Democrats and they are more business oriented.

Another Republican respondent added,

> *R10:* I always think of Republicans as for personal accountability—you're your own person, you have your own business. The onus is on you. You pay a little in taxes for stuff we need, but pretty much they aren't going to baby you. It's on you.

In the same vein, a Democratic respondent agreed with the Republican Party's association with tax cuts but had a different take on the issue, pointing out that the Republicans are

> *R11:* usually telling you they're going to reduce the taxes, but it's really reducing the taxes for the rich people and reducing the taxes to big businesses as opposed to reducing my taxes.

Similarly, a white female in a different focus group believed that

> *R12:* Republicans like to give [taxes] to the little people. . . . They like to give the good tax rates to businesses and to the

wealthy people—so in a way they're giving taxes to the more average Americans—better tax breaks go to the wealthier, and I think that if they do give a new tax, it will be more targeted toward things that most of their constituents would not affect.

Respondents also described the Republican Party as "prolife," "elite," "conservative, businessmen," and "middle-aged white males." Finally, the Republican Party was associated with opposition to gun control:

R10: definitely the Republicans are more the NRA type. They don't really like people—laws and restrictions against them. The Democrats . . . definitely—would like to see more laws keeping [guns] away from the kids and stuff.

R13: I don't know if they'd rather see more laws but the laws that are there [enforced]. And the Republicans would rather—because the NRA has a lot of pull in Washington—so they would rather make them happy than think about what actually goes on in the world—I think the military is definitely Republican-leaning. Gun manufacturers and all sorts of things like that are definitely Republican-leaning. And it kind of goes to push the Republican platform to more aggressive behavior. I just see the Democrats as more passive and willing to negotiate and to [do] more peaceful things than to just go bomb a country that's already—just like bombing a hole to make it bigger. [It] just doesn't really make sense.

Like African Americans, white respondents described the Democratic Party as socially liberal. One white female described the Democratic Party as being interested in

R12: environmental, social issues like social welfare, health concerns, health insurance, helping the people, helping the individual as opposed to helping big business.

A white male in the same focus group added that the Democratic Party reminded him of education. A white female in a different focus group believed that the Democratic Party represented "campaign finance [and] welfare—not so much welfare but the preservation of the ideas that go along with it." Comparing the Democrats to the Republicans, a female respondent indicated that the "Democrats tend to be more in trouble with their personal lives and Republicans are a little lousier on their ethics in relation to what they actually do." Finally, one Republican woman talked about

> R14: the running joke in my family because my mom is a Democrat and my dad is a Republican. My mom votes for schools, my dad votes for prisons. Republicans are more about crime. And Democrats want to build it up and Republicans, you know, want to tear it down. They cancel each other's votes.

Respondents were also asked what sorts of people were associated with the two parties. Overwhelmingly, respondents associated the Democratic Party with minorities and the Republican Party with white males. Members of the all-Republican focus group associated the Democratic Party with "upper 40s, lower 50s females," "more minorities, a lot of college kids," and generally with a larger variety of people. When asked to expand on this response, one man indicated that he believed that the Democratic Party was "younger, maybe more idealistic at times. They're more hip, for lack of a better word. 'Hey, I'm cool, I'm young, I'm a Democrat.' They're diverse, so everybody wants to get in on it."

Democratic respondents agreed, associating the Democratic Party with women and with minorities in general, including Arab Americans, Jewish Americans, Hispanics, Native Americans, and Asian Americans. Those interviewed also included unions and people with lower incomes in groups associated with the Democratic Party. When asked why, the Democratic respondents answered that the party believed in

> R12: equality . . . for all them—I'd say, for like the lower incomes, like welfare, financial aid, all those things apply and are important—things like unions that hire workers—all those things are usually better represented by Democrats, and I think richer white Americans are more concerned with finances and how it's going to affect them and what tax bracket, and traditionally I think most Republicans are older, so their views are different and more conservative to go along with Republicans.
>
> R11: What I've heard Republicans say is that they believe in supporting big business because it will have a trickle-down effect. That supposedly the theory is they try to help big businesses because they say big businesses are going to employ those

poor people, you know, and all those minorities and everything. But I just don't see that works. I don't think enough of
the benefits and the money really does trickle down. A lot of it
just gets sucked up by the people at the top.

In all of the focus groups, the white respondents believed that the
difference between the Republican and Democratic Parties were
becoming less distinct.

> *R11:* I think they are moving together . . . and it's harder to draw
> the line and say "You will be a Republican and this person
> will be Democrat," just looking at . . . you just wrote down a
> simple bio and someone would decide what they would be.
> I think it goes a lot deeper than that. And unless you have a
> very specific issue that comes to national attention and gets
> written into the platform, I think it's hard to vote along
> party lines. You have to actually know candidates because
> there's a lot of Republicans that if you read their records
> they look like Democrats, and vice versa.
> *R15:* I think it's definitely becoming harder to vote along party
> lines. I think pretty soon there's going to be an ultra-busi-
> ness-conservative guy but he's going to be very antiabortion
> or something like that . . . people are going to have to start
> voting on the actual candidate more than just party lines.

Following a more general discussion of the two parties, respondents
were specifically asked about the representation of African Americans.
For the most part, all of the respondents indicated that the Democratic
Party would better represent African Americans. One male Republican
believed that "based on the platforms alone, I think they'd be inclined
to go for the Democrats." Another male in the same focus group
added, "And that's the way most African Americans do go. With
Detroit being mostly African American, it's a strongly Democratic
city." When asked why, he responded that the Democrats "specifically
they want to improve inner-city schools where most African Americans
tend to go. Stuff like that." The other two respondents in this focus
group explained that Democrats better represent blacks because of

> *R9:* the whole affirmative action issue. It's a pretty clear line,
> most Democrats in favor, most Republicans against it—I
> mean they're not against diversity or anything like that! . . .

Also, in big urban cities like Detroit, there's a lot of African Americans who work for the auto industry, and maybe their union supports the Democrats. There's also a lot more poorer neighborhoods, so they're probably attracted to the Democrats with welfare programs and stuff like that.

R14: Well, I don't want to stereotype and say [that all African Americans need] welfare, but you know, a lot of people in inner cities need more social programs. . . . There's a lot of different things, not just welfare, medical stuff, too.

In addition, one Republican respondent believed that blacks believed that the Democratic Party better represented black interests based on the Democratic Party's affiliation with certain leaders.

R10: Something else is the people they look up to. Everybody admired Martin Luther King [Jr.] during the civil rights movement. Now Jesse Jackson has kind of assumed that, and he's very strongly for the Democrats. Also Al Sharpton—in fact, Al Sharpton is running for president as a Democrat. They probably think that if they agree with the Democrats and I agree with them, then I must agree with the Democrats—the people they hold in esteem.

Respondents were then asked how well they believed black Republicans could represent African American interests. Most white Democrats agreed that the answer would depend on the candidate. Some of those interviewed mentioned that a black Republican would do a better job than a white Republican. For the most part, however, the Democratic respondents remained skeptical. One woman argued that "if there was an African American Republican running, it might make [African American voters] look more at everyone running. It might make them get more involved, but not necessarily more Republican." In other words, she believed that the presence of black Republicans would have a mobilizing effect but that it would not necessarily operate in favor of the Republican Party.

The Republican respondents, however, were more optimistic. Said one man,

R10: I think [Republicans] can even represent [African Americans] better than black Democrats. Because they can't take them for granted. They won't get 90 percent of the black vote in their district. Because it will be like, "We took a chance voting on this black Republican. If he doesn't do it, then we'll go back to the Democrats."

The conversation then shifted to specific black Republican figures such as Clarence Thomas, Condoleezza Rice, and Colin Powell. Although a few Democratic respondents believed that some blacks would vote for Rice or Powell if they were to run for office simply because they were black, most indicated that the candidates' stance on issues would deter African American support. Republican respondents generally agreed, although they believed that Rice would have a better chance than Powell or Thomas. According to members of the Republican focus group,

> R9: I don't think [Powell would attract African American voters], because Colin Powell has some Republican beliefs. Like he's against affirmative action, I think. Clarence Thomas is the same way . . . and the whole thing with personal accountability. [Republicans] are strong into that and I'm not saying all [African Americans] aren't, but maybe some, a few here and there, might like that they can work but that the government will help them out too. . . . There might also be feeling that like Clarence Thomas and Colin Powell, some might think, "Whoa, what are you doing? Why are you turning your back on us?" They might feel kind of upset, not betrayed but upset. It's not coming across right.

> R10: I would agree that like with Colin Powell, maybe people don't see him as being on the same level as them. . . . Colin Powell has a different set of ideals. He conforms with the Republicans a lot . . . whereas Jesse Jackson is not. It's complete opposite ends of the spectrum. And, it just seems that—it's that you see Jesse Jackson active in the community, talking, going to schools, reaching out to people. You never see Colin Powell do that. . . . Jesse Jackson reaches out more to the community, so people trust him.

> R14: Jesse Jackson to me is more of an emphatic leader. He rallies everyone together . . . African Americans especially. Colin Powell doesn't seem to be like that. He's more of just military. If there was someone who was going to come talk to me and it seemed like he had good ideas, well, I'd probably follow him too.

Following this exchange, respondents were asked to talk more about Rice. As mentioned earlier, Republican respondents believed that Rice would be better than Powell at attracting blacks. One female believed that Rice would attract some African Americans but not an overwhelming majority. The males in the focus group believed that Rice would have the most impact on young black women.

> *R9:* Maybe Colin Powell won't [attract blacks] because people see him as going through the military and people see blacks as being—not forced—but there's a large number of blacks in the military, and there might be some resentment about that. But with Condoleezza Rice, she's incredibly powerful, and there might be a lot of young African American women who say, "Where's that in the Democratic Party?" They've got none of that. They've got Donna Brazile, but she lost. They might see Condoleezza Rice as the new face of African American women in the Republican Party.
>
> *R10:* I don't know. It's—I'd say Condoleezza Rice has more tendency to bring in blacks than Colin Powell just for the fact that she is a woman. All these children can be like, "Wow, look at her." I don't necessarily think that more blacks will come in. With Condoleezza Rice they should.

Respondents were then asked about the 2000 Republican National Convention. The Democratic respondents agreed with the African American respondents. One woman described the convention as a "joke" and then continued,

> *R11:* I watched the whole thing and it was just ridiculous. There were just these minuscule people within the framework of the Republican Party and they were paraded around. . . . I don't think I would've ever felt comfortable being those people because they were such—like they really have anything to do with the Republican Party. They know they are such a minority. And they were like showpieces. . . . There were a lot of people that were higher up and had a lot more to do with what actually goes on in the Republican Party, and they didn't get a chance to speak just to show a black face or an Asian face or whatever.

A male in the same focus group agreed.

R15: They were almost just throwing black people up there just hoping that black people will see a black presence and say, "I'll vote Republican," instead of maybe getting up there, even a white person, and saying how they would help black people. . . . They were just parading around people instead of really doing anything with meaning.

The Republican respondents were less cynical about the convention, viewing the Republican outreach as sincere. Only one Republican respondent questioned the convention activities.

R14: Instead of showcasing entertainers or athletes, they just need to encourage African Americans in general to vote and to be educated about their choices. They don't know. They're just like, . . . 'Maybe they'll vote because they see Michael Jordan supporting this guy,' but . . . statistics show that minorities don't vote, and not that many people vote in America anyway, but you know if you want to change something about it like the school system or whatever, get people educated about it so they will vote and then they get to use their choices.

Finally, respondents were asked what the Republican Party would have to do to attract more African Americans. Again, Republican and Democratic respondents disagreed. Democratic respondents believed that the Republican Party would have to change its platform.

R11: I think the only way the Republicans can get more African Americans in their party is by changing their party . . . by actually listening to the African Americans' concerns and actually having part of their platform addressing their concerns. And say you had a well-known African American who's a Democrat who switched parties and said, "I'm now a Republican." Let's say Jesse Jackson became a Republican. But the only reason they would do that is if the party changed and was more responsive to them.

R15: I don't really think that blacks are ever going to become as a group Republican. They just don't offer [African Americans] what they need. . . . Being a Democrat just has more of an advantage for them. . . . There are a lot of black people living in poverty that don't have a lot of money that I think the

Republicans almost don't always look to help as much as the rich white people. The Democrats are . . . always trying, I think, to help with programs like food stamps and stuff like that.

In contrast, the Republican respondents did not believe that changing the Republican platform was the answer. One male respondent argued, "I don't think they could change their platform that much, but still even if they did, people feel loyalty. Even though some people might change their views, most won't." Another male in the same focus group said, "I think there might be some gratitude, but I don't think most people think about the 1960s when they go in the voting booth." This respondent indicated that he believed that change would occur slowly because of a connection with the civil rights movement.

R9: I think it might take a generation when our generation takes over the leadership role. The tumultuous 1960s and '70s was a big experience with the civil rights movement. Our generation doesn't have that big uniting thing. So I think in 20 or 25 years there might be more diversity [in the Republican Party].

The female in this focus group believed that "unless more African Americans run as Republicans, I don't think they'll get more support from minorities."

Although the white respondents talked about the two parties in terms of race and racial groups, they only did so after much prompting. The black respondents, in contrast, freely and spontaneously discussed both parties in terms of race. These results suggest that differences between black and white perceptions of the two major parties are driven not just by the information contained in their party images but by the relative salience of this information. For African Americans, race is very salient; for white respondents, however, class seemed to be the most salient division between the two parties.

Conclusion

People have distinct perceptions of the two major parties that are rooted in issue positions, historical events, and group interests, especially with respect to race. The survey data suggest that individuals historically have distinguished the two parties along racial lines that correspond to the state of the times. Prior to 1960, the distinction between the two parties was not as prominent because the parties themselves were not making a substantial distinction. From 1960 to the present, individuals have consistently placed the Democratic Party as more liberal on race than Republicans. Moreover, the survey data indicate that blacks recognize a greater distance between the Democratic Party and Republican Party on the issue of race.

Unpacking the survey results with qualitative data revealed that at least contemporary party images align with party activities. Whereas the survey data link party behavior with individual perceptions post hoc, the qualitative data allow respondents to describe in their own words the origins of their perceptions of the two major parties. Many African American respondents offered the Republican Party's positions on affirmative action and education as reasons for believing that the party was racially conservative.

These perceptions became especially important when exploring the prospect of reshaping party images with respect to race, although more so for African Americans than whites. All of the African American respondents as well as several of the white respondents believed that the Republican Party would have to alter its position on many racial issues. In contrast, many white respondents believed that simply recruiting more African Americans into the party would help reshape images of the Republican Party. Moreover, all of the respondents agreed that while recruiting blacks into the Republican Party might not improve perceptions of the party on race, specific figures could. The respondents disagreed on which public figures would be particularly effective.

The results from this chapter provide the necessary backdrop for exploring the limitations of reshaping party images. First, these data reveal the relative weight blacks and whites place on race and race-related issues. Second, the results illustrate that differences of opinion exist regarding how the Republican Party can overcome its current reputation on race. I will test the relationship between race and party image in chapter 5. In the next chapter, however, I will explore how the media responded to the 2000 Republican National Convention as a way of determining whether media coverage of the convention played a role in the reshaping of party images.

4 A Different Spin

The Media's Framing of the 2000
Republican National Convention

WHEN ATTEMPTING TO reshape their images in voters' minds, parties must remain cognizant of potential sources of countervailing information. Encountering information that contradicts the party's newly projected image enables citizens to deflect partisan appeals. For this reason, it is important to examine not only a party's campaign communication but also how other institutions in the information environment respond to the campaign. With respect to the Republican Party's attempt to reshape its image along racial lines, one such institution to consider is the media.

Studies (e.g., Steeper 1978) have found that although campaign events may have little effect on public opinion, subsequent news coverage of those events does. The probability of attending a political convention or witnessing other political events is very small, but the presence of a multitude of mass media outlets capable of relaying such events to broad audiences increases the likelihood of encountering political information. As Graber (1989) explains, news stories "provide the nation with shared political experiences, such as watching presidential election debates or congressional investigations, that then form a basis for public opinions and for uniting people for political actions" (3). Dalton, Beck, and Huckfeldt (1998) argue that media coverage of political events becomes especially important during elections:

> Few voters attend a rally or have direct contact with the presidential candidates or their representatives. Instead, information presented in the media provides people with cues about the policy positions, qualities, and abilities of the candidates. From this infor-

mation, as well as other sources, the public forms its images of the candidates and its voting choices. (111)

As a result, the media play an important role in political elites' ability to convey their messages.

First, in determining that an event is newsworthy, the media decide the event's level of significance.

> Newspeople determine what is "news"—which political happenings will be covered and which will be ignored. Their choices affect who and what will have a good chance to become the focus for political discussion and action. Without media attention the people and events covered by the news might have no influence, or reduced influence, on decision-makers. (Graber 1989, 6)

The voters are the decision makers during the election cycle, and the media weight the importance of such events for subsequent electoral decisions by covering (or not covering) a political event (see also Iyengar and Kinder 1987).

Second, the media not only serve as vehicles through which elites speak to members of the electorate but also act as interpreters of the message being sent. In their framing of political events, the media clarify and translate what political elites attempt to transmit to would-be constituents. According to Graber (1989), "Most incidents lend themselves to a variety of interpretations, depending on the values and experiences of the interpreter. The kind of interpretation that is chosen affects the political consequences of media reports" (10). In other words, the political ramifications of a campaign event are somewhat contingent on the frames the media use to discuss it.

The effect of media coverage during campaigns also includes press coverage of campaign ads. Media coverage of campaign ads may have either a reinforcing effect (Ansolabehere and Iyengar 1995) or a diminishing effect (Cappella and Jamieson 1997).

Neuman, Just, and Crigler (1992) explain the process:

> Sources (government spokesmen, public affairs people, campaign managers, candidates, and officials) interpret news for reporters. They give the story a "spin" congenial with their goals, and hope to see their construction of reality incorporated into the news story. Journalists reconstruct reality for the audience, taking into account their organizational and modality constraints, professional

judgments, and certain expectations about the audience. Finally, the individual reader or viewer constructs a version of reality built from personal experience, interaction with peers, and interpreted selections from the mass media. (120)

This process suggests that the filtering of information to the public is two tiered and that any analysis of political information should include not only the original source of the message (in this case, party elites) but also the mediators of this message—the media.

Subsequent coverage of the 2000 Republican National Convention is especially important to examine given individuals' limited ability to experience the convention as it occurred. Only a tiny fraction of voting-age citizens attended the convention in person. Moreover, in 2000 the major networks limited coverage of both the Democratic and the Republican conventions. CBS, NBC, and ABC devoted less than an hour a day to the Republican convention, with the exception of the final evening, when the party's presidential nominee, George W. Bush, gave his acceptance speech. As a result, information about the convention most likely came from subsequent news coverage of the convention rather than from witnessing the convention from gavel to gavel.

Thus, this chapter seeks primarily to investigate whether the media recognized the increase in the number of African Americans present at the 2000 Republican National Convention, the amount of time the media devoted to highlighting this aspect of the convention, and the valence of this coverage. This chapter examines the dominant frames used by both the mainstream and the black media in their coverage of the 2000 Republican convention. I reveal the news media's potential role in the effectiveness of the Republican Party's strategy.

First, I determine the level of importance the media placed on the black convention attendees in 2000. To this end, I examine the amount of coverage the media devoted to the strategy relative to the amount of overall coverage. For the prevalence of blacks at the Republican convention to reshape party images, people would have to receive the campaign communication. Therefore, I examine whether the media conveyed this information. I hypothesize that the media will recognize the use of race during the convention and devote a considerable amount of coverage to this strategy. One criterion for story selection is novelty. For an event, situation, or condition to receive media coverage, "it must be something that has just occurred and is out of the ordinary, either in the sense that it does not happen all the time . . . or in the sense that it is not part of the lives of ordinary persons" (Graber 1989, 86). The fact that the convention only occurs once every four years should make it newsworthy. With the increase in the number of visible African Americans and other minorities, the Republican convention becomes novel.

I also expect that the African American press will devote a substantial portion of their convention coverage to the Republicans' race strategy. One theme found consistently in the black press is African American involvement in white events. For black newspapers, the only newsworthy part of white news events is blacks' participation (Wolseley 1990). Thus, inasmuch as the black press covered the 2000 Republican National Convention, this coverage should be devoted largely to highlighting the various aspects of the Republicans' inclusive message.

Another way to gauge the importance the media placed on the GOP's strategy is by examining the duration of the coverage. Because timeliness is another criterion of newsworthiness, I hypothesize that when the media cover blacks at the convention, this coverage should occur both during and shortly after the convention. Overall, coverage of the Republicans' diversity message before and after the convention should be significantly less than it is during the convention.

In addition, I look at the context in which the media discussed the convention. While the 2000 convention evidenced an increased African American presence, the party did not change its position on issues such as affirmative action. Accordingly, I determine whether the media highlighted this conundrum. Juxtaposing the Republican race strategy with its current policy positions potentially posed a barrier to the party's ability to meet the threshold of change in citizens' minds. I hypothesize that the media will highlight the policy positions of the Republican Party in conjunction with the overall discussion of the convention. Parties present their platforms for the next four years at the conventions; therefore, it seems only natural that the media will discuss platforms as part of their overall convention coverage. In this case, the media will act as a source of opposition without intending to do so.

Finally, I examine the valence of the convention coverage to assess how the media interpreted the convention events and whether the media opposed or supported the Republican campaign strategy. By responding to the convention with cynicism, the media could oppose the Republican message. Likewise, praising the convention's diversity and inclusion could bolster the strategy's effect.

I hypothesize that the coverage of the 2000 Republican National Convention will be mostly positive. This hypothesis rests on the assumption that "although the media regularly expose the misbehavior and inefficiencies of government officials, for the most part [the media] display a favorable attitude toward political leaders and the American political system" (Graber 1989, 100). This phenomenon results in part from the media's reliance on government officials as news sources. One analysis estimated that public officials were the source of 78 percent of foreign and domestic news stories appearing in the *New York Times* and the *Washington Post* (Gans 1979, 145). While trying to maintain some level of objectivity, news organizations must remain mindful of the impact of potentially alienating a news source. In describing the relationship between journalists and public officials, Gans (1979) argues that "sources have somewhat more power in the relationship than reporters, since they can punish reporters by withholding information, thereby putting them at a disadvantage with peers from competing news media" (134). In this respect, news organizations are constrained in the level of critical analysis they can publish.

I expect there to be an exception to the overall tone of the coverage when the black media are examined separately. Specifically, I hypothesize that black media outlets' coverage of the 2000 Republican National Convention will be mostly negative. The black press has a history of serving as a vehicle for protest and opposition to the status quo. Because of their experiences, African Americans tend to be more critical of American political institutions. Given the historic relationship between African Americans and the Republican Party (see Walton 1975; Weiss 1983), the black press should provide a more skeptical and negative assessment of the Republican Party's race strategy.

To test the validity of these propositions, I conduct a content analysis of the print media. Specifically, I analyze three nationally circulated newspapers—the *New York Times,* the *Los Angeles Times,* and the *Washington Post*—as well as a sample of African American newspapers. (See the appendix.) For each article included in the content analysis, I coded the frame used to describe the convention, the tone of the article, and when the article appeared in relation to the convention. (See the appendix for coding rules.)

General Descriptive Findings

Table 4 presents the total distribution of all convention-related articles during the eighteen-day period in the sample. This table indicates that of the 197 articles included in the sample, 78.2 percent were news stories, 4.6 percent were editorials, 3.6 percent were letters to the editor, 10.7 percent were opinion columns, and 3 percent were op-ed pieces.

Table 4 also indicates that approximately 60 percent of the convention-related articles appeared during the convention. In the week leading up to the 2000 Republican National Convention, 21 articles (11 percent of the sample) with "Republican convention" in the title or lead paragraph appeared in the news sources included in this study. During the convention, the number of articles increased to 118. In the week following the convention, the number of articles decreased to 58, or about 30 percent of the sample frame.

Figure 6 presents a daily account of the frequency of news coverage. A closer look at the convention coverage indicates that the majority of the coverage during the eighteen-day period occurred on the second, third, and fourth days of the convention (August 1–3, 2000). Cover-

TABLE 4. General Descriptive Statistics

	Number	Percent
Sources of articles in sample		
Black print media	17	8.6
Mainstream Media	180	91.4
Total	197	100
Type of print coverage		
Letters to the editor	7	3.6
Editorial	9	4.6
Opinion column	21	10.7
Op-ed	6	3.0
News articles	154	78.2
Total	197	100
Print news coverage in proximity to 2000 GOP Convention		
Before	21	10.7
During	118	59.9
After	58	29.4
Total	197	100

Source: New York Times, Los Angeles Times, Washington Post, Baltimore Afro-American, Los Angeles Sentinel, New York Amsterdam News, New York Voice, Oakland Post, Sacramento Observer, Speakin' Out News, Jacksonville Free Press, New York Beacon, Philadelphia Tribune, Tennessee Tribune, Voice, Washington Informer.

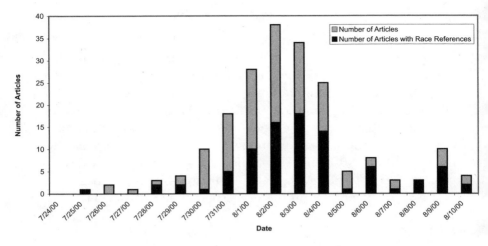

Fig. 6.   Number of print media articles covering the 2000 Republican National Convention featuring race references over sample frame. (Data from *New York Times, Los Angeles Times, Washington Post, Baltimore Afro-American, Los Angeles Sentinel, New York Amsterdam News, New York Voice, Oakland Post, Sacramento Observer, Speakin' Out News, Jacksonville Free Press, New York Beacon, Philadelphia Tribune, Tennessee Tribune, Voice, Washington Informer.*)

age seems fairly evenly distributed around those days. The number of articles about the convention appearing on any given day ranged between 0 and 10 in the week leading up the convention, between 18 and 38 during the convention, and between 3 and 10[1] after the convention.

Race References

One of this chapter's goals is to examine whether the media recognized the increased presence of African Americans at the convention. In general, 45 percent of the articles referred to some aspect of the Republican Party's message of diversity. Seventy-six percent of the black media's convention coverage mentioned the Republican race strategy, compared to 42 percent of mainstream media. A difference-of-means test indicates that this difference is significant at the $p < .01$ level.

1. August 4, 2000, the day immediately after the convention, constituted an exception: 25 articles appeared.

Complying with the timeliness criterion, a dramatic increase in race references occurred the day after Colin Powell's speech (August 1, 2000), with another increase on August 2, the day after Condoleezza Rice's speech. Prior to the convention, the media devoted very little attention to the strategy—that is, the media did not anticipate an increase in black participation at the convention. Nevertheless, following Powell's and Rice's speeches, the print media continued to highlight the race strategy until the day after the close of the convention (August 4). In the postconvention period, references to the GOP diversity message decreased along with overall convention coverage (see figure 6).

The frequency of race references is much smaller in coverage of previous conventions. In 1988, 13 percent of the articles coded referred to African American delegates or speakers at the convention. The coverage of the 1992 convention contained no race references, and only 28 percent of the print media coverage of the 1996 Republican National Convention contained race references. These figures seem to indicate that the increased presence of African Americans at the 2000 convention increased the media's attention on the black convention attendees as well as the convention's impact on black voters. This coverage is significantly greater than had previously been the case.

Valence

To understand how individuals reacted to the message of inclusion and diversity presented at the convention, it is important to examine not only whether the media recognized the message but also the tone of the coverage. Thus, in this section I examine the valence of the print media coverage of the Republicans' race strategy. I discern whether the media reacted skeptically to the campaign, thereby undermining it, or positively framed the convention, thereby increasing the campaign's impact.

Overall, the content analysis reveals that 79 percent of the convention coverage was neutral, 14 percent was negative, and only 7 percent was positive. Table 5 indicates that the distribution of tone varied by article type. Among the articles with race references, 20 percent were negative, 73 percent were neutral, and 8 percent were positive. In contrast, 10 percent of the articles without race references were negative, 84 percent were neutral, and 6 percent were positive. A chi-square test indicates that the tone of the articles and the presence of race references are not independent and that a statistically significant difference exists in tone between those articles with race references and those without. On average, the articles with race references tended to be more negative.

Table 6 illustrates how the valence of the 2000 coverage differs from the coverage of previous conventions. In 1988, the coverage of the Republican National Convention was completely neutral, regardless of race references. The coverage of the 1992 Republican convention contained no race references, although the majority of the print coverage was neutral. Print media coverage of the 1996 Republican National Convention varied slightly by the presence of race references. For example, 90 percent of the articles with race references were neutral, while 10 percent were positive. In contrast, 12 percent of the articles without race references were negative, 82 percent were neutral, and 6 percent were positive. A difference-of-means test, however, indicated that these differences were not statistically significant.

To get a sense of exactly how the media covered the Republican race strategy, I include a few of the dominant frames the media used to describe the convention. The positive articles tended to focus on reactions from Republican delegates. For example, an August 1 *Washing-*

TABLE 5.   Tone of Articles with and without Race References by Media Source (in percentages)

	Race References	No Race References
Both media sources		
Negative	20	10
Neutral	73	84
Positive	8	6
Mainstream print media		
Negative	22	8
Neutral	72	86
Positive	5	6
Black print media		
Negative	0	50
Neutral	75	50
Positive	25	0

Source: New York Times, Los Angeles Times, Washington Post, Baltimore Afro-American, Los Angeles Sentinel, New York Amsterdam News, New York Voice, Oakland Post, Sacramento Observer, Speakin' Out News, Jacksonville Free Press, New York Beacon, Philadelphia Tribune, Tennessee Tribune, Voice, Washington Informer.

ton Post article summarized interviews conducted with a number of delegates:

> But there was little talk of conservatism on the convention floor today as delegates were asked how they thought the GOP had been changed by Bush's rise to the party leadership. Open and inclusive, younger and more vigorous, were some of the words they used to describe the Bush-led party. (Walsh 2000, A11)

In addition to highlighting the excitement and enthusiasm of the black Republican delegates, an article featured in the *Baltimore Afro-American* also discussed some of the GOP's positive race-related activities:

> For Black voters who would suggest that the Republican convention holds no interest to them, consider these historical facts. A Republican president issued the Emancipation Proclamation, which outlawed slavery in this country. The first Black elected officials to serve in the Continental Congress were Republicans. A Republican Congress passed the Civil Rights Act of 1964. A Republican president initiated the Small Business Administration, which provides loans to minority businesses. Ironically, as important as it is, history is likely overlooked in the clamor of convention business—the platform debates, nominating speeches and state caucuses. (Erwin 2000, A1)

TABLE 6. Tone of Print Media Coverage of Past Republican Party Conventions (in percentages)

	All	Race References	No Race References
1988			
Negative	0	0	0
Neutral	100	100	100
Positive	0	0	0
1992			
Negative	15		15
Neutral	85		85
Positive	0		0
1996			
Negative	7	0	12
Neutral	85	90	82
Positive	7	10	6

Source: New York Times.

Negative references to the Republican message of inclusion either were discussed directly or could be found in articles that did not focus specifically on the race strategy. The strategy would sometimes be used to contrast other convention activities. An August 2 *Washington Post* news article pinned the Republicans' message of inclusion against the party's lavish treatment of its major financial contributors:

> Even as the GOP works aggressively to project an image of inclusiveness from the convention podium, the Regents [a group of 137 people and companies that contributed at least $250,000 each to the Republican National Committee during the 2000 election cycle] program shows how, off camera, the party provides special access and favors to its biggest givers. . . . Indeed, some GOP officials shudder simply at the group's name, which they feel undercuts the message of the minutely choreographed convention. (Allen 2000, A15)

I also assessed whether the distribution of valence differed by media source. For these analyses, the media sources were divided into mainstream media and black media. The *Los Angeles Times,* the *New York Times,* and the *Washington Post* were included as mainstream media sources, while all others were included as black media sources. I hypothesized that mainstream media coverage would be largely positive, while African American media coverage would be mostly negative; however, a difference-of-means test revealed no statistically significant difference in tone between articles appearing in black media sources and those appearing in mainstream newspapers, although the mainstream media sources' coverage on average was more negative.

I then examined whether these similarities remained when the analyses separated the articles with race references from those without. Of the articles appearing in the mainstream media sources, 42 percent referred to the GOP's race strategy; of this group, 22 percent were negative, 72 percent were neutral, and 5 percent were positive. In great contrast, among the mainstream media articles without race references, 8 percent were negative, 86 percent were neutral, and 6 percent were positive. Further, the Pearson chi-square indicates that these differences were statistically significant at the $p < .10$ level. The valence distribution of the articles differed substantially in the black news sources, where 75 percent of the articles with race references were neutral and 25 percent were positive and 50 percent of the articles with no race references were negative and 50 percent were neutral. The Pearson chi-square indicates that these differences were statistically significant at the $p < .10$ level.

These data suggest that a larger proportion of the mainstream media coverage of the Republican diversity message was negative. In general, the mean tone of the racialized media coverage was more negative in the mainstream media sources than in the black media sources. A difference-of-means test indicates that this difference is statistically significant at the $p < .05$ level. Approximately three-quarters of media coverage of the Republican race strategy was neutral, however.

Qualitatively, a closer examination of the articles indicates that the mainstream media tended to be more reactionary and overt, whereas the black media tended to be more subtle. Paragraphs from two black newspapers are illustrative. According to the *Sacramento Observer*,

> Kenteclad gospel groups, harmonic R&B singers, muscle-bound wrestlers—even a scowling rock group or two was thrown in for good measure.
>
> That was just a slice of this year's 2000 Republican Party Convention in Philadelphia attempt by the GOP's brass to update its image from the party of "old White guys" to one which makes claims of being inclusive of ethnic minorities, women and young people. ("GOP Stresses Inclusion" 2000, A4)

And an article in the *Baltimore Afro-American* noted

> that Blacks vote their interests and many of their most vital interests have been opposed by Republican lawmakers. There is no sign that Blacks, who rarely give Republican presidential candidates more than 10 percent of their votes, have forgotten the legacy of Ronald Reagan, who slashed funding for social programs, attacked Civil Rights leaders and the enforcement of the laws, and attempted to foster a new generation of conservative Black Republican leaders. (Walters 2000, A5)

African American newspapers, however, appeared to have delayed their responses. An examination of convention coverage just outside of the sampling frame revealed that later articles seemed to converge with the mainstream media's coverage. For example, several black newspapers printed an article under the title " 'New' GOP Unveiled at Convention . . . A Grand Oreo Party":

The Republican Convention in Philadelphia featured a rainbow coalition of African-American and other minorities elbowing each other in a mad dash to the podium to extol the virtues of petulant preppie George W. Bush and right-wing throwback Dick Cheney. The transparently pandering parade even stupefied political pundits, unprepared for the staged charade. The virtually lily-white auditorium, filled with delegates bedecked in cornball ten-gallon hats and assorted pachyderm ephemera, sat entertained by a mind-boggling troupe of pre-conditioned minstrel zombies mouthing the GOP line. (Williams 2000, A7)

In sum, the Republican Party benefited from generally neutral coverage of the convention. Although the presence of African Americans at the 2000 Republican National Convention encountered skepticism in some instances, the media—regardless of news source—generally did not pose a major obstacle when it came to the tone used to describe the convention.

Symbols versus Substance

One of the most important aspects of the media coverage of the 2000 Republican National Convention is whether the media discussed the GOP's platform as well as its convention participants. Doing so could potentially impede the Republican Party's ability to meet the criteria for becoming a "new" party. Highlighting the party's unchanged policy positions might signal to individuals that the GOP had not really changed.

In 1988, approximately 20 percent of newspaper coverage of the convention focused on the attendees. This figure decreased to 17 percent in 1992 but increased to 25 percent in 1996. In 2000, however, about 40 percent of the convention coverage focused on who attended.

In contrast, a reverse pattern occurs in the amount of coverage devoted to the Republican Party's platform. In both 1988 and 1992, 25 percent of convention coverage discussed the GOP's platform or at least its stance on specific issues. In 1996, the amount of coverage of the Republican platform decreased slightly, to 22 percent. Less than 10 percent of the 2000 coverage referenced the Republican Party's issue positions.

I also examine the number of articles that discussed both convention attendance and Republican issue positions. Less than 20 percent of the articles in 1988 discussed both the Republican Party's platform and the convention attendees. The percentage of articles discussing both issues and convention presence increased to approximately 30 percent in 1992 and remained at that level throughout the 1996 and 2000 conventions.

These analyses seek primarily to examine whether the media coverage of the 2000 Republican National Convention juxtaposed the Republican Party's outreach to African Americans with its platform. In chapter 1, I hypothesized that the success of the Republican Party's attempt to reshape its image would be contingent in part on whether the media highlighted the more policy-oriented political symbols associated with the GOP. The rationale is that the media's attention to the Republican platform would mute the effect of the Republican strategy because by bringing to readers' minds the part of the Republican Party that had not changed. The new images presented at the GOP convention would thus be less salient in individuals' evaluations of the party. To assess whether this was a possibility, I examined whether the coverage of the Republican race strategy included a discussion of the Republican Party's platform.

Table 7 presents the results. In 1988, the topic of African Americans attending the convention was discussed in terms either of their presence at the convention or of their status as potential convention viewers.[2] Discussion of African Americans in conjunction with the 1988 Republican National Convention did not include issues. In contrast, nearly 50 percent of the articles without race references discussed the GOP platform in some respect. As indicated in table 7, 29 percent of the articles discussed issues without mentioning the convention attendees, and 21 percent discussed both. The coverage of the 1992 Republican National Convention made no reference to race. Among the 1992 articles that did not discuss race, just over half discussed the Republican Party's issue positions—25 percent of the articles talked about the issues exclusively, and 31 percent discussed both issues and convention attendance. In 1996, the discussion of race reemerged. The articles without race references were fairly evenly distributed

---

2. Because of the coding rules, these types of articles appear in the excluded category, in which an article mentions neither the GOP platform nor the presence of any particular group or person at the convention.

across categories. Among the articles with references to race, 50 percent discussed the African American presence at the convention in conjunction with the Republican platform. In 2000, the discussion of African Americans and the convention focused almost entirely on their presence at the convention or on their presence at the convention in conjunction with the Republican platform. For example, 40 percent of the articles focused solely on the black presence, while only 5 percent of the articles with race references discussed Republican issue positions and 52 percent of the articles with race references discussed both the African American presence at the convention and the Republican Party's position on various public policy issues. Among the articles without reference to race, the articles were more evenly distributed across the categories. Although 40 percent of the articles focused only on who was at the convention, 14 percent of the articles discussed the Republican platform, and 19 percent discussed both.

In summary, print media coverage of Republican National Conventions shifted its focus away from discussing issues and toward examining convention attendees. That is not to say that media coverage of the Republican Party's platform completely disappeared. The results sug-

TABLE 7. Comparison of Print Media Focus on Attendees versus Party Platform in Coverage of Republican Conventions (in percentages)

	Attendees	Platform	Both
1988			
No Race Reference	14	29	21
Race Reference	50	0	0
1992			
No Race Reference	17	25	31
Race Reference	N/A	N/A	N/A
1996			
No Race Reference	24	22	24
Race Reference	27	21	50
2000			
No Race Reference	40	14	19
Race Reference	40	5	52

Source: *New York Times, Los Angeles Times, Washington Post, Baltimore Afro-American, Los Angeles Sentinel, New York Amsterdam News, New York Voice, Oakland Post, Sacramento Observer, Speakin' Out News, Jacksonville Free Press, New York Beacon, Philadelphia Tribune, Tennessee Tribune, Voice, Washington Informer.*

gest that a discussion of the issues was most likely to appear in conjunction with a description of who was attending the convention. This
was especially true when the print media were covering the message of
diversity featured at the 2000 Republican National Convention.
Hence, by discussing convention attendance and political issues in a
single article, the media might have inadvertently undermined the conveyance of the Republican Party's new image by highlighting aspects of
the party that had not changed.

Newsmagazines

Finally, I also examine the frames used by popular newsmagazines,
although these publications did not print enough articles to include in
the analysis. On the first day of the convention, *Time* featured an article covering protest activity, including the Shadow Convention (an
alternative convention held concurrently in Philadelphia) and other
expected protest groups. This particular article did not refer to the
Republican Party's show of diversity, and the tone of both of these articles was neutral (Lopez and Desa 2000).

A week before the convention, *Time* also featured a story devoted to
the image making of George W. Bush and the "new" Republican
Party. The article described what observers could expect to see at the
2000 convention:

> Everywhere the symbols will align to send a comfortable message.
> . . . Washington politicians will be shoved off to side stages and
> obscure time slots; and an entire classroom of inner-city school
> kids will spotlight Bush's education proposals. A final night
> devoted to testimonials to the candidate will feature an African-
> American preacher. (Carney and Dickerson 2000, 31)

This article thus mentioned the Republican Party's diversity message
before the convention occurred. But all three *Time* articles had a
mostly neutral tone, with the slightest hint of cynicism injected into
the description of the convention schedule.

Two weeks after the convention, both *Time* and *Newsweek* featured a number of articles highlighting the various aspects of the
Republican race strategy. In "The Ricky Martin Factor," *Newsweek*
discussed the impact of the appearances of George P. Bush (the
handsome Latino nephew of George W. Bush) and R & B recording
artist Brian McKnight:

Battleground 2000, a bipartisan poll, found that Bush went into last week's convention down 7 points among Latinos and ended it with an 18-point lead.

Black voters weren't nearly so impressed. Bush's fellow GOP governors rejoiced that Buchanan was gone, but the scars were evident; only 86—about 4 percent—of the delegates in Philly were black, up from 53 in 1996. (Bai 2000, 26)

Time ran an opinion piece about Colin Powell and his role at the 2000 convention. In the article, the author described her reaction to Powell's condemnation of his party's stance on affirmative action:

Isn't killing and burying affirmative action the signature cause of the G.O.P.? . . . Forget reality. With a raucous Chaka Khan, with rappers and wrestlers and a rocking gospel choir (hey, these Republicans do have rhythm), critics had taken to comparing the convention to a Utah Jazz home game, where everyone in the stands is white and most of the performers are black. (Carlson 2000, 35)

In general, newsmagazine coverage of the Republican convention coverage tended to be neutral. The convention coverage that focused on the Republicans' message of inclusion, however, ranged from slightly critical to overtly suspicious.

Conclusion

Thus, the print media recognized the use of race during the 2000 Republican National Convention; moreover, the media provided competing frames by which to interpret convention events.

In terms of recognizing the use of race during the 2000 convention, both the mainstream and black media devoted a considerable amount of coverage to this strategy. The black media, however, devoted significantly more of their convention coverage to the Republican race strategy. The proportion of coverage with race references in the black media was twice that of the mainstream media coverage.

With respect to valence, a statistically significant difference existed between the tone of the mainstream media's coverage of the Republican race strategy and that of the black media. In general, a greater proportion of the racialized coverage of the mainstream media was negative. When the comparison was limited to the racialized coverage, the difference was even greater. Contrary to my original expectations, however, mainstream media tended to be more critical of the Republican Party than did the black media, even when the newsmagazine sources are included. However, nearly 75 percent of both mainstream and black media coverage of the Republican race strategy was neutral.

Probably more important than tone, however, is what additional information the media provided readers. For example, the analyses indicate that the media did not simply convey the presence of African Americans at the 2000 Republican National Convention. Quite a large portion of media coverage juxtaposed African American attendance with the Republican platform. Highlighting the presence of African Americans at the convention as well as the Republican Party's position on issues potentially muted the effect of the Republican race strategy, giving readers multiple bits of salient information to use in subsequent evaluations of the Republican Party.

I would be remiss if I did not address some of the possible limitations of these analyses. First, this study has been confined to analysis of print media. Although they constitute only a subset of the information channels now available to the American electorate, print media provide an interesting snapshot of the frames surrounding the 2000 Republican National Convention. Furthermore, approximately 74 percent of the American electorate read the newspaper at least once a week, and 59 percent of this group read about the 2000 campaign.[3] These figures suggest that the print media's framing of the convention could have reached a substantial number of people.

There is also the question of generalizability, given that this analysis has been restricted primarily to three mainstream media sources, two newsmagazines, and a collection of African American media sources. The *Los Angeles Times,* the *New York Times,* the *Washington Post, Time,* and *Newsweek* represent five of the most widely circulated news periodicals. Further, the incorporation of all African American print media sources available online gives a fairly representative sample of the black presses that exist in the major cities across the United States. Finally, scholars have repeatedly demonstrated the consistency of news across organizations and outlets (Just et al. 1996).

---

3. 2000 American National Election Study. See the National Election Studies (www.electionstudies.org). The 2000 National Election Study [dataset]. Ann Arbor: University of Michigan, Center for Political Studies [producer and distributor].

This study also has not addressed the causal relationship between these frames and public opinion. There is no way to guarantee that these findings affected the way the electorate interpreted the convention events or if the frames used by the media affected evaluations of the Republican Party in general. This issue will be addressed in chapter 5.

But even independent of its effect on public opinion, media reaction to the Republican convention is crucial to understanding the way political events are interpreted. It is a reflection of the norms valued by a society. As Gamson (1992) argues,

> Media discourse, then, is a meaning system in its own right, independent of any claims that one might make about the causal effect on public opinion. Certain ways of framing issues gain and lose prominence over time, and some assumptions are shared by all frames. National media discourse, although only one part of public discourse, is a good reflection of the whole. We need to understand what this discourse says about an issue, since it is a central part of the reality in which people negotiate meaning about political issues. (27)

The fact that the media coverage of the convention was not uniformly positive indicates that at least part of the time, the media recognized a violation of a norm. News organizations are comprised of individuals. And as individuals, journalists bring to bear their experiential knowledge when framing the news. The cynical tone used in some of the convention coverage results from the media taking into account the Republican Party's history with respect to race. The media, like the public, have certain expectations regarding the Republican Party's behavior. When the party deviated from these expectations, the media responded by questioning its motives and sincerity. In this sense, the media do not act as a passive institution open to manipulation, as once thought (Patterson 1994). Rather, the media perform a watchdog function.

5 *Seeing Is Believing?*

Reactions to the 2000 Republican
National Convention

THE THEORETICAL MODEL of party image change depicted in figure 2 illustrates that reshaping partisan stereotypes is a function in part of individuals' predispositions and the media's framing of the party. The results presented in chapter 3 suggest that individuals vary in their perceptions of political parties: African Americans' pictures of the two parties' images along racial lines are more crystallized than those of whites. Furthermore, blacks' threshold for what constitutes change is also set higher than that of whites. Thus, the Republican Party's ability to reshape its image with respect to race should prove more difficult among blacks than whites. Likewise, reshaping the Republican Party's racial symbolism should also be harder when individuals encounter media messages that highlight aspects of the party that have not changed or contain no discussion of the elements of the party that have been altered. The data presented in chapter 4 show that citizens might have stumbled onto several alternative versions of the 2000 Republican National Convention. People could have read a basic account of the convention that included a description of the black attendees, media coverage that completely omitted mention of blacks at the convention, or an account that juxtaposed the attendance of many black speakers and entertainers with the fact that the party did not change is traditional conservative platform. Therefore, the media had the potential to serve as an obstacle to the Republican Party's attempt to modify its image with respect to race.

Chapter 5 seeks empirically to test these relationships. First, using survey data, I gauge general reactions to the 2000 Republican National Convention as well as the reactions of whites and blacks separately.

The data used in these analyses come from the Post–GOP Convention Poll, which was conducted by the Gallup organization shortly after the close of the convention. This poll seemed particularly well suited to test the correlation between convention exposure and perceptions of the Republican Party. First, the Post–GOP Convention Poll over-sampled African Americans, allowing me to examine black/white differences in reactions to the convention. Second, the Gallup poll was conducted almost immediately after the convention, minimizing the possibility that exogenous events could explain changes in perceived Republican Party images. Third, any other events that occurred between the convention and the survey would have muted rather than amplified the effect. Finally, there was no reason to believe that convention watchers and non–convention watchers would be affected differently by some intervening occurrence.

Still, using survey data rather than experimental data poses a potential measurement problem. In the real world, people self-select themselves into watching the convention. As a result, other unmeasured motivating factors may influence both convention watching and evaluations of the Republican Party. To overcome this problem inherent to using survey data, I conducted the 2002–2003 Party Image Study, which incorporated an experiment into its design. In an experiment, the researcher can control who is exposed to the treatment—in this case the convention—and who is not. Further, an experiment allows the researcher to control what type of information people receive about the convention. The 2002–2003 Party Image Study was, of course, conducted a few years after the convention, and numerous events occurred in the interim, including the contested 2000 election and the 2001 terrorist attacks on New York City and Washington, D.C. Consequently, convention events should be displaced in citizens' minds by other more recent salient activities of the Republican Party. Therefore, the ability to observe an effect of the experimental manipulations should be more difficult. Nevertheless, I used data from the 2002–2003 Party Image Study to establish the causal link between convention exposure and perceptions of the Republican Party's image with respect to race. Moreover, I utilized these data to determine how subtle changes in the media's interpretation of the convention might have moderated individuals' reactions to the convention.

To do so, I replicated some of the frames used by the news media when describing the convention. In the experiment, subjects were exposed to one of four scenarios: (1) a control with no mention of the Republican convention; (2) a race-neutral description of the Republican convention with no references to the presence of African American attendees; (3) a description of the many African American speakers and entertainers at the convention; or (4) a description of the many African American speakers and entertainers present at the convention supporting the Republican Party's traditional platform. (See the appendix for a more detailed description of the survey and experimental design.)

Tuning In

According to the Post–GOP Convention Poll, approximately 21.2 percent of the electorate watched none of the convention, 24.4 percent watched very little of it, 35.5 percent watched some of the convention, and 19 percent watched a great deal of the convention.

Table 8 presents a breakdown of the rate at which different demographic groups watched the convention.[1] Fifty-eight percent of whites and 48 percent of African Americans watched at least some of the convention. A comparison-of-means test indicates that this difference is statistically significant. A substantively large and statistically significant difference occurred in the average rate of convention watching between Democrats (47 percent) and Republicans (70 percent). Also significant (both substantively and statistically) was the difference between the college-educated (64 percent of whom watched at least some of the convention) and those without college degrees (50 percent). Finally, using analysis of variance, I examined differences in convention watching among a range of age categories. Compared to those respondents over the age of 65, 18–29 year olds, 30–49 year olds, and 50–64 year olds watched significantly less of the 2000 Republican convention.

Convention Exposure and Racial Symbolism

What impact did tuning in have on perceptions and evaluations of the Republican Party? Given the GOP's existing reputation with respect to race, I hypothesized that the use of racial images during the convention should be inconsistent with extant party images. Therefore, con-

---

1. For this part of the analysis, the watching the convention variable was dichotomized and coded 1 if the respondent watched at least some of the convention and 0 if the respondent watched none or very little of the convention.

vention exposure should incite a modification of the racial symbolism associated with the Republican Party. Investigating the validity of this claim required identifying a measure of the Republican Party's racial symbolism. Such an item would require respondents to make a summary judgment of the GOP with respect to race that was not tied to a particular candidate or policy stance. I used responses to the following question: "Would you say the Republican Party is generally doing a good job or a bad job these days of reaching out to blacks, Hispanics, and other minorities?" Because this question did not reference George W. Bush or any of the Republican Party's positions on racial issues, respondents were free to make an assessment of the GOP using whatever criteria they deemed applicable (either consciously or subconsciously) without any prompt from the interviewer. Responses to this question ranged from 0 to 1, where 0 indicated that the Republican Party did a bad job reaching out to blacks, Hispanics, and other minorities, .5 meant that the party did neither a good nor a bad job, and 1 indicated that the GOP did a good job.

Figure 7 presents the results of the survey analyses.[2] First, within the

TABLE 8.   Who Was Tuning In?

	Watched at Least Some of the Convention (%)	N
Blacks	47	369
Whites	57	887
Republicans	70	371
Democrats	47	532
Strong partisans	56	903
Weak partisans	51	395
Without college degree	50	856
With college degree	64	469
Male	52	739
Female	57	595
Age 18–29	46	258
Age 30–49	50	526
Age 50–64	59	316
Age 65+	65	217
Entire sample	55	1,370

Source: Post–GOP Convention Poll.

2. These figures are based on the regression analyses in table A2. All of the predicted values in this figure were calculated by holding gender and black (when applicable) at their modes and all other variables constant at their means.

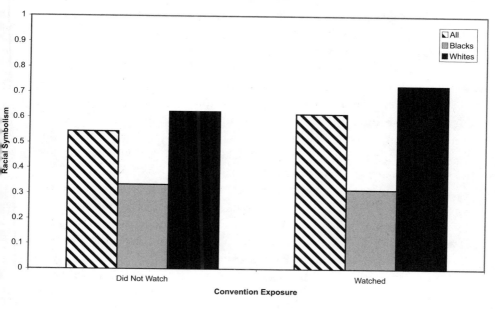

Fig. 7. Perceptions of the Republican Party's racial symbolism based on convention exposure. (Data from Post–GOP Convention Poll.)

entire sample, convention exposure led to a change in party images. Those respondents who watched none or little of the convention gave the Republican Party a racial symbolism score of .54, which essentially represents a neutral position. The GOP's racial symbolism placement increased to .61 among those who watched a great deal of the convention. On average, perceptions of the Republican Party's image with respect to race were positive among those exposed to the convention.

I speculated that the effect of watching the convention on perceptions of the Republican Party's image would be contingent on race. Specifically, I expected African Americans to be more resistant to the recent Republican campaign. To test for a race effect, I estimated the impact of convention watching on perceptions of the Republican Party's racial symbolism separately for African Americans and whites. As figure 7 indicates, whites' image of the Republican Party became more positive when they watched a great deal of the convention. When exposed to little or none of the convention, the mean placement of the Republican Party along the racial symbolism dimension was .62. Among those whites who watched a great deal of the convention, the GOP's placement increased by .11, to .73.

The Republican Party's perceived racial symbolism did not receive the same boost among African Americans. Blacks who did not watch a great deal of the convention placed the Republican Party at .33 on the racial symbolism dimension. Watching a great deal of the convention, however, resulted in a slight and statistically insignificant decrease among blacks. In other words, blacks who watched the convention and those who did not exhibited no difference in perceptions of the Republican Party's image with respect to race. Furthermore, the difference in reactions between blacks and whites was statistically significant at $p < .05$ (one-tailed test).

In general, the use of race at the 2000 Republican National Convention in Philadelphia left citizens with the impression that the Republican Party had become more inclusive. Nevertheless, the convention's impact was contingent on race. Not only did African Americans place the Republican Party significantly lower on the racial symbolism dimension, indicating that they did not believe that the GOP did a good job reaching out to minorities, but these perceptions did not improve after watching the convention.

Tweaking the Frames

Given the overall impact of convention exposure, I now turn to examining how the different framing of the convention influenced perceptions of the Republican Party. As stated earlier, these analyses seek to discern the intervening effect of the media's assessment of the convention and in so doing demonstrate the ways in which media outlets serve as barriers between a party projecting a new image of itself and the public's incorporation of this new version into its partisan stereotype.

Figure 8 presents the comparison of whites' and blacks' reactions to the different framing of the 2000 Republican National Convention.[3] Among whites, the media's framing of the convention had a direct impact on perceptions of the Republican Party's racial symbolism. As might be expected, when citizens read the article about the convention that omitted any discussion of the presence of blacks, their perceptions of the GOP's image with respect to race remained the same. In the control condition, subjects gave the Republican Party an average score

---

3. These figures are based on the regression analyses in table A3. All of the predicted values in this figure were calculated by holding gender at its mode and all other variables constant at their means.

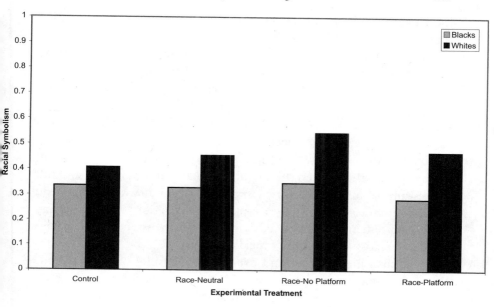

Fig. 8. The impact of convention frames on perceptions of the Republican Party's racial symbolism. (Data from 2002–2003 Party Image Study.)

of .41 on the racial symbolism item. In the race-neutral condition, the mean placement of the GOP was .46, an increase that is both substantively small and statistically indistinguishable from 0. When whites read about African American attendees, the Republican Party received a .55 score, a .14 increase in its perceived racial symbolism. This difference was statistically significant. Finally, the results suggest that when the media highlighted aspects of the party that did not change, they foiled the Republican Party's ability to alter perceptions of its image with respect to race. When white subjects read a version of the convention coverage that highlighted both blacks' presence and the fact that the GOP had maintained its traditional conservative platform, images of the Republican Party increased only by .01 to .47, a difference that was not statistically significant.

Much as was the case in their response to the convention in general, blacks' perceptions of the Republican Party's image with respect to race remained intact regardless of which version of the convention they read about. In general, figure 8 indicates that African Americans placed the Republican Party much lower on the racial symbolism dimension than did whites. Whereas whites' placement of the GOP hovered around the neutral to slightly positive side of the scale, blacks' perceptions of the party never surpassed .5, even when blacks read about the GOP's outreach efforts during the convention. In the control condition, African Americans' mean assessment of the Republican Party's racial symbolism was .34, which translates into negative perceptions of the GOP's image with respect to race. When blacks read a version of the convention coverage that highlighted the diversity of the convention program, they placed the Republican Party at .35, a small and not statistically significant increase. Similarly, when black subjects read about the convention in the race-platform condition, the Republican Party's placement on the racial symbolism dimension experienced a small and statistically insignificant decrease, to .29.

In summary, the survey and experimental results suggest that the ability to reshape party images largely depended not only on the individual's race but also on what information the individual received. The survey results show that convention exposure correlated positively with perceptions of the Republican Party's image with respect to race. Those who watched a great deal of the convention perceived the GOP as much better at reaching out to blacks and other minorities than did those who did not watch the convention. Further, the findings indicate that the Republican Party had greater success at modifying its image among whites. Regardless of the amount of convention exposure, blacks' Republican Party images remained intact. Moreover, although whites' party images altered as a result of convention exposure, the nature of information about the convention they received mattered. By excluding a discussion of the diversity of the Republican Party in 2000 or by juxtaposing the presence of blacks at the convention with a statement about the party's unchanged policy positions, the media made it difficult for the GOP to meet the threshold for what constitutes change.

Exploring the Alternatives

In the previous section, I demonstrated that the effect of watching the convention was contingent on the race of the individual. But was this really a race effect, or do alternative explanations account for why blacks and whites responded differently? This section answers this question.

Political Knowledge

Levels of political knowledge have long been associated with susceptibility to political communication and persuasion (see, e.g., Iyengar and Kinder 1987; Zaller 1992; Miller and Krosnick 1999, 2000). But would varying levels of political knowledge account for differences between blacks and whites? To answer this question, I composed an index of political knowledge using questions featured on the 2002–2003 Party Image Study.[4] The index comprised five measures, each representing the responses to questions about contemporary U.S. national politics.

1. What job or political office does Clarence Thomas hold?
2. How much of a majority is required for the U.S. Senate and House to override a presidential veto?
3. Who is the U.S. secretary of state?
4. Whose responsibility is it to decide if a law is constitutional or not? Is it the president, the Congress, or the Supreme Court?
5. What job or political office does Joe Lieberman hold?[5]

Using this scale, I compared the levels of political knowledge of blacks and whites. Although whites scored moderately higher than African Americans (.46 compared to .40), this difference was not statistically significant. While I do not argue that levels of political sophistication did not affect individuals' receptiveness to the Republican race strategy (see Philpot 2004), differences in political knowledge could not have accounted for the differences in blacks' and whites' susceptibility.

Alternatively, susceptibility might be contingent on issue-specific knowledge rather than on more general political knowledge. To explore whether this claim could be substantiated, I examined subjects' ability to answer the political knowledge questions that asked about African Americans. Specifically, I examined question 1, which asked about Clarence Thomas, and question 3, which asked about Colin Powell.[6]

4. Similar items were not available on the Post–GOP Convention Poll.

5. For each question, responses were coded 1 if the respondent answered the question correctly and 0 if the respondent did not. The scores for each question were then added together and scaled from 0 to 1. The interitem correlation between these measures ranged from .02 to .42. The Chronbach's alpha for these five items was .64. Overall, the mean score on this dimension was .42.

6. Again, responses were coded 1 if the respondent answered the question correctly and 0 if the respondent did not. The scores for each question were then added together and scaled from 0 to 1. The interitem correlation between these measures was .31. The Chronbach's alpha for these two items was .48, and the mean score on this dimension was .54.

As with general political knowledge, the variation between blacks' and whites' levels of issue-specific knowledge could not have accounted for the differences in levels of receptiveness to the Republican race strategy. African Americans' mean score was .53, while for whites that number was .56, a difference that was not statistically significant.

Party Identification

Finally, I examined whether party identification explains differences between blacks' and whites' susceptibility to convention exposure. Much like the national samples, 73 percent of the African Americans in the experimental sample identified as Democrats. Of the remainder, 7 percent identified as Republicans and 20 percent identified as independents. In contrast, 38 percent of the whites in the experimental sample identified as Democrats, an equal percentage identified as Republicans, and 25 percent identified as independents.[7] Thus, it is quite possible that the overwhelming number of Democrats in the black sample could be responsible for the differences between blacks and whites. Studies have shown that reactions to campaigns are very much contingent on the perceiver's party identification. Support for the importance of party identification dates back to early voting studies (e.g., Berelson, Lazarsfeld, and McPhee 1954; A. Campbell et al. 1960). Specifically, strong identifiers tend to resist campaign communication of the other party. If such is the case, blacks' party identification could be driving the differences found between blacks and whites. In other words, the disproportionate number of Democrats in the African American electorate may cause the race effect. Moreover, if blacks and whites with similar partisanship are compared, the race difference should disappear.

To explore whether party identification could account for the differences found between blacks and whites, I once again compared blacks' and whites' placement of the Republican Party on the racial symbolism dimension. This time, however, I restricted my comparisons to strong Democrats. As stated earlier, African Americans may resist the Republican Party's message of inclusion because they tend to be strong Democrats. As such, they should not be receptive to the Republican Party's campaign communication because of their partisanship rather than their race. If such is the case, partisanship should

---

7. Total exceeds 100 percent as a consequence of rounding.

also explain whites' receptivity to the Republican convention. In other words, strong Democrats, regardless of race, should be less affected by convention exposure.

Figure 9, which uses the Post–GOP Convention Poll data, shows that both blacks and whites who did not watch the convention perceived the Republican Party as having a negative racial symbolism.[8] Strong Democrats, regardless of race, apparently believed that the Republican Party did not do a good job reaching out to minorities. Although strong Democrats who were African American placed the Republican Party lower than strong Democrats who were white, this difference is not statistically significant and might be expected since, absent exposure to the convention, strong Democrats would not necessarily be primed to think about race when evaluating the Republican Party. Thus, no polarization should exist between blacks and whites. When strong Democrats watched the convention, whites placed the Republican Party .08 points higher on the racial symbolism dimension. In contrast, blacks lowered their placement of the GOP by .02, from .19 to .17. Moreover, the differences between black and white strong Democrats were statistically significant. When strong Democrats were exposed to the images of black supporters of the Republican Party at the convention, black and white perceptions of the GOP's racial symbolism diverged. However, neither group placed the Republican Party above .5 on the racial symbolism dimension.

As figure 10 indicates, a similar pattern emerges in the 2002–2003 Party Image Study.[9] Again, both black and white strong Democrats in all experimental treatment groups on average gave the Republican Party negative racial symbolism scores. In the control condition, blacks who were strong Democrats gave the Republican Party a mean racial symbolism score of .32. Whites with the same party identification placed the Republican Party at .05, a statistically significant difference. In the race-neutral condition, the difference between whites and blacks dissipated. Although blacks placed the GOP at .34 and whites gave the Republican Party an average racial symbolism score of .25, this differ-

---

8. This figure is based on the regression analyses in table A4. All of the predicted values in this figure were calculated by holding gender at its mode and all other variables constant at their means.

9. This figure is based on the regression analyses in table A5. As with the other figures, the predicted values in figure 10 were calculated by holding gender at its mode and all other variables constant at their means.

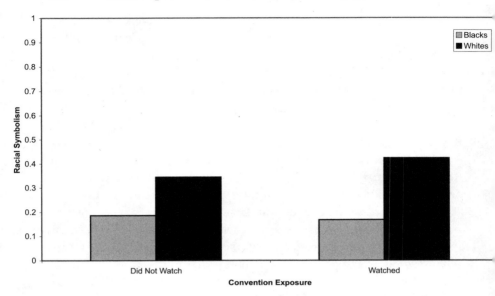

Fig. 9.   Perceptions of the Republican Party's racial symbolism based on convention exposure among strong Democrats. (Data from Post–GOP Convention Poll.)

ence was statistically indistinguishable from 0. When strong Democrats read about the diversity featured at the 2000 Republican National Convention, whites in the race–no platform condition placed the Republican Party .11 points higher on the racial symbolism dimension than did whites in the control condition. Conversely, blacks in the race–no platform condition lowered their placement of the party by .02. Further, the difference between blacks' and whites' reactions in this condition was statistically significant. Finally, in the race-platform condition, where subjects read about the black convention attendees and read that the GOP had not changed its platform, the difference between black and white partisans once again disappeared. Although a statistically significant difference existed between blacks and whites in general, no additional difference occurred between black and white partisans in this particular condition. Taken together, these results suggest that being strong Democrats cannot entirely explain why blacks were more resistant to the Republican appeal.

In summary, political knowledge (either issue specific or more general) and party identification fail to explain the differences found

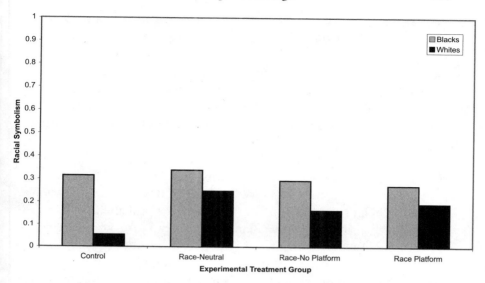

Fig. 10. The impact of convention frames on perceptions of the Republican Party's racial symbolism among strong Democrats. (Data from 2002–2003 Party Image Study.)

between blacks and whites. For the most part, blacks remained fairly constant, regardless of what type of information they received about the convention, in their perceptions of the Republican Party. In contrast, whites of both parties modified (to varying degrees) their Republican Party images with respect to race when exposed to the diversity featured at the 2000 Republican National Convention. Party identification unquestionably matters. Nevertheless, susceptibility to the Republican campaign was also contingent on race.

Racial Symbolism and Candidate Evaluation

As discussed in chapter 1, the ultimate goal of reshaping party images is electoral success. Consequently, I now examine the impact of convention exposure and improving party images on candidate evaluations. I speculated earlier that the same stimulus—in this case, the 2000 Republican National Convention—that altered party images with respect to race should also prime the use of this construct in subsequent candidate evaluations. Given that watching the convention affected whites' but not blacks' perceptions of the GOP's outreach efforts, I examined whether watching the convention primed the use of these perceptions when individuals were required to evaluate political candidates and whether the differences between blacks and whites persisted. If a priming effect occurred, the perception of the Republican Party's effort to reach out to minorities would be expected to be contingent on watching a great deal of the convention. I expected to find that convention exposure would increase the weight of the Republican Party's racial symbolism in subsequent evaluations of Republican candidates.

Figure 11 confirms my expectations. Using the results of a logistic regression (see table A5 in the appendix), I calculated the predicted probability of voting for George W. Bush in 2000 based on convention exposure.[10] Figure 11 presents the increase in the probability of voting for Bush when images of the Republican Party move from negative racial symbolism to positive racial symbolism. In other words, I subtracted the probability of voting for Bush among those with negative perceptions of the Republican Party's image with respect to race from the probability of voting for Bush among those with a positive perception. For African Americans, the difference between having negative and positive perceptions of the GOP's racial symbolism among non–convention watchers was only .17. Absent convention watching, if the Republican Party improved its image on race among blacks, it could expect only a modest increase in the probability of voting for its presidential candidate. Although the probability of voting for Bush increased by .34 among those who watched the convention, the difference between the two groups was not statistically significant. Stated another way, improving party images among blacks yielded the same boost in the probability of voting for Bush regardless of convention exposure.

Watching the convention increased the weight of the Republican Party's racial symbolism on white respondents' candidate evaluations. Specifically, improving the Republican Party's image with respect to race among those who did not watch the convention led to a .12 increase in the probability of voting for Bush. By improving party images among those whites who watched the convention, however, the Republican Party increased the probability of voting for Bush by .62, a statistically significant difference.

10. These analyses rely on the Post–GOP Convention Poll. Predicted probabilities were calculated by holding gender at its mode and all other variables constant at their means.

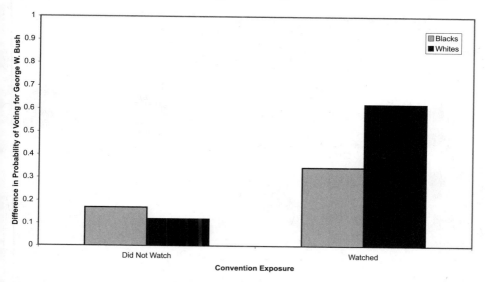

Fig. 11. The impact of improving the Republican Party's racial symbolism on the probability of voting for George W. Bush. (Data from Post–GOP Convention Poll.)

I conducted similar analyses using the 2002–2003 Party Image Study. Figure 12 presents the difference in Bush's feeling thermometer scores when the Republican Party improved its image in the different treatment groups.[11] In both the control and race-neutral conditions, improving party images led to a small and statistically insignificant decrease in Bush's mean feeling thermometer scores among both blacks and whites. Essentially, in these two conditions where subjects were not exposed to an account of the diversity of the 2000 Republican National Convention's program, the GOP's image with respect to race had no bearing on evaluations of Bush.

Conversely, improving party images among subjects in the race–no platform and race-platform conditions resulted in a substantial and statistically significant increase in Bush's feeling thermometer scores. Among blacks in the race–no platform condition, improving the

11. This figure is based on the regression analyses in table A7. The mean thermometer scores were calculated by holding gender at its mode and holding all other variables at their means.

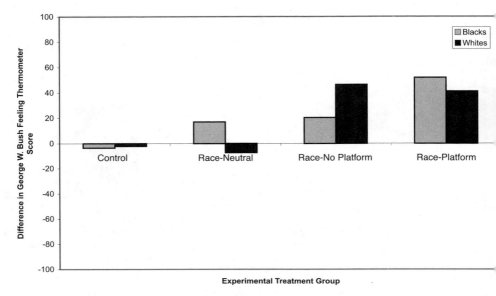

Fig. 12.   The impact of improving the Republican Party's racial symbolism on George W. Bush's feeling thermometer. (Data from
2002–2003 Party Image Study.)

Republican Party's racial symbolism yielded a 20-point increase in
Bush's feeling thermometer. This increase reached 52 points among
blacks in the race-platform condition. When whites read about the
African Americans present at the 2000 convention in the race–no platform condition and improved their images of the Republican Party's
racial symbolism, Bush's feeling thermometer increased by 46 points.
Likewise, Bush's feeling thermometer increased by 41 points when
subjects modified their party images in a positive direction in the race-
platform condition.

In sum, exposing people to information about the Republican
Party's diversity efforts during the 2000 national convention primed
the use of the party's racial symbolism in subsequent candidate evaluation. Bush received more positive evaluations from individuals whose
party images were modified as a result of convention exposure; however, party images did not improve in all cases. On average, blacks,
regardless of convention exposure, had negative perceptions of the
GOP's racial symbolism. Hence, evaluations of Bush remained quite
low. Moreover, evaluations of Bush became more negative when

blacks were primed to think about the Republican Party's racial symbolism. In the control condition, blacks with negative perceptions of the Republican Party's image with respect to race gave Bush a mean score of 42 on the feeling thermometer. Blacks who believed that the Republican Party did a bad job reaching out to minorities in the race—no Platform and race-platform conditions gave Bush average feeling thermometer scores of 23 and 16, respectively. In addition, whites' party images did not improve in the race-platform condition. Whites with negative perceptions of the Republican Party in the control condition gave Bush a mean thermometer score of 68. In the race-platform condition, whites with negative perceptions of the Republican Party's racial symbolism gave Bush a score of 38. Consequently, priming the section of the Republican Party's image that relates to race in candidate evaluations could adversely affect candidate evaluations among those who did not believe that the Republican Party did a good job reaching out to minorities.

Maintaining the Republican Party's Southern Base

Finally, I examined the impact of watching the convention on southern whites.[12] In chapter 1, I posited that to succeed, the 2000 Republican race strategy had to attract new voters without alienating its current electoral base. The results presented in this chapter suggest that exposure to the 2000 Republican National Convention significantly increased the likelihood of voting for Bush among both white and black voters provided that the convention convinced them that the Republican Party did a good job of reaching out to blacks, Hispanics, and other minorities. But how did southern whites react to the convention? To answer this question, I replicated the analyses among southern whites in the Gallup survey.[13]

Figure 13 presents the results.[14] On average, whites in the South placed the Republican Party at .67 on the racial symbolism dimension.

12. The South is defined as the eleven states of the Confederacy—South Carolina, Mississippi, Florida, Alabama, Georgia, Louisiana, Virginia, Arkansas, Tennessee, North Carolina, and Texas.

13. Analyses in this section are confined to the Post–GOP Convention Poll because subjects were not asked the state in which they resided in the 2002–2003 Party Image Survey, so there were no means of distinguishing between southerners and nonsoutherners.

14. Figures 13 and 14 are based on the analyses presented in table A8. As with the other figures in this chapter, the predicted values were calculated by holding gender at its mode and the rest of the variables constant at their means.

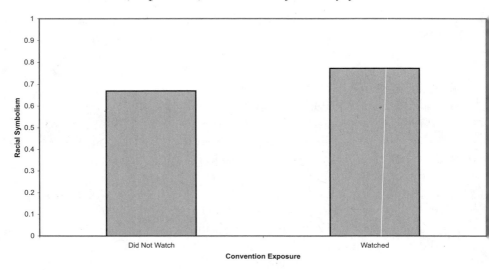

Fig. 13. Perceptions of the Republican Party's racial symbolism based on convention exposure among southern whites. (Data from Post–GOP Convention Poll).

Like whites in general, southern whites' significantly improved their party images, improving their placement of the Republican Party on the racial symbolism item by .10, to .77, when exposed to the convention.

Figure 14 indicates that watching the convention also primed the use of the Republican Party's racial symbolism in southern white vote preferences. For example, among southern whites who watched the convention, improving the Republican Party's image with respect to race increased the likelihood of voting for George W. Bush by 77 percentage points (from .21 to .98). Among southern whites who did not watch the convention, this increase amounted to only 3 percentage points. The probability of voting for Bush among southern whites with negative perceptions of the Republican Party's racial symbolism not exposed to the convention was .84. When this group had positive perceptions of the Republican Party's image with respect to race, the probability of voting for Bush was .87. Even though the Republican Party's image with respect to race did not play a significant role in the likelihood of voting for Bush among those who did not watch the convention, the probability of voting for Bush remained quite high. These

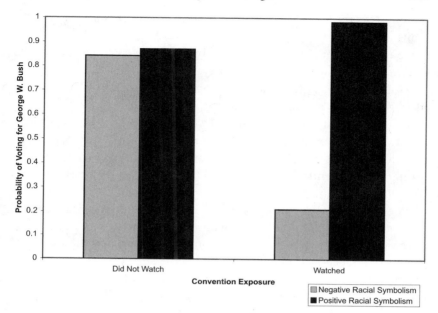

Fig. 14. The impact of improving the Republican Party's racial symbolism on the probability of voting for George W. Bush among southern whites. (Data from Post–GOP Convention Poll).

findings suggest that the Republican Party succeeded on both fronts—it increased its number of supporters and did not disrupt its current electoral base.

Conclusion

Convention watching apparently affected people's perceptions of the Republican Party's racial symbolism. Not everyone who watched the convention was affected in the same way, however. Susceptibility to convention exposure was contingent on an individual's race. As posited earlier, watching the 2000 Republican convention generally had no effect on African Americans' perceptions of the GOP, perhaps because African Americans' preexisting party images were so strongly rooted that the Republican Party's recent attempt to appear racially inclusive could not override the numerous other incidences of racial conservatism. For blacks, increasing the visibility of blacks in the party was not enough to change the Republican Party's image with respect to race because the party had not altered the policy positions that directly affected blacks. By failing to address the substantive components of their party images—the information these individuals used to make their interpretations—the Republican Party failed to address the objects that give meaning to the party.

Modifying party images also was largely contingent on what information individuals received about the convention. Convention exposure had only minimal effects on subjects exposed to mediated versions of the Republican Party's convention activities that deviated (even slightly) from the party's projected image. By spinning what transpired during the convention, the media created obstacles that impeded the process of party image change.

These findings also suggest that priming the Republican Party's racial symbolism in candidate evaluations proved to be a double-edged sword. Watching a great deal of the convention increased the weight of the GOP's racial symbolism on candidate evaluations. The ability to translate this phenomenon into electoral success, however, depended on the party's ability to improve its image. In cases where the Republican Party's image with respect to race remained negative, priming the use of this construct resulted in more negative evaluations of the Republican presidential candidate.

The results presented in this chapter suggest that when parties attempt to reshape their images along a particular dimension, they must do two things simultaneously—improve their party images with respect to that dimension and make that dimension relevant to candidate evaluations. Without accomplishing these two things concurrently, the process of altering party images might have unintended consequences.

6 *One Step Forward, Two Steps Back*

The Compassionate Conservative versus the Florida Recount

So FAR, I HAVE EXAMINED three obstacles—history, the predispositions of voters, and the media—that political parties face in attempting to reshape their images. Chapter 6 explores the role of one additional barrier—the parties themselves. Specifically, I investigate what happens when a political party does not convey a consistent image of itself. As discussed earlier, the incorporation of new information into individuals' party images depends on existing perceptions of the party. People more willingly encode information that is consistent with their extant partisan stereotypes. If citizens encounter both a new picture of a party and an alternative version of the party that conforms to the old, they will discount the new projected party image. Therefore, a party's attempt to modify its image is largely contingent on its ability to maintain the new projected version of itself. When the party retreats from its new image, citizens' perceptions of the party will revert back to the original picture.

With respect to the example used throughout this book—the GOP's attempt to reshape its racial symbolism—I examined the Republican Party's image in light of the dispute over the 2000 election. The Republican Party's alleged participation in activities aimed at disenfranchising minorities directly conflicted with the picture of the party painted during the 2000 Republican National Convention. As a result, the GOP's attempt to improve its racial symbolism was subverted.

Dimpled Chads and Disenfranchised Voters

On January 20, 2001, George W. Bush was inaugurated as the 43rd president of the United States of America. Not since the election of

1876, however, had a presidential election generated such controversy. George W. Bush received 50,456,002 votes, 47.87 percent of the popular vote. His opponent, Al Gore, received 48.38 percent of the popular vote. Nevertheless, Bush won the election by winning Florida's 25 Electoral College votes. Bush had won Florida, the state where his brother served as governor, by 537 votes. Ironically, Florida, one of the disputed states in the 1876 election, lay at the heart of the controversy 124 years later. As Walton and Smith (2003) explained,

> The 2000 election is controversial because in effect the "loser" became the "winner." It is also controversial because there were widespread allegations of voting irregularities and suppression of the black vote in Florida—the state that gave Bush his one-vote margin of victory in the electoral college. Finally, the 2000 election is controversial because the Supreme Court affected its outcome by stopping an ongoing recount of the Florida vote. (160)

Many observers argued that Bush's win was illegitimate and that the presidency had been stolen or at least bought.

The mainstream discussion of the election centered on miscast or uncounted ballots. As Kellner (2001) explained, "[I]t was revealed on November 8 that many usually Democratic Party voters in Palm Beach County, Florida, had accidentally voted for ultra-rightwing candidate Pat Buchanan because of the confusing, and allegedly illegal, 'butterfly' ballot that listed the candidates side by side with arrows pointing to the holes to be punched" (31–32). Furthermore, close to 20,000 ballots had been disqualified as a result of faulty voting equipment. Still-attached chads[1] prevented citizens' votes from being counted.

Along with the discussions of dimpled chads and butterfly ballots were allegations of corruption. Several media accounts indicated that Florida Secretary of State Katherine Harris "commissioned a Republican-connected firm to 'cleanse' voter lists of felons, and in so doing had wiped off around 100,000 legitimate voters, mostly African American and poor voters who tended to vote Democrat" (Kellner 2001, 39). Moreover, several reports indicated that African Americans had been harassed and denied the right to vote when they arrived at vari-

---

1. According to the *Merriam-Webster Collegiate Dictionary*, 11th ed., chads are "small pieces of paper or cardboard produced in punching paper tape or data cards."

ous voting sites (Kellner 2001, 33). Finally, *USA Today,* in conjunction with several other newspapers, found that "in precincts where blacks were the majority, 8.9 percent of the votes were uncounted compared to 2.4 percent in white majority precincts and 3 percent statewide." In addition, this study found that all of the precincts with the highest percentage of spoiled ballots had African American voting-age populations of 80 percent or higher (Walton and Smith 2003, 162). Thus, like the election of 1876, the 2000 election proved detrimental to African American voters.

African American leaders saw the Florida situation as just one of many incidents of election fraud. In an issue of *Crisis* published after the 2000 election, the National Association for the Advancement of Colored People (NAACP) listed several instances of vote suppression committed by the Republican Party over the preceding two decades. Each incident involved the intimidation of African American and Hispanic voters. The NAACP argued that "whether in the East, South, or far West, voter suppression of black and brown people is a favorite tactic of Republican strategists" (Strickland 2000, 13).

Members of the Congressional Black Caucus (CBC) protested the election results. During the certification of the Electoral College vote, 12 CBC members "tried in vain to block the counting of Florida's 25 electoral votes, protesting that black voters had been disenfranchised" (Mitchell 2001, 17). When Bush was formally elected, 20 members of the CBC protested by leaving the proceedings. In addition, several members of the CBC as well as thousands of other blacks protested Bush's inauguration by holding a demonstration outside the Supreme Court building (Walton and Smith 2003, 165).

The treatment of black and Hispanic voters certainly contradicted the theme of inclusion and diversity put forth by Bush and the Republican Party during the course of the election. How did these events affect the Republican Party? Did the dispute over the presidency undo the headway the Republicans had made during the 2000 convention? To answer these questions, I first examined the media's coverage of the Republican Party during this time. Using articles appearing in the *New York Times* (a mainstream news source) and the *New York Amsterdam News* (an African American news source) from Election Day 2000 until December 13, when Al Gore conceded the election, I explored the extent to which the media connected the GOP to the Florida recount and whether the media linked the recount to a discussion of race. Utilizing the 2002 American National Election Study, I then examined whether the election affected assessments of the Republican Party. Specifically, I explored whether questions of the election's legitimacy affected evaluations of the Republicans' ability to represent minorities.

The Media and the 2000 Election

In discussing the Republican Party in the postelection period, the media overwhelmingly focused on the party's role in the Florida recount efforts. Of the articles about the Republican Party in the sample, 63 percent discussed the Florida recount. For example, a *New York Times* article reported,

> In West Palm Beach, the canvassing board plodded through the recount here as a Republican rally of some 300 stopped traffic outside, waving signs that read, "Democrats Are Bottom Feeders" and "Al Gore Is a Liar" and others with clever obscenities. (Bragg and Holloway 2000, A1)

The discussion also included the Republican Party's use of absentee ballots and whether these ballots should be counted. In addition, the media focused on the partisan argument over whether all of the ballots should be recounted by hand or by machine and who should oversee the recount.

Media coverage of the Republican Party also featured discussions of the Republican convention, even though more than three months had passed since the convention's end. Specifically, 6 percent of the articles discussed the convention. Much of this coverage centered on the convention's role in the overall process of electing the president.

The Republican Party also was discussed in conjunction with different minority groups and the issue of diversity. For example, 25 percent of the articles discussed African Americans, 11 percent discussed Hispanics, 7 percent discussed Jewish Americans, and 5 percent discussed racial minorities and diversity in general. In addition, 11 percent of the articles discussed women and 4 percent discussed the poor. Most of the articles in the *New York Times* connecting the GOP to race speculated about presidential cabinet appointments:

> Mr. Bush, they said, would also like his cabinet to include at least one Hispanic, blacks and women—a desire heightened by the closeness of the election, the need to unite a divided country and

his sustained campaign pledge to put a new face on the Republican Party. (Bruni 2000, A27)

Other *New York Times* articles discussed the historical relationship between African Americans and the Republican Party and whether Latino voters would become a part of the party's electoral base.

In contrast, several articles in the *New York Amsterdam News* focused on the role of black and Hispanic voters in other races, such as the New York senatorial race. One example reported,

> All is not now sweetness and light in the state Republican Party. It has been virtually destroyed by a one-woman tidal wave, by the name of Hillary Clinton, who came into New York as a stranger, listened on a tour, did her homework, visited, learned and finally wound up in the Black church and in the Black community—for she found out that this was where she was most comfortable and could be herself. (Tatum 2000b, 1)

A number of articles also analyzed the electoral fate of black Republican candidates in 2000.

I then examined the juxtaposition of race against the discussion of the Florida recount. These analyses sought to discern whether the media's coverage of the dispute over the election was framed in a way in which citizens could connect it to the racial symbolism of the Republican Party. Of the articles discussing the Florida recount, 20 percent discussed African Americans. Another 20 percent included a discussion of diversity and racial minorities. Regardless of source, these articles were not particularly flattering, as in this example from the *New York Amsterdam News*.

> But we begin the millennium in America, which is, by the way, a very young country, not knowing who the next president of the United States will be. We do know that Al Gore won. What we are not certain of at this point is how the Bush forces, including father George, brother Jeb, George W., the CIA and the Republican Party and the wealthiest white men in America, will try to convince Black people that the election for president that is being stolen in Florida is not really a theft at all. It is merely, to their way of thinking, a more honest way to decide who the president of the United States is or should be, based upon a whole system of rationaliza-

tion, lies, deceit and more duplicity than can be named. (Tatam 2000a, A51)

Several articles referred to members of the Republican Party as crooks and criminals who had stolen the election. Moreover, the articles discussed the disenfranchisement of black and Latino voters.

Finally, 6 percent of the media coverage mentioned the Republican convention in conjunction with the Florida recount. According to a November 2000 *New York Times* article,

> During the G.O.P. convention in Philadelphia we were treated to the view of a Republican Party that had become less white, less elitist, more multiracial, led by a Texas governor who promised to be a uniter, not a divider, and who would distance himself from the mean-spiritedness of the Newt Gingrich/Tom DeLay era.
>
> During the post-election, however, we have seen a Republican Party dominated by elderly elite white men and women, who will delegitimize any court, any judge and any ruling that stands in the way of Mr. Bush's presumed right to govern. The Bush aides will question the patriotism of anyone who raises doubts about confusing military ballots, but they evince no concern for blacks, Jews and Hispanics who wrongly voted for Pat Buchanan, or no one, because of their confusing ballots. So much for the Spirit of Philadelphia. (Friedman 2000, A29)

These findings suggest that the Republican Party's image in the media was connected to the Florida recount. Moreover, this discussion was linked in many instances to race, directly conflicting with the image of compassionate conservatism the party had painted in the preceding months. The media's postelection coverage of the party may have aided in undoing the improvement in perceptions that the Republican Party had enjoyed in the postconvention period.

The Public, the Republican Party, and the 2000 Election

The previous section discussed the media's perception of the Republican Party in the postelection period. But how did the American electorate perceive the Republican Party during this time?

Chapter 3 showed that people perceive parties to have distinct reputations for the ability to represent different constituencies. With respect to which party was better for different groups in society in

2002, individuals recognized similar relationships. (See the appendix for the exact questions respondents were asked.) Table 9 indicates that people believed that the Democratic Party was best for blacks. Specifically, 42 percent of respondents indicated that the Democrats were better for African Americans, while only 5 percent believed that the Republican Party was better and 53.2 percent believed that no differences existed. When it came to which party was better for white Americans, the Republican Party had the advantage, but not overwhelmingly so: 21.9 percent of respondents believed that the Republican Party was better for whites, while 5.3 percent indicated that the Democratic Party was better; however, 73 percent saw no difference between the two parties.

Differences also existed along gender lines. The Republican Party was perceived to be better than the Democratic Party for men. While the vast majority of respondents saw no difference between the two parties with respect to men, 21 percent indicated that the Republican Party was better, compared to 6 percent who indicated that the Democratic Party was better. In contrast, about 29 percent of respondents thought the Democratic Party was better for women, while less than 7 percent believed the Republican Party was better for women and nearly two-thirds saw no difference between the two parties.

Finally, respondents thought that the Democratic Party was better for the poor and that the Republican Party was better for the rich. Specifically, just over half of the respondents indicated that the Democratic Party was better for poor people, while 8.7 percent chose the Republican Party and 39 percent saw little difference between the two parties. In contrast, 56.8 percent of respondents believed that the GOP better served the interests of the rich, 37.7 percent saw no difference between the parties, and only 5.5 percent thought that the Democratic Party was better.

TABLE 9. **Perceptions of Which Party Is Better for Different Groups in Society (in percentages)**

	Blacks	Whites	Women	Men	Poor	Rich
Democrats	41.8	5.3	28.7	6.2	52.7	5.5
Republicans	5.0	21.9	6.8	20.9	8.7	56.8
Not much difference between them	53.2	72.8	64.5	73.0	38.6	37.7

Source: 2002 American National Election Study.

The 2002 American National Election Study asked, "All things considered, would you say that the 2000 presidential election was decided in a way that was fair or unfair?"[2] Table 10 presents the distribution of responses. In general, 60 percent believed that the 2000 election was decided in a fair manner. Approval of the election, however, varied by race and partisanship. Whereas 66 percent of whites believed that the election was decided fairly, only 21 percent of blacks agreed. Republicans were also more likely than Democrats and independents to approve of the way the 2000 election was decided. Specifically, 30 percent of Democrats, 61 percent of independents, and 92 percent of Republicans approved of the election.

How did the perceived fairness of the 2000 election relate to the GOP's party image? In the aftermath of the election, responses to this question were significantly correlated to the Republican Party's image along a number of dimensions. In particular, perceptions of which party better represented the interests of different groups in society were moderated by the election's perceived fairness. Evaluations of the Republican Party, however, were affected only when they called into question the effectiveness of the GOP's representation of minority groups. For example, figure 15 examines differences in evaluations of the two parties' racial symbolism—that is, which party was best for blacks, based on attitudes toward the 2000 elections.[3] The y-axis represents a scale from 1 to 0 where 1 means that the Democratic Party does a better job representing a particular group and 0 means the Republican Party is best for that group. A value of .5 means that no difference exists between the two. Among whites, no difference existed between those who believed the 2000 election was fair and those who did not—evaluations ranged from .43 to .45, with the Republican Party having a slight advantage over the Democratic Party in representing whites. Regardless of perceptions of the 2000 election, respondents believed that the Democratic Party better represented African Americans. Those who believed that the election was unfair, however, indicated that the Democratic Party was 16 percentage points better at representing blacks than those who believed the election was fair. Evaluations moved from .61 to .77 as perceptions of the election became more negative, a statistically significant difference.

2. See the appendix for information on how this variable was coded.

3. The predicted values used in this figure were calculated using the results presented in table A9. Female was held at its mode, and all other variables were held at their means.

TABLE 10. The 2000 Election Was Decided in a Way That Was Fair (in percentages)

	All	Blacks	Whites	Men	Women	Democrats	Republicans	Independents
Approve strongly	41.3	12.0	45.0	43.4	39.7	14.8	72.7	37.2
Approve not strongly	19.0	9.0	20.8	19.8	18.4	15.6	19.7	23.9
Disapprove not strongly	7.6	10.0	7.2	6.5	8.5	10.6	1.4	9.1
Disapprove strongly	32.0	69.0	27.0	30.3	33.3	59.1	6.3	29.8

Source: 2002 American National Election Study.

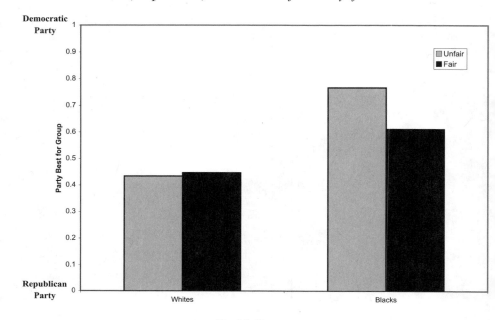

Racial Group

Fig. 15.   Impressions of the Republican Party's image on race based on perceived fairness of the 2000 election. (Data from 2002 American National Election Study.)

The same pattern emerges with respect to other minority groups. As figure 16 illustrates, respondents overwhelmingly believed that the Republican Party does a better job of representing the interests of the rich.[4] Although a modest difference existed between respondents who believed that the election was fair and those who did not, this difference was not statistically significant. In contrast, respondents perceived the Democratic Party as better representing the poor. Those who believed the election was unfair, however, gave the Democratic Party a larger advantage—on average, a statistically significant 9 percentage point difference.

Respondents believed that the Republican Party better represented men and that the Democratic Party better represented women. When asked to evaluate the parties' ability to represent men, respondents

4. The calculated predicted values for this figure were derived from the regression analysis results presented in table A10. Again, these estimates were calculated by holding the variable for gender at its mode and all other variables at their means.

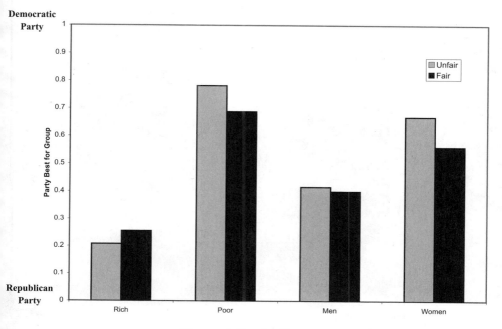

Class and Gender Group

Fig. 16.   Impressions of the Republican Party's image on gender and class based on perceived fairness of the 2000 election. (Data from 2002 American National Election Study.)

gave the Republican Party about a 10 percentage point advantage, regardless of perceptions of the 2000 election. With regard to the representation of women, however, a statistically significant 11 percentage point difference existed between those who believed that the election was fair and those who did not.

Perceptions of the 2000 election also mattered when it came to evaluations of George W. Bush. Figure 17 presents the results.[5] This time, the y-axis represents average feeling thermometer scores. Higher scores indicate warmer feelings toward Bush. On average, those with negative perceptions of the 2000 election gave Bush a feeling thermometer score of 56, just higher than neutral. Among those with more positive perceptions of the election, Bush's feeling thermometer score increased to 76. This 20-degree difference is statistically significant.

5. The predicted values used in this figure were calculated using the results presented in table A11. Female was held at its mode, and all other variables were held at their means.

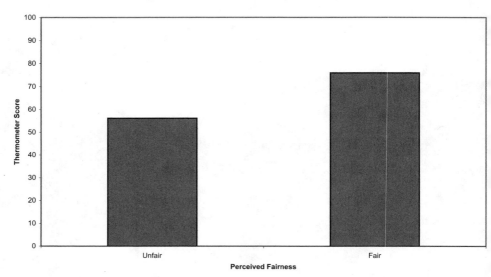

Fig. 17.   George W. Bush feeling thermometer based on perceived fairness of the 2000 election. (Data from 2002 American National Election Study.)

Conclusion

Scholars have only just begun to gauge the impact of the 2000 election. Studies have already found that the election did not undermine "the overall level of expressed public confidence in either the presidency or the [U.S. Supreme] Court" (Price and Romantan 2004, 952). Nevertheless, I find that the perceived fairness of the 2000 election factored into the calculus of citizens' evaluations of the parties. The events surrounding the 2000 election remained salient in voters' minds two years later. The perceived fairness of the election affected beliefs regarding the Republican Party's ability to adequately represent minority groups as well as positive or negative feelings toward Bush. The perceived fairness of the election did not correlate with all assessments of the parties. This was not just a matter of people making general partisan evaluations. Citizens linked the election to particular (relevant) aspects of the parties' images.

The results presented in this chapter also confirm that the process of shaping and reshaping party images is an uphill battle. Elites face constant opposition from their competitors, from the media, and from everyday politics. At times, elites face opposition—not all of it intentional—from within their party ranks. Nevertheless, reshaping party images is an iterative process that sometimes requires elites to take one step forward and two steps back.

7 *The Second Time Around*

Race and the 2004 Republican National Convention

> The 2004 Republican National Convention will celebrate the president's record of improving the quality of life for all Americans. Under the leadership of President Bush, the Republican Party celebrates diversity and is strengthening its ties to ethnic communities throughout the nation.
> —Republican National Committee, 2004

WHILE POLITICAL PARTIES FACE several obstacles when attempting to reinvent themselves in the minds of the public, there is at least one way in which a party can smooth the road ahead of it—repeat the effort. Continuing to project its new image through an additional election cycle demonstrates a certain level of sincerity and commitment to voters. Whereas a party projecting an inconsistent version of itself undermines its ability to convey change, sustaining the new image increases a party's credibility and bolsters its ability to alter its image. Thus, by repeating the effort, political parties are better able to modify existing partisan stereotypes.

The Republican Party's ability to reshape its racial symbolism depends on its willingness to repeat the message of inclusion and diversity featured during the 2000 election cycle. And in fact, the GOP did just that in 2004. As in 2000, the 2004 Republican National Convention in New York City featured a number of African American speakers and entertainers.

In this chapter, I examine whether a political party has more success when voters realize that its attempt to reshape its image is part of an ongoing endeavor. To do so, I once again rely on experimental data. Specifically, I use the 2005 Party Image Study to examine whether highlighting the fact that the Republican Party's outreach to black voters was a repeated effort succeeded in reshaping the party's image. As part of the 2005 Party Image Study, subjects were exposed to four dif-

136

ferent versions of a question wording experiment. In the control condition, subjects were just required to answer the following question: "How much do you think the Republican Party has changed over the last few years?" Before answering this question in the other experimental treatment groups, subjects were asked to read one of three brief scenarios about the 2004 Republican National Convention—one that was race-neutral, one that described the GOP once again reaching out to black voters, and one that described the Republican Party's outreach efforts in conjunction with its unchanged platform. (See the appendix for exact question wording.) In all three versions, subjects read, "This outreach effort is an ongoing strategy that began at the 2000 Republican National Convention." After answering the experimental question, subjects were asked how well they thought the Republican Party did in reaching out to blacks, Hispanics, and other minorities. Responses to this question, which is the same item used in both the Post–GOP Convention Poll and the 2002–2003 Party Image Study, were coded 1 if subjects believed that the Republican Party did a good job, 0 if the party did a bad job, and .5 if the GOP did neither a good nor bad job.

I examine the differences in subjects' mean placement of the Republican Party on the racial symbolism dimension based on experimental condition. I argue that two campaigns are better than one—that is, that political parties' attempts to modify their images are more persuasive when they are replicated. By picking up where they left off, political parties are in a better position to meet the threshold for what constitutes change in voters' minds. Therefore, I hypothesized that the Republican Party would have more success in reshaping its image in 2004 than was the case in 2000.

Pulling out the Stops

The presence of African Americans at the 2004 Republican National Convention met and in some instances exceeded the levels experienced in 2000. As table 11 illustrates, the number of black delegates increased from 85 (4.1 percent) in 2000 to 167 (6.7 percent) in 2004. The number of black alternates also increased, from 76 in 2000 to 124 in 2004. The convention featured notable African American celebrities such as 2003 Miss America Erika Harold and NFL Hall of Famer Lynn Swann. Musical guests included the Harlem Boys Choir and gospel recording artist Donnie McClurkin.

The Republican Party clearly was quite proud of its delegate diversity. According to the official Web site for the 2004 convention, "[W]hen the Republican Party hosts its first-ever national convention in New York City next month, it will welcome the most diverse group of delegates in party history."[1] The Web site spotlighted the minority delegates, profiling several black, Latino, and Asian American attendees.

In addition, the party provided background information on how it had increased its minority support and had done so at a rate that exceeded that of the Democratic Party. According to the Republican National Committee, the "Republican Party is celebrating a milestone achievement in [the] party's connection with America's minorities."[2] The GOP also took pride in the fact that during his first term in office, Republican president George W. Bush had appointed one of the most diverse cabinets in history. Finally, the Republican Party detailed how the Bush administration's record on education, home ownership, and unemployment had greatly benefited minorities.

After the convention, the Republican Party's outreach efforts continued. In subsequent weeks, the GOP expended substantial resources on targeting minority voters. From September 7 to November 2, the Bush-Cheney campaign spent just under $2 million on media targeting minority voters; in contrast, the Kerry-Edwards campaign spent slightly more than $600,000 on minority media during the same period. As a proportion of cumulative media expenditures, the Republican Party spent about 2 percent on minority media buys, while the Democratic Party spent 1.5 percent (Shaw 2006). These figures suggest that in 2004, the Republican Party engaged in a number of activities aimed at attracting traditional Democratic-leaning voters.

TABLE 11. African American Presence at the 2004 Republican National Convention

Delegates	167
	(6.7%)
Speakers	12
	(12.8%)
Musical entertainers	3
	(16.7%)

Source: Republican National Committee.

1. www.gopconvention.com.
2. www.gopconvention.com.

Even the Republican Party's 2004 platform received a bit of a facelift. Although the party did not change its position on racial issues, it made the discussion of racism and diversity slightly more prominent. Whereas in 2000 the GOP devoted only one paragraph to addressing racism and three paragraphs to minority interests, four years later the platform contained two paragraphs about racism and seven paragraphs about minorities. The 2004 Republican platform vowed to focus on America's most needy students, especially minority students, and denounced bigotry and prejudice and celebrated the nation's diversity. Still, with respect to affirmative action, the Republican Party's platform "reject[ed] preferences, quotas, and set-asides based on skin color, ethnicity, or gender, which perpetuate divisions and can lead people to question the accomplishments of successful minorities and women" (Republican National Convention 2004). As in previous years, the Republican Party did not support affirmative action. Nevertheless, diversity and inclusion clearly numbered among the Republicans' themes throughout the 2004 election cycle.

The Second Time Is the Charm

How did these activities resonate among voters? Figure 18 indicates that repeating the diversity effort improved the Republican Party's racial symbolism. In the control condition, where subjects received no information about the 2004 convention, the mean racial symbolism was .29. The GOP's racial symbolism improved in all three experimental conditions. When subjects were informed that the Republican Party was reaching out to Democratic-leaning voters or that the party was specifically trying to court African American voters, the mean placement of the GOP along the racial symbolism item increased a statistically significant .10, to .39.[3] In the experimental condition where subjects read that the Republican Party had reached out to blacks but that the party had not changed its platform, the racial symbolism increased to .36, but this increase was not statistically significant.

The results presented in figure 18 suggest that repeating the effort may have convinced some of those who were less swayed by the 2000 effort. In the control condition, blacks on average gave the Republican Party a racial symbolism score of .23. When blacks read that the Republican Party was trying to attract African American voters as part of an ongoing effort that began in 2000, the GOP's racial symbolism

---

3. This difference is statistically significant at the $p < .10$ level (one-tailed test).

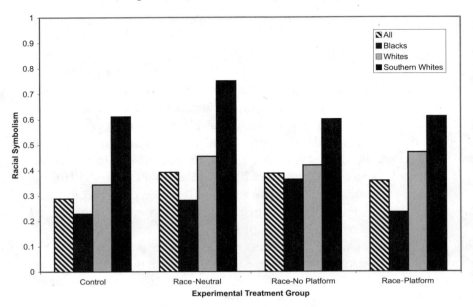

Fig. 18.   Perceptions of the Republican Party's racial symbolism. (Data from 2005 Party Image Study.)

increased to .36. The difference between the control and the race–no platform condition was statistically significant. The Republican Party also received a modest boost in the other two conditions, but those differences were not statistically significant.[4]

Figure 18 illustrates whites' reactions to the experimental treatments. Whites in the control group, on average, placed the Republican Party at .34 on the racial symbolism dimension. Unlike blacks' perceptions, however, whites' perceptions of the Republican Party did not improve in the race–no platform condition. Although the Republican Party's racial symbolism increased to .45 and .42 in the race-neutral

4. Another reason why there would be an observed effect in the 2005 Party Image Study that was absent in the 2002–2003 Party Image Study was that samples were recruited from different places. As a result, the 2005 sample might have a greater propensity to support the Republican Party. A brief examination of the party identification of both samples indicates that such is not the case. Seventy-three percent of the African Americans in the 2002–2003 Party Image Study identified with the Democratic Party, compared to 82 percent in the 2005 Party Image Study. Thus, blacks in the 2005 sample should have been more resistant to a message about the Republican Party's attempt to reshape its image with respect to race (see Philpot 2004).

and the race–no platform conditions respectively, these differences were not statistically significant. Only when whites read that the GOP was reaching out to black voters and that the party had not changed its platform did they place the party .13 points higher on the racial symbolism dimension.[5]

The Republican Party was less successful at reshaping party images among southern whites, however: those in the control group gave the GOP an average racial symbolism score of .61. In the race-neutral condition, the mean placement on the racial symbolism dimension increased by .14 to .75, a difference that was not statistically significant. When respondents were exposed to the racialized versions of the convention descriptions, perceptions of the Republican Party's image with respect to race also remained unchanged. In the race–no platform condition, the GOP's mean placement was .60. Likewise, respondents in the race-platform condition gave the Republican Party an average racial symbolism score of .61. Neither of these conditions yielded a statistically significant difference in perceptions of the Republican Party's image with respect to race. This, however, is not necessarily bad news for the party. Southern whites, regardless of experimental treatment condition, believe that the Republican Party does a good job reaching out to minorities. Thus, repeating minority outreach efforts in 2004 did not alienate the Republican Party's electoral base.

Conclusion

By repeating the message of diversity that was present during the 2000 convention, the Republican Party continued to reshape its image with respect to race. Just as the dispute over the 2000 election undermined the progress made during the 2000 Republican National Convention by providing an alternative and contradictory version of the GOP's image, the 2004 Republican National Convention illustrated some consistency by the party. Generally speaking, this repeated effort left individuals with the impression that the Republican Party did a better job than Democrats at reaching out to blacks, Hispanics, and other minorities. However, mention of the party's unchanged platform impeded this process of party image change.

The repeated diversity effort apparently also gave the Republican strategy among blacks a sense of legitimacy that had been absent in 2000. Projecting the same image in 2004 enabled the party to con-

---

5. This difference is statistically significant at the $p < .10$ level (one-tailed test).

vince African Americans that it had changed. While the average placement of the Republican Party on the racial symbolism dimension across all conditions remained negative, the GOP's image with respect to race substantially improved in the minds of blacks in the race–no platform condition. Making blacks aware that the inclusive message featured at the 2004 Republican National Convention was a part of an ongoing effort that began in 2000 allowed the GOP to begin chiseling away at blacks' crystallized party images with respect to race. Nevertheless, when black subjects were informed that the GOP had not changed its platform, their party images remained unmodified. Here, blacks were reminded that although the Republican Party continued to project a racially diverse image, it had not changed its position on public policy issues—the most salient components of blacks' party images.

In contrast, white subjects' Republican Party images with respect to race only improved in the race-platform condition. While the data employed in this chapter do not permit an exploration of this seemingly counterintuitive result, I speculate that the race-platform condition was the only condition that provided enough context for the GOP's 2004 outreach efforts. Building electoral coalitions is a balancing act. Moving too far in one direction might allow a party to attract a particular group of voters, but this gain might well come at the expense of another group. Informing whites that the Republican Party was initiating yet another attempt to reach out to minority voters might have left whites uncertain about the party's direction and about how far it was willing to go to include minority groups into its party base. Hence, the race–no platform condition showed an increase in the Republican Party's placement on the racial symbolism dimension, but standard errors were too large to confirm that this difference is statistically significant. In the race-platform condition, where subjects read about the Republican Party reaching out to blacks but not changing its platform, whites were convinced that the GOP has changed without changing too much.

All in all, the Republican Party came out ahead in 2004. It maintained its support among southern whites while continuing to foster a better relationship with blacks. The Republican Party certainly still has a long way to go before it convinces all Americans that it has a positive racial symbolism. But as long as the party continues to project a diverse image, it will slowly gain momentum in this process.

8 *Working in Reverse*

Reshaping the Democratic Party

> Two hundred summers ago, this Democratic Party was
> founded by the man whose burning pen fired the spirit
> of the American Revolution—who once argued we
> should overthrow our own government every 20 years
> to renew our freedom and keep pace with a changing
> world. In 1992, the party Thomas Jefferson founded
> invokes his spirit of revolution anew.
> —1992 Democratic Party Platform

How applicable is the theory of party image change beyond the activities of the Republican Party? What happens when the Democratic Party tries to appear more racially conservative? Answering these questions is the goal of chapter 8. While the preceding chapters have focused primarily on the circumstances under which the Republican Party can reshape its image with respect to race, there is no reason why the same theoretical approach could not apply to the Democratic Party as well.

Many of the same phenomena that impede the Republican Party's ability to alter the way citizens view the party work the same way for the Democratic Party. For some people, cosmetic changes will be enough; for others, the bar for proving that the party has changed is set much higher. Historically, when it comes to modifying their images with respect to race, the two parties have appealed to a continuum of voters, with blacks on one end and racially conservative whites in the South at the other end. Given the current party images, the Republican Party has found it difficult to prove to African Americans that it is now more racially inclusive. As chapter 5 demonstrated, the Republican Party had the most success with those voters located somewhere in the middle of the continuum. I anticipate that the Democratic Party will encounter the same difficulty when it tries to portray itself as more racially conservative. Southern whites should be the most resistant to

Democratic attempts to reframe the party's racial symbolism. Southern whites left the Democratic Party because of its stance on racial issues. Not only is race a salient construct in the partisan alignments of southern whites relative to nonsouthern whites, but quite a bit of distance currently exists between southern whites and the Democratic Party on racial issues. Thus, the Democratic Party will find it difficult to meet the burden of proof when trying to appear more racially conservative among southern whites relative to other groups in society.

Bill Clinton: A "New" Democrat?

The idea that the Democratic Party would reshape its racial symbolism is not without precedent. The 1992 election cycle and the emergence of Bill Clinton as the Democratic presidential candidate marked the beginning of a new Democratic Party. In the weeks leading up to the 1992 Democratic National Convention in New York City, Clinton trailed both George H. W. Bush and H. Ross Perot. Thus, it was imperative to create an image of the Democratic Party and its presidential candidate that would appeal to voters in ways that past Democratic candidates had not.

Democratic strategists sought to paint Clinton as the "candidate of fundamental change" (Goldman et al. 1994, 679). Clinton was a Democrat who was anti–big government, pro–personal responsibility, and generally against "politics as usual," positions traditionally reserved for Republican candidates. He focused on bread-and-butter issues such as reinvigorating the economy and promised to put the needs of middle-class Americans first (Goldman et al. 1994).

The 1992 Democratic National Convention was part of the transformation of the Democratic Party. Ron Brown, the Democratic National Chairman in 1992, "was determined that this was going to be a different kind of convention" (Germond and Witcover 1993, 336). According to Germond and Witcover (1993), Brown carefully orchestrated a convention that would maximize the momentum needed to continue through Election Day:

> [T]he convention offered a program designed to send the clear message that the Democratic Party of 1992 was a different party from what it had been, and its nominee truly "a different kind of Democrat," independent of the constituency groups—the "special interests," according to the Republicans—and committed to middle-class Americans worried about their jobs and health care. There

were all the usual Democratic touches of political correctness; one night the benediction was offered in English and then in Navajo. But the first priority clearly was projecting an image that would not repel independents and Reagan Democrats watching in their homes across the nation. (342)

Table 12 illustrates African Americans' presence in the 1992 Democratic National Convention program. At least since 1988, African Americans have had a greater presence at Democratic conventions than at Republican conventions. In any given year, the number of black delegates attending Democratic conventions has been at least six times the number attending Republican conventions. Blacks constituted between 18 and 23 percent of delegates at Democratic National Conventions from 1988 to 2004, while the percentage of African American delegates ranged between 3 and 7 percent at Republican National Conventions over that period.

A slight decrease occurred in African Americans' presence at the 1992 Democratic convention, from 962 four years earlier to 771; the number of black speakers also decreased, from 36 in 1988 to 27 in 1992 and 19 in 1996. Although he was among the few blacks allowed to give a speech during the 1992 convention, Jesse Jackson complained that Clinton was trying to distance himself from African Americans (Germond and Witcover 1993, 339). Although the number of blacks who addressed the convention decreased in 1996, the number of black delegates returned to approximately 20 percent, a figure that remained constant in 2000.[1] By 2004, the number of African Ameri-

TABLE 12. African American Presence at Democratic National Conventions

	1988	1992	1996	2000	2004
Delegates	962	771	908	872	871
	(23.1%)	(17.9%)	(21.0%)	(20.1%)	(20.1%)
Speakers	36	27	19	4	57
	(16.2%)	(16.3%)	(9.0%)	(16.7%)	(20.5%)
Musical entertainers	0	1	2		9
	(0.0%)	(50.0%)	(66.7%)		(47.4%)

Source: Official Proceedings of the Democratic National Convention, 1988, 1992, 1996; Democratic National Committee; Joint Center for Political and Economic Studies; C-SPAN Archives.

1. The number of black speakers in 2000 is a low estimate. At the time these figures were compiled, the Democratic National Committee had not yet assembled a complete list of convention attendees.

can speakers had reached 57, exceeding the pre-Clinton level, while the convention included 871 black delegates and 9 black musical entertainers.

Racial issues were not very prominent in the Democratic Party platform during this sixteen-year period. The number of paragraphs devoted to race and racial issues in the Democratic platform was comparable to that in the Republican platform. In recent presidential election years, however, race has figured more notably. In 1988 only one paragraph was devoted to racism, a number that increased to 9 in 2000 before falling again to 6 in 2004. The discussion of diversity also expanded in 2000 but returned to its 1996 level in 2004.

Other issues that rose in salience during this period included education, crime, and welfare. In 1988, only seven paragraphs discussed education. In 1996, 2000, and 2004, however, no fewer than 25 paragraphs were devoted to education. Welfare also ascended in prominence in the 1990s before all but disappearing by 2004, a development that is consistent with the scope of the welfare reform debate that occurred during the same period. Crime as an issue also experienced the same rise and fall in importance from 1988 to 2004. Prior to 1992, fewer than 10 paragraphs were devoted to crime in any Democratic platform. In 1996 and 2000, this number jumped to 23 and 22, respectively. By 2004, however, crime was no longer a prime issue.

Regardless of importance, however, the Democratic Party's positions on racial issues have remained the same. Table 13 summarizes the Democratic Party's platform on racial issues. From 1988 to 2004, the Democratic Party has supported affirmative action: its 2004 platform language on the subject reads, "We support affirmative action to redress discrimination and to achieve the diversity from which all Americans benefit," capturing the Democratic Party's sentiment on affirmative action in all five years that I examine. Likewise, the Democratic Party consistently condemned racism and any discrimination based on race, gender, religion, disability, or sexual orientation. Like the Republican Party, the Democrats celebrated U.S. diversity, but the Democratic Party platform included more detailed statements about how the party would protect the rights of minority groups. For example, the Democratic Party took stands against environment racism, against the rash of African American church bombings in the 1990s, against racial profiling, and in favor of the adoption of an Equal Rights Amendment.

The notable change to the 1992 Democratic Party platform was not to the party's issue positions per se but to some of the more rhetorical statements about personal responsibility and unresponsive government. For example, the Democratic Party posited that

> government must once again make responsibility an instrument of national purpose. Our future as a nation depends upon the daily assumption of personal responsibility by millions of Americans from all walks of life—for the religious faiths they follow, the ethics they practice, the values they instill, and the pride they take in their work. (Democratic National Convention 1992)

The 1992 Democratic Party Platform also promised to empower the poor by moving them "away from subsistence and dependence and toward work, family and personal initiative and responsibility."

Much of this rhetoric was featured during Clinton's acceptance speech, in which he vowed to "end welfare as we know it." Furthermore, Clinton criticized President George H. W. Bush's record on crime, claiming that he "talked a lot about drugs, but [had not] helped people on the front line to wage that war on drugs and crime" (Clinton 1992). Clinton promised to pick up where Bush fell short. Observers of the 1992 convention contended that "there was nothing subtle about [Clinton's] appeal to the political center" (Germond and Witcover 1993, 346). Clinton's policy initiatives would prove to be less conservative than the ones that would emerge out of a majority Republican Congress in the mid-1990s (Bane and Ellwood 1994; Danziger and Gottschalk 1995). On their face, however, excerpts of Clinton's speech could have easily been mistaken for a speech delivered at the Republican National Convention.

Clinton's advisers were well aware of the pitfalls of moving too far to the right. At around the time of the 1992 Georgia primary, senior campaign adviser Stan Greenberg warned the Clinton camp against enacting the southern strategy:

> The campaign will have to make a strategic judgment about the anti-liberal message. Clinton's support rises from 45–51 in the white community when he is anti-liberal, but that is balanced in part by slippage in the black community, from 25 down to 19 percent. . . . On balance, the anti-liberal theme only marginally enhances Clinton's candidacy; other additions will make more of a

TABLE 13. Democratic Platform on Racial Issues

	1988	1992	1996	2000	2004
Racism	• Believes equal access to government services should not be denied on the basis of race.	• Condemns anti-Semitism, racism, homophobia, bigotry, and negative stereo-typing of all kinds.	• Vows to continue to lead the fight to end discrimination on the basis of race, gender, religion, age, ethnicity, disability, and sexual orientation. • Deplores the recent wave of burnings that has targeted African American churches in the South. • Vows to renew efforts to stamp out hatred of every kind.	• Believes that there is a chasm created by income disparity, discrimination by race and gender, and the abandonment of our inner cities. • Vows to continue to lead the fight to end discrimination on the basis of race, gender, religion, age, ethnicity, disability, and sexual orientation. • Believes growing racial segregation of our schools and neighborhoods must be combated. • Supports a vision of an America healed of hatreds and misunderstanding. • Supports creation of a commission of distin-guished scholars and civic	• Vows to fight racial and ethnic health care disparities. • Believes all patriotic Americans should be able to serve in the armed forces without discrimination. • Believes racial and religious profiling is wrong.

Diversity

- Honors the nation's multicultural heritage.
- Takes special pride in our country's emergence as the world's largest and most successful multiethnic, multiracial republic.
- Pledges to help all Americans understand

- Believes that America is uniquely suited to lead the world into the twenty-first century because of its great diversity.
- Believes it is possible to draw strength

- leaders to examine the history of slavery, discrimination, and exclusion.
- Supports increased funding for civil rights enforcement.
- Recognizes new forms of discrimination, such as environmental injustices and predatory lending practices.
- Vows to fight for full funding and full staffing of the Equal Employment Opportunity Commission and other civil rights enforcement agencies.
- Opposes language-based discrimination in all its forms.
- Embraces diversity.
- Believes diversity of views is a source of strength, not a sign of weakness.
- Recognizes that tolerance is a virtue.
- Believes America's

- Rejoices in diversity.
- Believes all Americans benefit from diversity.
- Supports measures to ensure diversity, competition, and localism in media ownership.

(continues)

TABLE 13.—Continued

	1988	1992	1996	2000	2004
		the diversity of the culture. • Affirms that immigrants have contributed to the American tapestry.	from both diversity and constant values. • Believes the Democratic Party is a party of inclusion and respects the conscience of all Americans on the capital punishment issue.	diversity is expanding yet there is still widespread evidence of persistent discrimination. • Believes in celebrating diversity and in focusing on strengthening common American values. • Believes American schools must be funded to handle the diverse student body. • Believes pursuing excellence means including a diverse administration.	• Views diversity of views as a source of strength.
Affirmative action	• Believes the lingering effects of past discrimination should be eliminated by affirmative action, including goals, timetables, and procurement set-asides.	• Supports affirmative action.	• Believes in mending it, not ending it. • Supports affirmative action that is improved and promotes opportunity but does not accidentally hold others back in the process.	• Strongly opposed to rolling back affirmative action programs. • Believes in continuing to expand opportunities for everyone who wants to achieve.	• Supports affirmative action to redress discrimination and to achieve the diversity from which all Americans benefit.

Minorities				
• Seeks to recruit minority teachers. • Supports bilingual education and historically black and Hispanic institutions. • Believes the voting rights of all minorities should be protected. • Resists English-only pressure groups. • Supports the adoption of the Equal Rights Amendment. • Believes reproductive rights should be ensured regardless of ability to pay. • Believes treaty obligations with Native Americans should be enforced. • Pledges that women and minorities should have full and equal access to elective office and party endorsement. • Believes in the return of federally held foreclosed lands to minorities.	• Believes the voting rights of all minorities should be protected. • Resists English-only pressure groups. • Supports the adoption of the Equal Rights Amendment. • Vows aggressively to prosecute hate crimes. • Pledges to deal with other nations in such a way that Americans of any origin do not become scapegoats or victims of foreign policy disputes. • Believes treaty obligations with Native Americans should be enforced. • Believes reproductive rights should be ensured regardless of ability to pay.	• Deplores those who use the need to stop illegal immigration as a pretext for discrimination. • Strongly opposes divisive efforts like English-only legislation. • Committed to strengthening the government-to-government relationship between the federal government and Indian and Alaskan native tribal governments. • Supports an Equal Rights Amendment.	• Vows to end Republican delays in the Senate that have kept qualified nominees, especially women and minorities, waiting for a Senate vote. • Committed to equal treatment of all service members and believes all patriotic Americans should be allowed to serve their country without discrimination, persecution, or violence.	• Supports more minority students entering the sciences. • Vows to bring environmental justice to low-income, rural, and minority communities using federal resources to improve public health and spur economic development by cleaning up polluted sites.

Source: Democratic Party Platforms, 1988–2004.

difference without costing Clinton in the black community. (Goldman et al. 1994, 625)

In the end, the Democratic Party's move to the middle paid off. Clinton continued to focus primarily on the middle-class and on those moderate voters who had defected to the Republican Party during the Reagan-Bush administration. He also gained the support of nearly 85 percent of black voters. As a result, Clinton gained a 20 percentage point lead over Bush in the postconvention period (Goldman et al. 1994, 286) and won the presidency in 1992 and reelection in 1996.

Reclaiming the Democratic Party's Conservative Roots

Ideally, I would examine what impact the Democratic Party's attempt to co-opt Republican-owned issues in 1992 had on perceptions of the Democratic Party's image with respect to race. Adequate data from this period, however, were not available. In the absence of such data, I re-created a contrived instance where the Democratic Party tried to alter its racial symbolism in 2004. To explore the conditions that facilitated the Democratic Party's ability to reshape citizens' perceptions of its image, I employed the 2005 Party Image Study, which exposed subjects to a question-wording experiment in which they read about the Democratic Party reaching out to Republican-leaning voters. As with the experiment described in chapter 7, participants in the study were required to answer the following question: "How much do you think the Democratic Party has changed over the last few years?" Before answering this question, some subjects read a brief paragraph that gave a fictitious account of the 2004 Democratic National Convention. One paragraph described a race-neutral version of the convention that described the Democratic Party as attempting to reach out to conservative voters. Others read a racialized version of the convention that described the Democratic Party as reaching out to conservative voters by distancing itself from African Americans. In the control condition, participants read no paragraph about the convention. (See the appendix for exact question wording.) After answering the experimental question, subjects were asked how well they thought the Democratic Party reached out to blacks, Hispanics, and other minorities. Responses were coded 1 if subjects believed the Democratic Party did a good job, 0 if the party did a bad job, and .5 if the Democratic Party did neither a good nor a bad job.

Figure 19 presents the mean placement of the Democratic Party on the racial symbolism dimension by experimental treatment group. Overall, when subjects read about the Democratic Party reaching out to Republican-leaning voters, perceptions of the Democratic Party's racial symbolism became more negative. In the control condition, the mean placement of the Democratic Party was .7. As might be expected, absent any information that suggests otherwise, people associated the Democratic Party with positive racial symbolism. This is consistent with the findings presented in chapter 2 that in contemporary American politics, the Democratic Party is the party considered racially liberal. Nevertheless, when exposed to a description of the 2004 Democratic National Convention that described the party as reaching out to Republican-leaning voters, the mean placement of the Democratic Party on the racial symbolism scale decreased in both the race-neutral and the racialized conditions. The average racial symbolism score was .53 in the race-neutral condition and .52 in the racialized condition. A difference-of-means test indicated that both of these scores differed significantly from the control condition.

A closer examination of the response to the experimental treatments showed that race played a moderating role. Blacks in the control condition gave the Democratic Party an average racial symbolism score of .76. This placement decreased by 26 percentage points in the race-neutral condition and 23 percentage points in the racialized condition. Further, a *t*-test revealed that both of these differences were statistically significant. These results suggest that blacks resented the Democratic Party attempts to reach out to Republican-leaning voters, regardless of whether the Democratic Party distanced itself from African Americans. Blacks' perceptions of the Democratic Party's image with respect to race went from positive to neutral.

Whites' perceptions of the Democratic Party, in contrast, differed from the control condition only when they read the racialized version of the 2004 Democratic National Convention. In the control condition, whites' placement of the Democratic Party on the racial symbolism dimension was .68, a positive score. Although whites in the race-neutral condition gave the Democratic Party a mean racial symbolism score of .59, this difference was not statistically significant. When exposed to the racialized version of the experimental wording question, however, the Democratic Party's average placement on the racial symbolism item among whites was .56, a statistically significant differ-

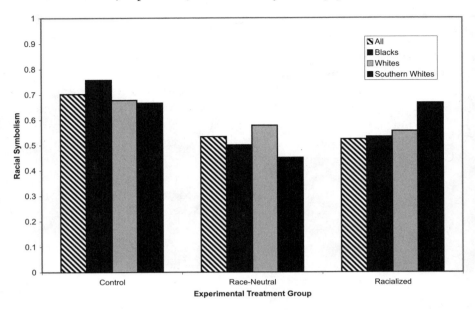

Fig. 19. Perceptions of the Democratic Party's racial symbolism. (Data from 2005 Party Image Study.)

ence of 12 percentage points. Like their black counterparts, whites in this condition indicated that, on average, the Democratic Party did neither a good job nor a bad job of reaching out to minorities.

Throughout this book, I have discussed the tension political parties have experienced when trying to recruit both black and southern white voters. These two groups have had conflicting interests and thus have found it difficult to coexist in sustainable political coalitions. Consequently, the Democratic Party, which was once the party of the Solid South, is now the party perceived as more racially inclusive. Moreover, the Democratic presidential candidates in both 2000 and 2004 failed to win any of the southern states despite winning more than 90 percent of the black vote. Thus, when the Democratic Party proves to the electorate that it is more racially conservative, southern whites are expected to be most resistant to this appeal.

Table 14 shows why such might be the case. With respect to racial issues, particularly affirmative action, southern whites were more likely than nonsouthern whites to believe that affirmative action was extremely important. While affirmative action never reached the same level of importance as it did among African Americans, southern whites were 5 percentage points more likely than nonsouthern whites to indicate that this issue was extremely important. At the same time, southern whites were more likely than both blacks and nonsouthern whites to see a difference between themselves and the Democratic Party on this issue. Ninety percent of African Americans and 59 percent of nonsouthern whites saw no difference between themselves and the Democratic Party on the issue of affirmative action; in contrast, only 46 percent of southern whites saw no difference. Whereas fewer than 10 percent of blacks and 37 percent of nonsouthern whites were more conservative than the Democratic Party, 50 percent of southern whites were more conservative than the Democratic Party on affirmative action.[2] Given the relative importance of racial issues coupled with the distance between southern whites and the Democratic Party on these issues, I expected members of that group to be the most resistant to a Democratic attempt to appear more racially conservative by distancing itself from blacks.

The results presented in figure 19 confirm this expectation. Southern whites in the control condition placed the Democratic Party at .67, indicating that they believed that the party did a good job of reaching out to minorities. In the race-neutral condition, this score decreased to

TABLE 14. **Importance of and Placement on Affirmative Action, by Race and Region**

	Importance of Affirmative Action	
	Percentage	N
African Americans	51.0	25
Non-southern whites	9.1	35
Southern whites	14.2	20

	Placement on Affirmative Action Relative to the Democratic Party			
	No Difference		More Conservative	
	Percentage	N	Percentage	N
African Americans	90.2	37	9.8	4
Nonsouthern whites	58.7	186	36.6	116
Southern whites	46.1	59	50.0	64

Source: 2002 American National Election Study.

2. The differences observed between southern whites and nonsouthern whites are statistically significant at the $p < .10$ level (one-tailed test).

.45, a statistically significant difference. Reading that the Democratic Party was reaching out to Republican-leaning voters apparently convinced southern whites that the party no longer had positive racial symbolism. The racialized condition, however, yielded no similar change in the Democratic Party's mean placement on the racial symbolism item. In this condition, the Democratic Party's average placement was .67, the same as in the control condition.

Conclusion

As is the case when the Republican Party tries to appear more racially liberal, when the Democratic Party attempts to appear racially conservative, some people will accept the changes while others will not. In general, perceptions of the Democratic Party's racial symbolism become negative when people read that the party is reaching out to Republican-leaning voters. Intuitively, whites' pictures of the Democratic Party with respect to race changed only in the racialized condition, when they read that the party was trying to distance itself from African Americans. This finding makes sense, considering that this experimental manipulation explicitly described the Democratic Party's relationship with blacks. Because the race-neutral condition omitted the information about the Democratic Party distancing itself from blacks, people would not be expected to connect the fictitious information about the 2004 Democratic National Convention to the party's racial symbolism.

The exception to whites' reactions to the Democratic Party's attempt to reshape its image occurred among southerners. Just as blacks were most resistant to the Republican Party's appeals, southern whites were least accepting of Democratic appeals when it came to race. Without any information other than the fact that the Democratic Party was trying to distance itself from blacks in 2004, southern whites were not convinced that the party was more racially conservative. When it comes to altering Democratic Party images among this group, the threshold for change is set much higher.

Blacks' party images, in contrast, were affected by both experimental manipulations. The results presented in this chapter suggest that blacks are particularly sensitive to the Democratic Party becoming too conservative. When blacks read about the Democratic Party reaching out to Republican-leaning voters, even absent information regarding the party distancing itself from African American voters, blacks no longer believed that the Democratic Party did a good job of reaching out to minorities. This finding identifies an important potential problem associated with the Democratic Party trying to modify its image with respect to race: in so doing, the party runs the risk of alienating African American voters. Although I do not further explore this possibility here, exposure to the experimental treatments also led to a decrease in blacks' support for John Kerry, the 2004 Democratic presidential candidate. Whereas the experimental treatments had no impact on whites' evaluation of Kerry in general, exposure to the racialized treatments led to a modest boost in support for Kerry among southern whites.

Although having the Democratic Party become too conservative may not lead blacks to defect to the Republican Party, such a change could demobilize black voters. Either situation, however, could be detrimental to the Democratic Party. In 2004, African Americans constituted between 9 percent of Kerry's vote share (California) and 62 percent (South Carolina) (Bositis 2004, 5). Without the support of African American voters, Democratic presidential candidates would fail to reach the majority needed to win key electoral votes. In the short run, appealing to Republican-leaning voters would not yield the net gain in votes needed to win a presidential election, since the party would be unlikely to pick up southern white voters to replace the lost black voters. Nevertheless, the results presented in chapter 7 suggest that a long-term repeated effort may succeed in redefining the Democratic Party as the party of the South. In the interim, however, it is likely that the Democratic Party will remain the party perceived to be better at representing minority interests.

9 *The Final Tally*

Race, Party Image, and the American Voter

> It is . . . unintelligent to insist on a single explanation of
> anything so complex as the American party system, and
> it is difficult or impossible to assign relative weights to
> all the factors that must be taken into account in a gen-
> eral explanation.
> —E. E. Schattschneider, "United States:
> The Functional Approach to Party Government"

AT ANY GIVEN TIME, a multitude of interests attempt to exert
power on the U.S. political system. Moreover, it is extremely difficult
to know with absolute certainty the source of observed political outcomes. Nevertheless, two competing interests in particular have been
exploited throughout American history in the quest for political pay-
offs—racially conservative whites in the South and African Americans.
As both of these groups have sought economic, social, and political
benefits, the two major political parties have used this competition to
their advantage. As a result, American society possesses a seemingly
permanent racial divide. Exploited by political elites, this divide can
determine which policies, parties, and candidates the American people
support.

Scholars have only just begun to explore the extent to which this
divide can be narrowed. Most argue that the key to obliterating the
racial divide lies in the laps of political elites (Kinder and Sanders 1996;
White 2005). But inasmuch as political elites continue to play the race
card, must voters continue to respond? I argue that the answer is no.
Citizens possess the ability to resist elite messages, as previous research
has shown (Berelson, Lazarsfeld, and McPhee 1954; A. Campbell et al.
1960; Iyengar and Kinder 1987). In this book, I have sought to further clarify the circumstances that assist in an individual's ability to
resist elite messages.

Choosing to focus primarily on political parties, I explored whether party elites can reshape the electorates' party images. Specifically, I answered two central questions related to party images. First, are party images malleable? Second, if party images are malleable, do elites face obstacles in attempting to reshape party images?

The theoretical proposition asserted in this book is that reshaping party images is a continuous journey along which elites face many obstacles. Inherent in this argument is the fact that voters do not exist as tabulae rasae. At the start of any given campaign, it is highly likely that voters have already accumulated information about parties through firsthand, informal, and/or mediated experiences with the political system. Individuals amass information from the parties themselves as well as from competing sources of information. The information that ultimately resonates with the electorate is determined by perceived importance, which can be determined by individuals' life experiences or by heightened media attention. When it comes to playing the race card—using racial images and racially coded symbols and words—to reshape party images, the new information being presented to the electorate must outweigh existing information. For some, these superficial gestures are convincing enough to signal change. For others, the use of racial images constitutes no more than smoke and mirrors.

Overview

Battling History

In exploring the boundaries of strategies that seek to reshape party images, I have focused on the part of one's party image that relates to race. People associate the two major parties with a variety of political symbols, which incorporate all candidates, issue positions, and political events that an individual links to a political party. The totality of these symbols represents an individual's party image. Political elites attempt to alter which symbols are associated with their parties as well as the interpretation individuals assign to those symbols to yield positive evaluations and electoral outcomes in their favor. Over the years, political parties have used racialized images and issues to divide the electorate and gain political power. Associating the two parties with different racial symbols helps the electorate distinguish between a party that is racially liberal and one that is racially conservative.

In the past, political parties could win electoral success by being overtly racially conservative. But in the post-civil-rights era, a shift in racial attitudes prevents political parties and candidates from being explicitly racist. While subtle race cues are still used and the racial divide continues to be exploited, the use of race in campaign communication must appear to adhere to the norm of egalitarianism.

The violation of this norm can have negative political consequences, as the modern-day Republican Party discovered. Conservative candidates such as Barry Goldwater, Richard Nixon, Ronald Reagan, and Pat Buchanan coupled with racialized campaigns such as the 1988 Willie Horton ad firmly solidified the Republican Party as the party of racial conservatives. These political symbols associated with the GOP repelled moderate/liberal whites and African Americans. As a result, in 1992 the Republican Party was unable to assemble a winning coalition to sustain the presidency even though the party benefited from an incumbent presidential nominee (Speel 1998).

Chapter 3 examined the extent to which this history resonated with voters. Using survey data collected over the past fifty years, I found that people have distinct perceptions of the parties when it comes to race. The survey data suggest that individuals historically have distinguished the two parties along racial lines that correspond to the state of the times. Prior to 1960, the distinction between the two parties was not as prominent because the parties themselves did not make a substantial distinction. From 1960 to the present, individuals have consistently identified the Democratic Party as more liberal on race than the Republican Party.

The qualitative results echoed the results found in the survey data. Regardless of gender or race, people identified the racially conservative and racially liberal parties. However, the willingness to discuss the parties in terms of race differed for blacks and whites. Specifically, race was much more salient among blacks, whereas the class division between the two parties was more salient among whites. This difference guided perceptions of the two major parties and provided insight into the obstacles that must be overcome to change party images with respect to race. In general, African Americans' perceptions of the Republican Party's racial image were quite fixed and were rooted in the party's position on such racial issues as affirmative action. As a result, African American respondents believed that the Republican Party would have to alter its position on many racialized issues to change its image. In contrast, many white respondents believed that simply recruiting more

African Americans into the party would help reshape images of the Republican Party.

Battling the Media

In chapter 4, I suspended the examination of public opinion to explore the media's reaction to the 2000 Republican National Convention. This chapter was based on the assumption that in covering political events, the media have the ability to amplify and/or distort political elites' messages. Because many people cannot witness political events firsthand, the media serve as conveyors and interpreters of political information. Thus I examined whether the media recognized the use of race cues at the Republican convention and how they portrayed the use of such cues to the public. By conducting a content analysis of three nationally circulated newspapers, thirteen black newspapers, and two newsmagazines, I revealed that the media recognized the use of race during the 2000 Republican National Convention. Nearly half of all convention coverage discussed some aspect of the Republican race strategy. Nevertheless, the media in some cases also juxtaposed the presence of blacks at the convention with the unchanged issue positions of the Republican Party.

These results suggest that the Republican Party faced some opposition from the media, which did not simply convey the events of the 2000 Republican National Convention as they occurred. Rather, the media provided their own interpretation of the events, including information about the party's platform and history with respect to race that contradicted the Republican Party's projected image and made it more difficult for the GOP to prove to the electorate that it had changed.

A Battle Won?

Using the results of the content analysis, chapter 5 tested the effect of these varying frames by conducting an experiment. Moreover, I tested the generalizability of the experimental results by analyzing survey data collected shortly after the 2000 Republican National Convention. The results generally revealed that watching the convention affected people's perceptions of the Republican Party's image with respect to race. Susceptibility, however, was contingent on the individual's race. Specifically, African Americans' perceptions of the GOP were largely unaffected by watching the 2000 Republican convention. These results were also contingent on which version of the 2000 Republican

National Convention individuals received. When blacks and whites read about the racial outreach featured at the convention and these accounts explicitly stated that the Republican platform had not changed, perceptions of the Republican Party's image with respect to race did not improve.

Chapter 5 also examined the extent to which convention exposure primed the use of the Republican Party's racial symbolism in candidate evaluations. The assumption behind these analyses was that reshaping the Republican Party's image with respect to race should result in more positive evaluations of the party's presidential candidates. These findings suggest that making the GOP's racial symbolism applicable to candidate evaluations was a double-edged sword. Watching a great deal of the convention increased the weight of the GOP's party image with respect to race in both whites' and blacks' candidate evaluations. A problem occurred, however, when the Republican Party failed to prove to the electorate that the party did a good job of reaching out to minorities. Priming the party's racial symbolism among those with negative perceptions of the Republican Party led to negative evaluations of George W. Bush. The opposite was true when the GOP improved its image with respect to race. Thus, when attempting to reshape party images, political parties must simultaneously modify their images on a particular dimension and make this dimension a salient construct in candidate evaluation. Without doing both, a party cannot expect to receive an increase in support for its presidential candidates.

Chapter 8 further explored the idea that in the process of party image change, cosmetic changes to the party's image without corresponding changes to the party's platform will resonate among some citizens better than others. I examine the reverse case of party image change with respect to race by gauging reactions to a fictitious instance where the Democratic Party was attempting to appear more racially conservative. As discussed throughout this book, southern whites and African Americans have competing interests that the political parties have exploited. As a result, southern whites are firmly entrenched within the Republican Party's electoral coalition, while blacks form part of the Democratic Party's electoral base. Similar to blacks' reaction to the Republican Party's effort to appear more inclusive, southern whites resisted a Democratic appeal to conservatives. Chapter 8's results reconfirm that parties have the most difficulty reshaping their images in a particular issue domain among people with the most crystallized conceptions of the party on that dimension.

Chapter 6 examined the fragility of altering party images by exploring the extent to which the Republican Party suffered as a result of the disputed 2000 presidential election. By employing the 2002 American National Election Study, I found that perceived fairness of the 2000 election constituted a salient piece of information when citizens were asked to evaluate the Republican Party's ability to represent minorities in 2002. Specifically, as perceived fairness of the election decreased, so too did the Republican Party's perceived ability to represent blacks, the poor, and women. However, the election had no impact on whether respondents believed that the Republican Party could represent whites, men, and the rich better than the Democratic Party could. Furthermore, attitudes toward the election affected presidential evaluations. Feelings toward George W. Bush became increasingly colder as the perceived fairness of the 2000 election decreased. These findings suggest that success in the area of improving party image can easily be undone.

Finally, chapter 7 presented the upside of party image change. Once again relying on experimental data, I examined what happened when individuals encountered a party projecting a new image and were informed that the new image constituted part of a sustained strategy that had begun in a previous election cycle. I found that exposure to a description of the 2004 Republican National Convention where the GOP once again reached out to black voters—a group unmoved by the 2000 strategy—reshaped blacks' perceptions of the Republican Party's racial symbolism. The results in this chapter suggest that maintaining a consistent message lends a sense of legitimacy to a party's attempt to reshape its image.

Where Do We Go from Here?

The discussion of party image in this book has been limited to the discussion of blacks and whites, but there is no reason that the theory and approach cannot be transported to other societal groups. I have demonstrated that the ability to change one's party image with respect to race becomes more difficult (1) as race becomes more important to an individual and (2) as the parties' previous race-related activities become more entrenched in an individual's existing party image. At one end of the spectrum are African Americans, a group that often uses race as a lens through which to view the political world and that has a long history with the two parties. At the other end are whites, who do not necessarily place high levels of importance on race. While whites have knowledge of the political parties, the race-related activities in which the parties engage are not salient pieces of whites' party images. In between these two groups are individuals who may hold race salient but who lack the same historical relationship with the two parties that African Americans possess.

One such group of voters is Latinos, who currently constitute roughly 12.5 percent of the U.S. population. In 2000, Latinos surpassed African Americans as the largest minority group in the United States, and census estimates show that by 2050, Hispanics will constitute nearly a quarter of the U.S. population. Furthermore, relatively large Latino populations—15 percent or more of the total population—are present in such politically significant states as New York, Florida, Texas, and California.

Political strategists recognize the political importance of this group. As Lionel Sosa, a media consultant for George W. Bush in 2000, argued,

> Hispanic voting power is huge. There are more Hispanics in the United States than there are Canadians in Canada, about 35 million. If you were to take the U.S. Hispanic population and consider it a Latin American country, it would be the fourth largest. And it would be the richest. Period. Hispanics are becoming more involved in the political process, more educated, and more aware of their power. It is a voter group that's becoming so large that the Democrats can no longer take the group for granted and the Republicans can no longer ignore it. (Jamieson and Waldman 2001, 155–56)

As with African Americans, the Republican Party has targeted Latino voters in recent presidential elections. Republican strategists believe that many Latinos are "natural" Republicans. Republican Frank Guerra, producer of Spanish-language ads for the Bush campaign, believes that the Latino voter

> is somebody who has left their country. They've traveled far away to try to earn money, so that they can support their families. And when they earn that paycheck, they want to keep as much of it as

they can. And depending on where they're from, sometimes there's a fundamental mistrust of government. And that's very Republican. (McChesney 2004)

Thus, the Republican Party has targeted both older Latino voters, who may be more conservative, as well as newly immigrated Latino voters. The 2000 Republican National Convention featured many Latino leaders and entertainers, including George P. Bush, nephew of George W. Bush. Because of a demographic shift in the Hispanic community, "fully 50 percent of today's Hispanic voters have Spanish as their primary language" (McChesney 2004). As a result, Bush strategists "produced thirteen spots for the 2000 campaign in both English and Spanish, and also a Hispanic video for the convention" (Jamieson and Waldman 2001, 159). Early in 2004, Bush spent more than $1 million on ads targeting Latino voters (McChesney 2004).

Evidence suggests that Republican appeals have met with marginally more success among Hispanics than among African Americans. According to exit polls conducted by the Voter News Service, Republicans experienced the most dramatic increase in votes from the Latino community. In 1996, Republican presidential candidate Bob Dole received 18 percent of the Latino vote; four years later, George W. Bush received 35 percent of the Latino vote. According to Sosa,

> In the end, Bush got 1½ million more Hispanic votes than Dole got four years ago; 850,000 more votes than Clinton/Gore got four years ago; and 6,500 more Latino votes in Florida than Gore did. Without the Latino vote in Florida, Bush would have surely lost the state, and thus the presidency. All with no recounts. (Jamieson and Waldman 2001, 163)

But as scholars recognize, understanding the political behavior of Latinos is more complex than may at first appear to be the case. First, "the one voter subsegment that goes into Election Day by the largest margin undecided is the Hispanic voter" (McChesney 2004). More importantly, Latinos include many different ethnic groups—Mexicans, Puerto Ricans, and Cubans, among others—all of which have different political histories. Moreover, each of these ethnicities encompasses various generations: some Latinos are recent immigrants, while others are third-generation U.S. citizens. All of these factors influence how Latinos are socialized into the U.S. political environment and the extent to which they have contact with the two major parties (Hero 1992; DeSipio 1996).

These intragroup differences have political ramifications. National origins and levels of cultural identity affect support for public policies (Newton 2000; Bedolla 2003), ideology and partisanship (McClain and Stewart 1999), and turnout (Stokes 2003). Puerto Ricans and Cuban Americans, for example, tend to be more conservative than Mexican Americans (de la Garza et al. 1992). In terms of partisanship, Latinos in general strongly support the Democratic Party, but not to the extent that blacks do (McClain and Stewart 1999). And again, such support varies across national origin. Sixteen percent of Mexican Americans and 14 percent of Puerto Ricans identify themselves as Republicans, compared to 64 percent of Cuban Americans (de la Garza et al. 1992).

Given the variations among the different Latino subgroups, Latinos' relative size as a minority group, and recent efforts to mobilize their votes, examining elites' ability to reshape Hispanics' party images seems like a logical next step. Doing so requires identifying the salient political symbols that give meaning to political parties for Latinos. Furthermore, scholars must determine the extent to which these symbols vary across ethnicities. Keeping with the theoretical framework outlined in earlier chapters of this book, elites should have the most success in changing the party images of Latinos who have recently immigrated to the United States and who lack crystallized perceptions of the political parties. As with blacks, altering party images with respect to race should become more difficult as perceived levels of economic, social, and political discrimination increase and as individuals come to perceive one party as better able to eradicate those conditions.

The theory and framework presented in this book can also be applied to another important cleavage in American politics, the gender gap. Although not a racial or ethnic group, women and their party images seem like a promising avenue for future research. Unlike blacks and to some extent Latinos, women do not behave as a politically cohesive group (Gurin 1985). However, a consistent but modest gap has existed between men's and women's preferences for political parties and support for presidential candidates (Frankovic 1982; Wirls 1986; Kaufmann and Petrocik 1999; Norrander 1999a, b). As Kaufmann and Petrocik (1999) argue, this cleavage "cuts across every demographic characteristic except for race" (870). Specifically, more women than men identify with the Democratic Party, and more men than women identify with the Republican Party (Kaufmann and Petrocik 1999). The source of the gap is disputed—the disparity is said to result from anything from attitudes toward the use of military force (Frankovic 1982; Gilens 1988; Conover and Sapiro 1993) to support for social welfare issues (Shapiro and Mahajan 1986; Chaney, Alvarez, and Nagler 1998; Kaufmann and Petrocik 1999; Norrander 1999b).

Most recently, scholars have identified partisan racial appeals as another source of the gender gap (Hutchings et al. 2004). Hutchings et al. cite a number of reasons why race seems a likely culprit. First, as noted earlier, the use of race in political campaigns is widespread (Edsall and Edsall 1991; Kinder and Sanders 1996; Gilens 1999; Mendelberg 2001). Second, women tend to be more liberal than men on racial issues (Schuman et al. 1997; Norrander 1999b). Finally, the gender gap emerged as the parties diverged considerably on the issue of race and as white males defected from the Democratic Party (W. Miller and Shanks 1996; Norrander 1999a). As in this volume, Hutchings et al. examine the impact of positive racial appeals in 2000 on evaluation of George W. Bush, finding that women exposed to the "compassionate conservative" strategy were more likely to believe that Bush was more compassionate and better able to handle race relations. As a result, women were more likely to support him.

Given the success of such appeals, future research should examine whether these effects translated into fundamental changes in the perception of the Republican Party or if the effects were candidate-specific. Such studies would have to account for the heterogeneity of women. The ability to change women's racial symbolism would depend on the salience of race to each woman as well as the crystallization of her existing party images.

Beyond racial symbolism, exploring women's party images provides an excellent opportunity to test whether gendered appeals carry the same weight as racial appeals. The 2000 Republican National Convention featured a number of female speakers and entertainers, but the party did not change its position on gendered issues such as abortion. In this instance, women who value the presence of other women in the ranks of the Republican Party may believe that the GOP is the party for women. Conversely, women who believe that abortion is a salient issue and who do not agree with the Republican Party's position on this issue will not be affected by the presence of women at the convention.

Conclusion

As Trilling (1976) has offered, the study of party image is relevant because it allows us to explore the extent to which political parties "continue to have meaning for voters and continue to arouse interest and concern among them" (4). Furthermore, party image is an intricate link to understanding political behavior and partisan loyalties (Matthews and Prothro 1964; Trilling 1976). Inasmuch as people engage in limited information processing, party images allow them to compensate by using previously stored knowledge to reach judgments and make decisions.

According to Lippmann (1922),

> Inevitably our opinions cover a bigger space, a longer reach of time, a greater number of things, than we can directly observe. They have, therefore, to be pieced together out of what others have reported and we can imagine. (53)

Lippmann (1922) also argued that we compensate for our lack of knowledge by picking recognizable signs out of our environment that proxy for ideas and use these ideas to fill out "our stock of images" (58–59). In other words, in times when "there is neither time nor opportunity for intimate acquaintance" we use "a trait which marks a well known type, and fill in the rest of the picture by means of the stereotypes we carry about in our heads" (Lippmann 1922, 59). Thus, drawing on one's party image allows an individual to interpret the actions of a political party even though that individual may have limited information about the party or the activity in which it is engaging.

If such is indeed the case, then it is important to explore the factors that facilitate or impede party elites' ability to change the meaning of their parties. This book takes up this task. Knowing when it is possible to change one's party image may help to predict when party elites can induce deviations in voting behavior and partisan loyalties. Discovering instances where people do not update their party images helps explain why overall party preferences tend to remain quite stable. Furthermore, such nonfindings have implications for the success of the strategies and tactics employed by political parties in recruiting new supporters.

This study sought to examine the circumstances that moderated party image modification. In other words, I explored the politics and process of altering the meaning individuals assign to political parties. In general, I found that a cosmetic makeover unaccompanied by platform modifications can reshape party images. As long as people perceive the newly projected image of the party as different from the old, they will update their pictures of the party to correspond with the party's new image. Political elites, however, must be aware that some citizens have differing notions of what constitutes real change. When trying to convey to voters that the party has changed in some way, elites must realize that some aspects of a party image are easier to change than others. Finally, party image change is also contingent on what other information people possess at the time they are asked to update their perceptions of the political party.

To relate this finding to the issue of race, when parties seek to reshape their racial symbolism without changing their positions on issues such as affirmative action and reparations for slavery, the parties can expect some success, but not among those to whom the policies are most important. These findings help explain why the Republican Party has failed to attract more African Americans even in the face of greater heterogeneity in income and education among that group. In addition, the Republican Party not only had to overcome the importance that blacks already placed on policy positions on racialized issues but also encountered opposition from the media, which further highlighted the fact that the party had not completely changed. Media opposition served as a barrier to change among blacks and whites. Finally, the findings suggest that success can be temporary. Political elites' ability to make lasting changes in party images relies on their ability to sustain these projected changes. The Republican Party made substantial headway among blacks when they read that the Republicans' attempts to reach out to blacks constituted an ongoing effort. Furthermore, elite strategies that seek to alter party images will work only to the extent that they do not contradict themselves, as was the case with the dispute over the 2000 election.

By focusing on the section of party image associated with race-related activities, this book furthers scholars' knowledge of race, political communication, and party politics in three previously ignored areas. First, this book focuses on positive rather than inflammatory racialized images. Most of the examinations of racialized campaigns focus on negative, stereotypical images. The few exceptions include Valentino, Hutchings, and White (2002) and Peffley, Hurwitz, and

Sniderman (1997), who have examined whether counterstereotypical racial images prime white racial attitudes when evaluating African Americans. These studies, however, have not empirically examined whether these images can alter the meaning of political parties, candidates, and issues. Thus, this project begins to fill this void by examining the impact of positive racial images on perceptions and evaluations of political parties and their candidates.

Second, this book focuses on both African American and white public opinion when discussing race and campaign communication. To date, examinations of the impact of racialized campaigns have neglected black public opinion, thereby painting an incomplete picture of how the injection of race in campaigns affects all voters. Discussing black public opinion is an important inclusion because images of African Americans racialize campaigns. Incorporating a discussion of black public opinion helps to explain why African Americans often feel alienated from and distrustful of the American political system.

Third, I demonstrate that examining campaign communication in isolation does not wholly explain the impact of the campaign. After all, elections do not occur in vacuums. Thus, this book included a discussion of how competing sources of information in the campaign environment created opposition to a party's ultimate goals. Specifically, I demonstrate that parties must battle the media as well as party history when attempting to reshape reputations for handling racial issues. Unlike previous studies, this project contextualizes the use of racial images within electoral discourse as a means of gaining a better understanding of the campaign's impact. Doing so not only helps us understand whether a campaign will reach its goal but also why it does or does not achieve its intended impact.

In the end, however, this book is not just a story about race and party image. It is a story about politics and how parties adapt to changing political environments. This book discerns how political parties attempt to assemble winning coalitions and when and why they will succeed. As the demographic makeup of the United States shifts and incorporates more and different voters into the electorate, parties will have to adapt to the changing political landscape. The future composition of party coalitions depends on whether different groups of voters will include political parties' outreach efforts in their decision-making calculus or whether these voters will dismiss this information as illusionary.

Appendix

This appendix provides detailed information on the multiple data sources and methodology used to obtain the findings discussed in the text.

Chapter 3

To examine party images over time, I employ survey data collected over the past fifty years. Since 1952, the American National Election Study (ANES)[1] has included open-ended questions that have solicited respondents' perceptions of the two major parties. While the same questions have not been asked for every survey year, two comparable questions permit the examination of respondents' images of the two major parties with respect to race over time. The first pair of questions, originally used by Matthews and Prothro (1964) and employed in subsequent studies of party image (see, e.g., Trilling 1976), asks respondents if there is anything in particular that they like/don't like about the Democratic/Republican Party. The second question asks respondents whether they perceive any differences between the Democratic

1. The American National Election Study (ANES) is a series of national surveys fielded continuously since 1948. The ANES is designed to collect data on Americans' social backgrounds, political predispositions, social and political attitudes, perceptions and evaluations of groups and candidates, opinions on questions of public policy, and political participation. Carried out by the Survey Research Center (SRC) or the Center for Political Studies (CPS) of the Institute for Social Research at the University of Michigan, the ANES is based on representative cross-section samples of between 1,000 and 2,000 voting-age citizens living in private households. Each study contains information from interviews conducted with 1,000–2,000 respondents interviewed before and after presidential elections and occasionally after congressional elections (ANES).

and Republican Parties and, if so, what these differences are. Both questions are coded similarly, denoting when a respondent perceived either party as having a positive or negative position toward racially identified groups. By positive, I mean responses indicating that a party was problack or racially liberal. Similarly, negative responses denoted when a respondent indicated that a party was bad for blacks and other minorities or was racist. For each year, responses from the entire sample were aggregated, and the percentage of negative responses was subtracted from the percentage of positive responses to give a summary response. The frequency of these responses permits discussion of the clarity of popular perceptions of the parties' racial symbolism.

I also use responses to the following question:

Some people feel that the government in Washington should make every possible effort to improve the social and economic position of blacks and other minority groups. Others feel that the government should not make any special effort to help minorities because they should help themselves. Where would you place the Democratic/ Republican Party on this scale?

The scale runs from 1 to 7, where 1 is "Government should help minority groups" and 7 is "Minorities should help themselves." This question has appeared repeatedly on the ANES since 1970. For each year, I compared the mean placement of each party on this scale for all respondents and then compared the mean placement for blacks and whites separately. I use responses to this question for a couple of reasons. First, it is the only question that asks respondents to evaluation the two parties on race in multiple years. Second, this item is not tied to any particular policy. Rather, it requires respondents to make a general assessment of the parties' willingness to address social and economic inequalities.

To examine contemporary party images, I conducted a series of focus groups and qualitative interviews. Focus groups and interviews seem particularly well suited given the task at hand. Because I am trying to allow people to define in their own words what the two major parties stand for, I need a format that facilitates unrestricted inquiry. I need to assess the full range of considerations people bring to bear when evaluating a party. Unlike survey questions, including open-ended questions, focus group and qualitative interview questions permit me to probe and follow up on responses to get at such issues.

Moreover, the incorporation of focus group data is essential because it facilitates the interaction among participants and encourages them to challenge and probe each other's ideas and responses. Naturally, while the qualitative portion of this study cannot match the polling data in sample size (thereby sacrificing the ability to generalize), the depth of qualitative research allows a kind of "pattern-matching" (D. Campbell 1975, 182). As Lin (1998) argues, this type of research permits researchers to uncover people's conscious and unconscious explanations for what they do or believe. The qualitative data allow me to ask respondents' specifically about their perceptions of the two major parties on race. In addition, this inquiry allows me to examine what it means when a respondent indicates that a party is "bad for African Americans" or is "racist."

As mentioned earlier, the qualitative data presented in this chapter are the product of a series of focus groups and qualitative interviews. To get a broad range of responses, I recruited subjects by race, sex, and partisanship. The participants in each of the focus groups were matched according to their race and partisanship. Given that the questions were somewhat racially sensitive, interviewers were also matched by race.

The first African American group consisted of four women between the ages of 35 and 60 whom I recruited while attending a public policy conference in Washington, D.C., in the early fall of 2000. Two of the women were from the Midwest, and two were from the South. All of the women had baccalaureate degrees. The second focus group also consisted of four African American women, but these women were much younger, ranging in age from 18 to 20. All were students at the University of Michigan: two were from Michigan, one was from New Jersey, and the fourth was from Colorado. This focus group was conducted in Michigan, also in the early fall of 2000. Both focus groups lasted approximately two hours.

To balance out the female focus groups, I also conducted interviews with three college-educated African American males between the ages of 23 and 31. One man was from Michigan, one was from South Carolina, and the third was from New York. The interviews were conducted during November 2000, and each interview lasted between 30 and 40 minutes.

The first white focus group was conducted during the fall of 2001. This group consisted of one female and two male University of Michi-

gan students between the ages of 18 and 21 recruited from an intro-
ductory world politics course. The second focus group also consisted
of University of Michigan undergraduates. To ensure ample representation of Republican views, I solicited the help of an assistant to recruit
Republican students—two male and one female—to participate in this
group. Again, the students' ages ranged from 18 to 21. The third focus
group consisted of nonstudent participants recruited from an Ann
Arbor business. Participants in this group ranged in age from 21 to
about 45. The second and third focus groups were conducted during
the spring of 2003. With the exception of one student in the first white
focus group who was from New York, all of the participants were from
Michigan. None of the participants in the white focus groups had completed college. Each of the focus groups lasted approximately two
hours. Table A1 summarizes the characteristics of the respondents
quoted in chapter 3.

Chapter 4

To examine the media's framing of the 2000 Republican convention,
I conducted a quantitative content analysis of the media's coverage of
the convention. According to Riffe, Lacy, and Fico (1998),

> Quantitative content analysis is the systematic and replicable exam-
> ination of symbols of communication, which have been assigned

TABLE A1.   Summary of Respondent Characteristics

Respondent Number	Age	Race	Sex	Education
1	18–21	Black	Female	Some college
2	18–21	Black	Female	Some college
3	21–35	Black	Male	College degree
4	18–21	Black	Female	Some college
5	35+	Black	Female	College degree
6	35+	Black	Female	College degree
7	21–35	Black	Male	College degree
8	21–35	Black	Male	College degree
9	18–21	White	Male	Some college
10	18–21	White	Male	Some college
11	35+	White	Female	High School
12	18–21	White	Female	Some college
13	18–21	White	Female	Some college
14	18–21	White	Female	Some college
15	21–35	White	Male	Some college

numeric values according to valid measurement rules, and the analysis of relationships involving those values using statistical methods, in order to describe the communication, draw inferences about its meaning, or infer from the communication to its context, both of production and consumption. (21)

Thus, I quantified the frequency with which the media referred to the Republicans' race strategy, the tone the media used in their overall coverage of the convention, and the relationships between these two factors as well as how these factors interacted with the source of the coverage and the proximity to different convention events.

This chapter relies on print media coverage of the 2000 Republican convention. The data are drawn from three nationally circulated newspapers (the *New York Times,* the *Los Angeles Times,* and the *Washington Post*) and a sample of thirteen African American news sources (the *Baltimore Afro-American,* the *Jacksonville Free Press,* the *Los Angeles Sentinel,* the *New York Amsterdam News,* the *New York Beacon,* the *New York Voice,* the *Oakland Post,* the *Sacramento Observer,* the *Speakin' Out News,* the *Philadelphia Tribune,* the *Tennessee Tribune,* the *Voice,* and the *Washington Informer*). The analyses includes news articles, editorials, opinion columns, and letters to the editor from July 24 (one week before the convention) through August 10 (one week after the convention). Articles from the two nationally circulated newspapers were downloaded from LEXIS-NEXIS Academic Universe.[2] Articles appearing in black newspapers were obtained from Ethnic NewsWatch.[3] Articles were included in the sample if "Republican convention" appeared in the headline or in the lead paragraph. This coding rule allowed me to confine the sample of articles to those whose primary focus was the Republican convention. Each article was assigned a unique identification number and then coded for the story's tone, racial references, and appearance relative to the convention. The sample included 197 articles. As table 5 shows, 8.6 percent of the articles were drawn from the black newspapers, and 91.4 percent of the articles were drawn from the *Los Angeles Times,* the *New York Times,*

2. LEXIS-NEXIS Academic Universe is an electronic collection of news and other reference information.

3. Ethnic NewsWatch is also an electronic collection of news information, but the information contained on this site is restricted to ethnic and minority news sources. To maximize the number of articles in the sample, all African American newspapers available online were included in the search.

and the *Washington Post*. To draw comparisons to other Republican National Conventions, I also include content analyses of print news coverage of the 1988, 1992, and 1996 conventions.[4]

Each article was coded for valence, race references, presence of discussion of platform, and presence of discussion of conference attendees. To code valence, an article was coded as negative if the author of the article explicitly criticized or used quotes from outside sources (without rebuttal) to criticize the Republican Party or its candidates. An article was coded as positive if the author of the article explicitly praised or used quotes from outside sources (without rebuttal) to praise the Republican Party or its candidates. An article was coded as neutral if the article contained neither criticism nor praise or presented both sides of an argument. For these analyses, only the news articles were examined, since editorials, letters to the editor, and so on are expected to have some biases. An article contained a race reference if the article discussed the race of the convention delegates, the race of the performers or speakers appearing during the convention, the reaction (or anticipated reaction) of African American/minority voters to the convention, or the Republican Party's emphasis on inclusion or diversity. To gauge the amount of coverage devoted to the Republican Party's platform relative to coverage of those present at the convention, the articles were coded 1 if the article discussed the GOP's platform or its position on a specific issue and 0 if the article did not. Similarly, articles were coded 1 if the article mentioned the presence of any specific constituencies, delegates, speakers, or entertainers at the convention and 0 if the article did not.

As Holsti (1969) argues, "[I]f research is to satisfy the requirement of objectivity, measures and procedures must be reliable; i.e., repeated measures with the same instrument on a given sample of data should yield similar results" (135). Thus, to ensure reliability in coding, an additional coder was solicited to code a subsample of 50 randomly

---

4. The content analysis for past conventions was confined to one newspaper, the *New York Times*. However, the same coding rules applied. The 1988 Republican National Convention was held August 15–18 in New Orleans. Articles for this year appeared between August 9 and August 24. The 1992 convention was held in Houston on August 17–21. The coding period for this year was August 11–27. Finally, the 1996 Republican National Convention in San Diego was held August 12–15. Articles in 1996 were coded from August 6 through August 21. A total of 103 articles were coded—16 from 1988, 36 from 1992, and 51 from 1996.

selected articles independently of the primary coder. The results from the two coders were then compared. Overall, the agreement between the two coders was fairly high. According to Riffe, Lacy, and Fico (1998), the standard minimum level of agreement should be 80 percent. Of the 50 articles selected from the sample, 90 percent were coded the same for platform, 90 percent of racial references were coded consistently, 92 percent were coded the same for tone, and 96 percent were coded the same for presence. To control for the possibility of agreement by chance, the Scott's pi was calculated for the four variables. When controlling for chance, a Scott's pi of 70 percent or greater is an acceptable level of reliability. The percentage of expected agreement by chance—that is, the level of agreement expected if the two coders randomly assigned the articles to categories—for the platform variable is 50 percent. The coding results for this study yielded a Scott's pi of .80. For the race reference variable, the expected agreement by chance is .65 and the Scott's pi is .72. With respect to tone, the expected agreement by chance is 49 percent and the Scott's pi is .84. Finally, the expected agreement by chance for the presence variable is 50 percent and the Scott's pi is .92. Even controlling for chance, the coding met the generally accepted standard of agreement.

Chapter 5

In chapter 5, I rely on two data sources to increase both the internal and external validity of my results. First, to get a general sense of how convention exposure resonated in the electorate, I use secondary analysis of the Gallup Organization's Post–GOP Convention Poll,[5] which was conducted by telephone on August 4–6, 2000, only a few days after the close of the Republican convention. The polling sample included a national probability sample of 1,051 adults. In addition, the poll also included an oversample of 319 African American adults, resulting in a total N of 1,370. Respondents were asked a series of questions about politics, including their level of attentiveness to the convention; how well they believed the Republican Party reached out to blacks, Hispanics, and other minorities; and their likelihood of voting for George W. Bush.

To get at the precise causal relationship between convention exposure and subsequent perceptions and evaluations of the Republican

---

5. This data set was obtained from the Roper Center for Public Opinion Research.

Party, I conducted the 2002–2003 Party Image Study, which incorporated an experiment into its design. The experiment sought to replicate exposure to the 2000 Republican National Convention and to incorporate the different framing of the convention people might have encountered in the media. Using data from the content analysis, the experiment incorporates three versions of the convention. In this experiment, subjects were asked to read a series of three newspaper articles that they were told had originally appeared in various newspapers over the preceding couple of years. The first and third articles were actual newspaper articles slightly edited to establish length uniformity. The second article took one of four forms, three of which were contrived and one of which was a real article used as a control.

The three contrived articles discussed the 2000 Republican convention. The headline of the first read, "Republicans Open Convention." The body of the article contained the following information: (1) the Republican Party was finally catching up with the Democrats in the art of appealing to swing voters; (2) the 2000 convention program featured numerous speakers and entertainers in support of the GOP's platform; (3) the 2000 convention was part of an ongoing outreach effort to increase support among the electorate; (4) swing voters generally agreed with the Republican Party on moral and education issues but would vote Democrat if the election were held tomorrow; (5) Theodore Williams, chairman of the Voters Project, believed that the Republican outreach effort constituted an unprecedented attempt to reach out to swing voters but admitted that he was unsure about how voters would respond; and (6) GOP leaders were aware that they had little chance of winning the majority of the swing vote but knew that every vote would count in what was predicted to be a tight election. The article was accompanied by a picture of convention attendees captioned, "Excitement sweeps convention attendees at the opening of the 2000 Republican National Convention." This article sought to recreate convention events, absent any references to the show of diversity displayed during the convention.

The second article was nearly identical to the first except that it depicted the Republican Party as reaching out to African American voters rather than swing voters. The headline read, "Republicans Open Convention, with a More Diverse Look." The body of the article contained the following information: (1) the Republican Party was finally catching up with the Democrats in the art of appealing to black voters;

(2) the 2000 convention program featured numerous African American speakers and entertainers in support of the GOP's platform; (3) the 2000 convention was part of an ongoing outreach effort to increase support among the black electorate; (4) black voters generally agreed with the Republican Party on moral and education issues but would vote Democrat if the election were held tomorrow; (5) Theodore Williams, chairman of the Black Voters Project, believed that the Republican outreach effort constituted an unprecedented attempt to reach out to black voters but admitted that he was unsure about how black voters would respond; and (6) GOP leaders were aware that they would have little chance of winning the majority of the black vote but knew that every vote would count in what was predicted to be a tight election. The article was accompanied by a picture of about thirty well-dressed African American men and women on stage at the 2000 Republican National Convention captioned, "Prominent African American leaders gather on stage at the opening of the 2000 Republican National Convention." This article is sought to re-create the Republican Party's attempt to appear racially inclusive at the convention.

The third contrived article was identical to the second except that it explicitly stated that the Republican Party had not changed its platform despite its attempt to appear racially inclusive. The body of the article contained the following additional information: (1) the 2000 convention program featured numerous black speakers and entertainers in support of the GOP's *traditional* platform; (2) Ed Jones, convention coordinator, was quoted as saying, "We've got a great message *and our ideas and principles remain unchanged*"; (3) Jones also stated that although the party's policy positions remained the same, the display of diversity illustrated the Republican Party's enthusiasm about sharing its message with black voters; (4) Theodore Williams, chairman of the Black Voters Project, believed that the Republican outreach effort constituted an unprecedented attempt to reach out to black voters but admitted that he was unsure about how black voters would respond *since Republicans hadn't actually changed their platform*. This manipulation sought to examine whether differences in media framing affect individuals' reactions to the GOP outreach effort. Specifically, this manipulation examined whether explicitly highlighting that the changes in the Republican Party were cosmetic rather than substantive minimized the effect of this campaign strategy.

As stated earlier, the fourth article is a control treatment. This particular article is about the effects of acid rain and contains absolutely no information about the Republican Party or political party conventions. The purpose of the control is to determine attitudes when subjects are not primed to think about the Republican Party or the convention.[6]

To obtain enough variance in the demographic characteristics and political predispositions within the sample, I recruited nonstudent subjects from a number of locations, including various hotel lobbies in Washtenaw County, Michigan. In addition, I oversampled among African Americans to make interrace comparisons across subjects. To ensure the inclusion of enough African Americans, subjects were recruited from a number of black venues, including churches, barbershops, and hair salons. The study was in the field from September 2002 to March 2003. Including the black oversample, I recruited 302 subjects (172 whites and 130 blacks) for the experiment.

The subjects were randomly assigned to one of the four treatments. The experiment was embedded in a questionnaire. In addition to reading the articles, the subjects were asked a number of questions designed to assess their level of media usage, political interest and participation, party identification, and ideological orientation. Subjects were also asked to answer questions about their racial attitudes, policy preferences, the political parties' policy preferences, and their affective response to the political parties. Finally, the subjects were asked to provide standard demographic information such as education, age, gender, race, and religion.

I am primarily interested in whether watching the convention

---

6. Before administering the experiment, the treatments were pretested on a group of undergraduates from the University of Michigan. Included in the student sample were 52 students recruited from various political science courses. The purpose of the pretest was to ensure that the subjects could observe the subtle differences among the manipulations. The results of the pretest indicated that 76 percent of the subjects who received one of the two articles about the GOP's outreach efforts to African Americans correctly indicated that the Republican convention featured many African Americans. Only 4 percent of the subjects who read either the control article or the swing voter article indicated that they read an article indicating that the 2000 Republican National Convention featured many African Americans. Of the subjects who received the swing voter article, 85 percent correctly indicated that they read an article about the Republican Party reaching out to swing voters, compared to 17 percent who did not read that article. All of the subjects in the control group recognized that they had read an article about acid rain, and none of the subjects in the other three treatment groups indicated that they had read an article about acid rain. Finally, 64 percent of the subjects who read the article explicitly stating that the Republican Party had not changed its platform indicated that the Republican Party had not changed its platform in 2000, compared to 0 percent in the control treatment group and 54 percent in the other two treatment groups.

affected people's perception of the racial components of the Republican Party's image. Measuring these perceptions required a question that asked respondents to interpret the racial meaning of the party's activities (i.e., whether the party is problack). This meaning should be derived without any mention of specific policies or personas in the actual question wording. To measure this concept, I use an item included on the Gallup survey: "Would you say the Republican Party is generally doing a good job or a bad job these days, of reaching out to blacks, Hispanics, and other minorities?" Responses were coded 1 for a good job, 0 for a bad job, .5 if a response was mixed/neither. For consistency, this measure was included on the experimental questionnaire.

These analyses also sought to examine the impact of convention exposure on candidate evaluations and vote preference. Discovering that the Republican Party altered people's perceptions of its racial symbolism represents only an intermediate step in the causal chain leading to vote choice. To gauge candidate preference in the survey analyses, I use the responses to the following question: "Now, if Al Gore were the Democratic Party's candidate and George W. Bush and Dick Cheney were the Republican Party's candidates, who would you be more likely to vote for?" A vote for Bush/Cheney was coded 1, while a vote for Gore was coded 0. Because the experiment was conducted two years after the 2000 presidential election, I used responses to a George W. Bush feeling thermometer instead of vote choice. In this question, subjects were asked to rate Bush on a scale from 0 to 100, where 0 to 49 meant that the subject did not feel favorably toward Bush, 50 was neutral, and 51 to 100 meant that the subject had particularly warm (favorable) feelings toward Bush.

The primary independent variable in these analyses is convention exposure. In the survey, convention exposure is measured by self-reported convention watching. If respondents watched a great deal of the convention, their responses were coded 1; if respondents watched none or little of the convention, their responses were coded 0. Responses were dichotomized in this way because it was assumed that maximum exposure to the convention would ensure that convention watchers were exposed to the Republican race strategy. Because exposure to the convention is manipulated directly in the experiment, degrees of exposure to the convention are represented by the experimental conditions.

Studies have found that political inference tends to be a function of an individual's political preferences (Conover and Feldman 1989). Therefore, in examining the impact of watching the GOP convention on perceptions of the Republican Party on racial outreach, I also included several measures of the respondents' political predispositions and demographic characteristics.

First, I included the respondents' party identification and ideology as additional measures of political predispositions. Party identification in the Post–GOP Convention Poll was coded using a two-part question, resulting in a 5-point scale running from Republican (0) to Democrat (1). In the experiment, party identification is measured using a 7-point scale that ran from Republican (0) to Democrat (1). I include party identification because I expect any evaluation (not just affective evaluation but evaluation in terms of propensity to do something, i.e., reach out to minorities) of a party to be a function of prior evaluations of that party (Downs 1957; Jackson 1975; Fiorina 1981). Because the data are cross-sectional and there is no measure of perceptions of the Republican Party before the convention, party identification proxies as a measure of previous evaluations. I also include the respondents' ideology as an additional measure of political predispositions. Ideology is measured in the Post–GOP Convention Poll using a 5-point scale running from very conservative (0) to very liberal (1). In the 2002–2003 Party Image Study, ideology is measured with a similarly coded 7-point scale.

Finally, I include demographic variables that measure gender, race, income, education, and age. The inclusion of the respondents' race is particularly important, given the relevance of the Republican campaign appeals to the African American community.[7] Because of previous interaction and experience with the GOP, I expect the race variable to act as a political predisposition, anchoring the effect of watching the convention (see chapter 1).

Tables A2–A8 present the results.

Chapter 6

The content analysis in this chapter relies on print media coverage of the 2000 election. The data are drawn from the *New York Amsterdam*

---

7. The survey sample included 390 African Americans and 954 non–African Americans, of whom 859 were white. Hispanics, Asians, and other minority groups were included only in the analyses utilizing the entire sample. Otherwise, the analyses only included blacks and whites.

TABLE A2. Perceptions of the Republican Party's Racial Symbolism

	All	Whites	Blacks
Watching the convention	.070	.103	−.018
	(.03)	(.04)	(.06)
Gender	.044	.067	−.035
	(.03)	(.03)	(.05)
Age	−.001	−.002	.000
	(.00)	(.00)	(.00)
Education	−.011	−.020	.009
	(.01)	(.01)	(.02)
Income	−.030	−.026	−.037
	(.01)	(.01)	(.02)
Party identification	−.473	−.394	−.631
	(.03)	(.04)	(.07)
Ideology	−.142	−.283	.006
	(.06)	(.08)	(.08)
Black	−.123		
	(.03)		
Constant	1.135	1.221	.953
	(.08)	(.10)	(.12)
N	1,096	712	329
R-squared	.27	.23	.20

Source: Post–GOP Convention Poll.

Note: Estimates are OLS coefficients with robust standard errors. Standard errors appear in parentheses under coefficient estimates. Bold coefficients are significant at the $p < .10$ level (one-tailed test).

News and the *New York Times*. The analyses include news articles, editorials, opinion columns, and letters to the editor for the period November 7 (Election Day) through December 13 (when Al Gore conceded the election). Articles from the *New York Times* were downloaded from LEXIS-NEXIS Academic Universe. Those from the *New York Amsterdam News* were downloaded from Ethnic NewsWatch. Articles were included in the sample if "Republican Party" appeared in the headline or in the lead paragraph. This coding rule allowed me to confine the sample of articles to those whose primary focus was on the Republican Party. One hundred articles were included in this sample— 88 from the *New York Times* and 12 from the *New York Amsterdam News*. Each article was assigned a unique identification number and then coded for the presence of different themes, including the Florida recount and the discussion of racial minorities.

To gauge public opinion, I rely on the 2002 ANES, which consists of pre- and postelection surveys. Data collection for this study began in

TABLE A3.   The Impact of Convention Frames on Perceptions of the Republican Party's Racial Symbolism

	Whites	Blacks
Race-neutral	.048	−.008
	(.08)	(.09)
Race–no platform	**.138**	.012
	(.09)	(.11)
Race-platform	.062	−.050
	(.08)	(.08)
Gender	**.079**	−.013
	(.06)	(.07)
Age	.000	**−.004**
	(.00)	(.00)
Education	**.068**	−.022
	(.04)	(.04)
Income	**−.021**	−.022
	(.01)	(.02)
Party identification	**−.264**	−.001
	(.15)	(.15)
Ideology	**−.441**	.004
	(.14)	(.12)
Constant	**.565**	**.754**
	(.18)	(.21)
N	135	90
R-squared	.22	.15

Source: 2002–2003 Party Image Study.

Note: Estimates are OLS coefficients with robust standard errors. Standard errors appear in parentheses under coefficient estimates. Bold coefficients are significant at the $p < .10$ level (one–tailed test).

September 2002 and ended in December 2002. The survey was conducted by telephone, and the sample included a national probability sample of 1,807 adults who participated in the 2000 ANES and an additional 1,175 adults interviewed in 2002. Respondents were asked a series of questions about politics, including whether they voted and for whom, their attitudes toward the 2000 election, and their evaluations of different candidates and groups in society.

I was interested in whether attitudes toward the 2000 election affected people's perceptions of the Republican Party and its ability to represent different groups. To measure these perceptions, I used a series of questions that asked respondents to evaluate whether the

TABLE A4. The Joint Effects of Race and Party
Identification on Perceptions of the Republican Party's
Racial Symbolism by Convention Exposure

	Did Not Watch	Watched
Party identification	**−.414**	**−.455**
	(.04)	(.08)
Black	−.035	.106
	(.09)	(.12)
Black × Party identification	−.124	**−.362**
	(.10)	(.14)
Gender	.038	.027
	(.03)	(.05)
Age	**−.002**	.002
	(.00)	(.00)
Education	−.015	.016
	(.01)	(.02)
Income	**−.035**	−.006
	(.01)	(.02)
Ideology	**−.150**	−.105
	(.07)	(.13)
Constant	**1.187**	**.750**
	(.09)	(.18)
N	837	204
R-squared	.23	.42

Source: Post–GOP Convention Poll.

Note: Estimates are OLS coefficients. Standard errors appear in
parentheses under coefficient estimates. Bold coefficients are significant at the $p < .10$ level (one-tailed test).

Republican or Democratic Party was better for a particular group.
Specifically, I used questions that asked respondents to evaluate the
parties' ability to represent blacks, whites, women, men, the poor, and
the rich. Responses were coded 1 for Democrat, 0 for Republican, and
.5 if a respondent saw little difference between the two parties.

I also examined the impact of attitudes toward the 2000 election on
attitudes toward George W. Bush. To do so, I used responses to a
Bush feeling thermometer. In this question, subjects were asked to rate
Bush on a scale from 0 to 100, where 0 to 49 meant that the subject
did not feel favorably toward Bush, 50 was neutral, and 51 to 100
meant that the subject had particularly warm (favorable) feelings
toward Bush.

The primary independent variable in these analyses is attitudes
toward the 2000 election. To measure these evaluations, I used

TABLE A5. The Joint Effects of Race and Party Identification on Perceptions of the Republican Party's Racial Symbolism by Experimental Treatment Conditions

	Control	Race-Neutral	Race–No Platform	Race-Platform
Black	**.324**	.134	.230	.143
	(.15)	(.22)	(.22)	(.20)
Party identification	**–.691**	**–.306**	**–.602**	**–.466**
	(.16)	(.22)	(.23)	(.21)
Black × Party	–.063	–.043	**–.100**	–.064
identification	(.05)	(.07)	(.06)	(.06)
Constant	**.745**	**.555**	**.766**	**.659**
	(.09)	(.13)	(.13)	(.11)
N	64	68	68	70
R-squared	.25	.03	.10	.08

Source: 2002–2003 Party Image Study.

Note: Estimates are OLS coefficients. Standard errors appear in parentheses under coefficient estimates. Bold coefficients are significant at the $p < .10$ level (one-tailed test).

responses to the following question: "All things considered, would you say that the 2000 presidential election was decided in a way that was fair or unfair? Do you feel strongly or not strongly that it was fair/unfair?" Responses were coded 1 if a respondent believed strongly that the election was fair, .67 if his or her approval of the election was not strong, .33 if the respondent disapproved not strongly of the 2000 election, and 0 if the respondent disapproved strongly.

I also included several measures of the respondents' political predispositions and demographic characteristics. First, I included the respondents' party identification and ideology as additional measures of political predispositions. Party identification was coded using a two-part question, resulting in a 7-point scale running from Republican (1) to Democrat (7). I also included the respondents' ideology as an additional measure of political predisposition. Ideology was measured using a 7-point scale running from very conservative (1) to very liberal (7). Finally, I included demographic variables that measured gender, race, income, education, and age.

Tables A9–A11 present the results.

Chapter 7

Chapter 7 relies on experimental data collected as part of the 2005 Party Image Study, which took place in June–August 2005. This study

TABLE A6.   Voting for George W. Bush Based on Convention Exposure and Perceptions of the Republican Party's Racial Symbolism by Race

	Whites	Blacks
Racial symbolism	.571	1.483
	(.33)	(.53)
Watching the convention	−1.491	1.014
	(.72)	(.64)
Racial symbolism × Watching the convention	2.617	.192
	(.93)	(1.40)
Gender	.351	−1.076
	(.30)	(.63)
Age	−.007	−.006
	(.01)	(.01)
Education	−.200	−.546
	(.11)	(.22)
Income	.246	.071
	(.10)	(.15)
Ideology	−2.966	3.029
	(.73)	(.96)
Party identification	−4.924	−5.662
	(.42)	(1.07)
Constant	4.473	3.880
	(.98)	(1.90)
N	616	282
Log pseudo-likelihood	−164.01	−67.35

Source: Post–GOP Convention Poll.

Note: Estimates are logistic regression coefficients with robust standard errors. Standard errors appear in parentheses under coefficient estimates. Bold coefficients are significant at the $p < .10$ level (one-tailed test).

sought to expose people to a scenario in which a political party attempted to reshape its image without changing its platform and to measure the extent to which people perceived differences in the party. To do so, I conducted an experiment. There were two versions of the experiment—one for the Democratic Party (which is used in chapter 8) and one for the Republican Party (chapter 7). Each version presented subjects with one of three scenarios. Table A12 provides the exact question wording for the Republican version of the experiment. The first scenario, which is the race-neutral condition, simply informed subjects that the party was attempting to reach out to voters who did not currently align with that party. In the race–no platform condition, the Republican Party was reaching out to African Americans, while the

TABLE A7.   George W. Bush Feeling Thermometer Based on Convention Exposure and Perceptions of the Republican Party's Racial Symbolism by Race

	Whites	Blacks
Race-neutral treatment	−32.755	−8.381
	(12.78)	(19.00)
Race–no platform treatment	−27.917	−19.322
	(11.40)	(11.78)
Race-platform treatment	−29.521	−25.560
	(9.41)	(10.71)
Racial symbolism	−2.075	−3.445
	(5.53)	(13.16)
Racial symbolism ×	−5.150	20.307
Race-neutral treatment	(7.66)	(23.31)
Racial symbolism ×	**48.298**	**23.745**
Race–no platform treatment	(12.73)	(14.86)
Racial symbolism ×	**43.042**	**55.223**
Race-platform treatment	(12.62)	(19.03)
Gender	−4.796	3.399
	(3.85)	(7.02)
Age	−.030	.002
	(.14)	(.21)
Education	**−5.445**	−.586
	(2.52)	(3.25)
Income	.472	1.674
	(.74)	(1.18)
Party identification	**8.781**	1.033
	(2.52)	(7.07)
Ideology	**−35.581**	−9.222
	(10.67)	(11.63)
Constant	**47.501**	**37.321**
	(8.55)	(23.27)
N	117	83
R-squared	.51	.20

Source: 2002–2003 Party Image Study.

Note: Estimates are OLS coefficients with robust standard errors. Standard errors appear in parentheses under coefficient estimates. Bold coefficients are significant at the $p < .10$ level (one-tailed test).

Democratic Party was attempting to distance itself from African Americans. The race-platform condition was identical to the race–no platform condition except that subjects were told explicitly that the parties had not changed their platforms. Finally, I included a control group where subjects did not read anything about the parties.

To obtain enough variance in the demographic characteristics and

TABLE A8. The Effects of Watching the Convention among Southern Whites

	Racial Symbolism	Vote Intent
Racial symbolism		.232
		(.70)
Watching the convention	**.103**	**−3.002**
	(.06)	(1.71)
Racial symbolism × Watching the convention		**5.284**
		(1.90)
Gender	.058	.184
	(.06)	(.70)
Age	**−.002**	.02
	(.00)	(.02)
Education	−.030	−.185
	(.02)	(.19)
Income	−.021	.273
	(.02)	(.23)
Party identification	**−.409**	**−5.917**
	(.08)	(.97)
Ideology	**−.250**	−.740
	(.15)	(1.28)
Constant	**1.312**	2.841
	(.18)	(2.27)
N	185	169
R-squared	.24	
Log pseudo-likelihood		−36.34

Source: Post–GOP Convention Poll.

Note: Estimates are OLS coefficients with robust standard errors for the racial symbolism model and logistic regression coefficients with robust standard errors for the vote intent model. Standard errors appear in parentheses under coefficient estimates. Bold coefficients are significant at the $p < .10$ level (one–tailed test).

political predispositions within the sample, I recruited nonstudent subjects from a number of locations, including hotel lobbies in Austin, Texas, and an art fair in Ann Arbor, Michigan. In addition, I oversampled among African Americans to make interrace comparisons across subjects. To ensure the inclusion of enough African Americans, subjects were recruited from the Conference on Christian Education, which is part of the National Baptist Convention, a historically black denomination. Including the black oversample, I recruited 436 subjects for the experiment (226 blacks, 59 southern whites, and 151 nonsouthern whites).

TABLE A9.   Impressions of the Republican Party's
Image on Race Based on Perceived Fairness of the
2000 Election

	Blacks	Whites
Perceived fairness of 2000 election	−.156	.013
	(.04)	(.04)
Age	.001	**.002**
	(.00)	(.00)
Party identification	**.032**	.009
	(.01)	(.01)
Income	−.001	−.006
	(.01)	(.01)
Black	−.008	−.079
	(.05)	(.05)
Female	−.031	.035
	(.03)	(.03)
Education	.009	−.007
	(.01)	(.01)
Ideology	.013	.013
	(.01)	(.01)
Constant	**.535**	**.286**
	(.10)	(.10)
N	398	398
Adjusted *R*-squared	.19	.027

Source: 2002 American National Election Study.

Note: Estimates are OLS coefficients. Standard errors appear in parentheses under coefficient estimates. Bold coefficients are significant at the $p < .10$ level (two-tailed test).

As stated earlier, the subjects were randomly assigned to one of six treatments or a control. The experiment was embedded in a questionnaire. In addition to reading the experimental treatment, the subjects were asked a number of questions designed to assess their level of political participation, party identification, and ideological orientation. Subjects were also asked to answer questions about their racial attitudes and the political parties. Finally, the subjects were asked to provide standard demographic information such as education, age, gender, race, and religion. The entire questionnaire took approximately 20 minutes to complete. After subjects completed the study, they received $10 in cash for their participation.

Figure 18 presents the means of the Republican Party's placement on the racial symbolism dimension. To determine the statistical

Table A10. **Impressions of the Republican Party's Image on Gender and Class Based on Perceived Fairness of the 2000 Election**

	Women	Men	Rich	Poor
Perceived fairness of 2000 election	**−.109**	−.016	.047	**−.094**
	(.04)	(.04)	(.03)	(.03)
Age	**−.002**	**.003**	.000	.000
	(.00)	(.00)	(.00)	(.00)
Party identification	**.037**	.006	**−.041**	**.059**
	(.01)	(.01)	(.01)	(.01)
Income	.005	.003	−.004	.003
	(.01)	(.01)	(.01)	(.01)
Black	−.020	**.103**	.055	−.026
	(.06)	(.06)	(.04)	(.04)
Female	−.032	.004	.024	−.011
	(.03)	(.03)	(.02)	(.02)
Education	.014	.009	**−.017**	.010
	(.01)	(.01)	(.01)	(.01)
Ideology	**.023**	.016	−.008	**.026**
	(.01)	(.01)	(.01)	(.01)
Constant	**.458**	**.346**	**.449**	**.418**
	(.09)	(.09)	(.07)	(.07)
N	389	390	788	790
Adjusted *R*-squared	.22	.03	.13	.29

Source: 2002 American National Election Study.

Note: Estimates are OLS coefficients. Standard errors appear in parentheses under coefficient estimates. Bold coefficients are significant at the $p < .10$ level (two-tailed test).

significance, I conducted *t*-tests between the control condition and the race-neutral and racialized conditions. The significance level for all analyses was $p < .10$ (one-tailed test).

Chapter 8

Chapter 8 relies on experimental data collected as part of the 2005 Party Image Study. As discussed in chapter 7, the 2005 Party Image Study sought to expose people to a scenario in which a political party attempted to reshape its image and measure the extent to which people perceived differences in the party. (See the preceding section for a more detailed discussion of the experiment.) Chapter 8 uses the Democratic version of the question wording experiment.

Table A13 provides the exact question wording for the Democratic

TABLE A11. George W. Bush Feeling Thermometer

Perceived fairness of 2000 election	**19.775**
	(1.94)
Age	−.002
	(.04)
Party identification	**−3.552**
	(.43)
Income	.066
	(.34)
Black	−2.138
	(2.59)
Female	1.685
	(1.27)
Education	**−.846**
	(.45)
Ideology	**−3.037**
	(.53)
Constant	**83.470**
	(4.59)
N	784
Adjusted *R*-squared	.50

Source: 2002 American National Election Study.
Note: Estimates are OLS coefficients. Standard errors appear in parentheses under coefficient estimates. Bold coefficients are significant at the $p < .10$ level (two-tailed test).

version of the experiment. The first scenario, which is the race-neutral condition, simply informed subjects that the party was attempting to reach out to voters who did not currently align with that party. In the race–no platform condition, the Democratic Party was reaching out to Republican-leaning voters while distancing itself from black voters. The race-platform condition was identical to the race–no platform condition except that subjects were told explicitly that the party had not changed its platform. Finally, I included a control group where subjects did not read anything about the party. For the analyses in this chapter, I combined both racialized treatment groups into one. Before doing so, I estimated the effect of each treatment group on the dependent variable. The difference between the two racialized treatment groups relative to the control group was statistically indistinguishable from zero.

TABLE A12. 2005 Party Image Study Experimental Treatment Groups

Control	How much do you think that the Republican Party has changed over the last few years?
Race-neutral	During its 2004 national convention, the Republican Party tried to appeal to Democratic-leaning voters. The 2004 convention program featured a number of liberal Republican leaders. At the same time, many of the conservative speakers featured at past conventions were not asked to give speeches at the 2004 convention. This outreach effort is an ongoing strategy that began at the 2000 Republican National Convention. How much do you think that the Republican Party has changed over the last few years?
Race–no platform	During its 2004 national convention, the Republican Party tried to appeal to Democratic-leaning voters by reaching out to African Americans. The convention program featured a number of black Republican leaders. At the same time, many of the conservative speakers featured at past conventions were not asked to give speeches at the 2004 convention. This outreach effort is an ongoing strategy that began at the 2000 Republican National Convention. How much do you think that the Republican Party has changed over the last few years?
Race-platform	During its 2004 national convention, the Republican Party tried to appeal to Democratic-leaning voters by reaching out to African Americans. While the party's principles and platform remain unchanged, the convention program featured a number of black Republican leaders. At the same time, many of the conservative speakers featured at past conventions were not asked to give speeches at the 2004 convention. This outreach effort is an ongoing strategy that began at the 2000 Republican National Convention. How much do you think that the Republican Party has changed over the last few years?

The dependent variable used throughout this chapter was an item similar to the one used to measure the Republican Party's racial symbolism. Specifically, I used responses to the following question: "Would you say the Democratic Party is generally doing a good job or a bad job these days reaching out to blacks, Hispanics, and other minorities?" Responses were coded 1 if subjects believed that the Democratic Party did a good job, 0 if the party did a bad job, and .5 if the party did neither a good nor bad job. The figures in this chapter present the means of the Democratic Party's placement on the racial symbolism dimension. To determine the statistical significance, I conducted t-tests between the control condition and the race-neutral and racialized conditions. The significance level for all analyses was $p < .10$ (one-tailed test).

TABLE A13.   2005 Party Image Study Experimental Treatment Groups

Control	How much do you think that the Democratic Party has changed over the last few years?
Race-neutral	During its 2004 national convention, the Democratic Party tried to appeal to Republican-leaning voters. The convention program featured a number of conservative Democratic leaders. At the same time, many of the liberal speakers featured at past conventions were not asked to give speeches at the 2004 convention.
	How much do you think that the Democratic Party has changed over the last few years?
Race–no platform	During its 2004 national convention, the Democratic Party tried to appeal to Republican-leaning voters by distancing itself from African Americans. The convention program featured a number of conservative Democratic leaders. At the same time, many of the black speakers featured at past conventions were not asked to give speeches at the 2004 convention.
	How much do you think that the Democratic Party has changed over the last few years?
Race-platform	During its 2004 national convention, the Democratic Party tried to appeal to Republican-leaning voters by distancing itself from African Americans. While the party's principles and platform remain unchanged, the convention program featured a number of conservative Democratic leaders. At the same time, many of the black speakers featured at past conventions were not asked to give speeches at the 2004 convention.
	How much do you think that the Democratic Party has changed over the last few years?

References

Adams, Greg D. 1997. "Abortion: Evidence of an issue evolution." *American Journal of Political Science* 41 (3): 718–37.

Aistrup, Joseph A. 1996. *The Southern Strategy Revisited: Republican Top-Down Advancement in the South.* Lexington: University Press of Kentucky.

Aldrich, John Herbert. 1995. *Why Parties? The Origin and Transformation of Political Parties in America.* Chicago: University of Chicago Press.

Allen, Mike. 2000. "For 'Regents', a special class of party favors." *Washington Post,* August 3, A15.

Allsop, Dee, and Herbert F. Weisberg. 1988. "Measuring change in party identification in an election campaign." *American Journal of Political Science* 32 (4): 996–1017.

The American National Election Study (www.electionstudies.org). 2005. The 1948–2004 ANES Cumulative Data File [dataset]. Stanford University and the University of Michigan [producers and distributors].

Ansolabehere, Stephen, and Shanto Iyengar. 1994. "Riding the wave and claiming ownership over issues: The joint effects of advertising and news coverage in campaigns." *Public Opinion Quarterly* 58 (3): 335–57.

Ansolabehere, Stephen, and Shanto Iyengar. 1995. *Going Negative: How Attack Ads Shrink and Polarize the Electorate.* New York: Free Press.

Bai, Matt. 2000. "The Ricky Martin factor." *Newsweek,* August 14, 26.

Bane, Mary Jo, and David T. Ellwood. 1994. *Welfare Realities: From Rhetoric to Reform.* Cambridge: Harvard University Press.

Bartels, Larry. 1997. "How campaigns matter." Paper presented at the meeting of the Committee on Campaign Reform, Washington, D.C.

Bedolla, Lisa Garcia. 2003. "The identity paradox: Latino language, politics, and selective dissociation." *Latino Studies* 1 (2): 264–83.

Berelson, Bernard R., Paul F. Lazarsfeld, and William N. McPhee. 1954. *Voting: A Study of Opinion Formation in a Presidential Campaign.* Chicago: University of Chicago Press.

Bolce, Louis, Gerald DeMaio, and Douglas Muzzio. 1993. "The 1992 Republican 'tent': No blacks walked in." *Political Science Quarterly* 108 (2): 255–70.

Bositis, David A. 2000a. *Blacks and the 2000 Republican National Convention.* Washington, D.C.: Joint Center for Political and Economic Studies.

Bositis, David A. 2000b. *National Opinion Poll, 2000: Politics.* Washington, D.C.: Joint Center for Political and Economic Studies.

Bositis, David A. 2004. *The Black Vote in 2004.* Washington, D.C.: Joint Center for Political and Economic Studies.

Bragg, Rick, and Lynette Holloway. 2000. "Counting the vote: The recount; tempers flaring under pressure." *New York Times,* November 26, A1.

Bruni, Frank. 2000. "Contesting the vote: The Texas governor; advisers to Bush say he would use appointments to send a message about diversity." *New York Times,* November 30, A27.

Bullock, Charles S., III, and Mark J. Rozell. 1998. "Southern politics at century's end." In *The New Politics of the Old South: An Introduction to Southern Politics,* edited by C. S. Bullock III and M. J. Rozell, 3–24. Lanham, Md.: Rowman and Littlefield.

Bunche, Ralph J. 1939. *Report on the Needs of the Negro (for the Republican Program Committee).* Washington, D.C.: Howard University.

Burnham, Walter Dean. 1967. "Party systems and the political process." In *The American Party Systems: Stages of Political Development,* edited by W. N. Chambers and W. D. Burnham, 277–307. New York: Oxford University Press.

Bush, George W. 2000. "Speech at NAACP annual convention." Baltimore, Md.

Campbell, Angus, Philip Converse, Warren Miller, and Donald Stokes. 1960. *The American Voter.* New York: Wiley.

Campbell, Bruce A. 1977. "Patterns of change in the partisan loyalties of native southerners: 1952–1972." *Journal of Politics* 39 (3): 730–61.

Campbell, Donald T. 1975. "'Degrees of freedom' and the case study." *Comparative Political Studies* 8 (2): 178–93.

Cannon, Carl M., Lou Dubose, and Jan Reid. 2003. *Boy Genius: Karl Rove, the Architect of George W. Bush's Remarkable Political Triumphs.* New York: Public Affairs.

Cappella, Joseph N., and Kathleen Hall Jamieson. 1997. *Spiral of Cynicism: The Press and the Public Good.* New York: Oxford University Press.

Carlson, Margaret. 2000. "The Man who wore the white shirt." *Time,* August 14, 35.

Carmines, Edward G., and James A. Stimson. 1986. "On the structure and sequence of issue evolution." *American Political Science Review* 80 (3): 901–20.

Carmines, Edward G., and James A. Stimson. 1989. *Issue Evolution.* Princeton: Princeton University Press.

Carney, James, and John F. Dickerson. 2000. "The selling of George Bush: An unlikely troupe of message makers want you to meet their man 'W.' Can a winning personality win in November?" *Time,* July 24, 30–33.

Carter, Dan T. 1996. *From George Wallace to Newt Gingrich: Race in the Conservative Counterrevolution, 1963–1994.* Baton Rouge: Louisiana State University Press.

Chaney, Carole K., R. Michael Alvarez, and Jonathan Nagler. 1998. "Explaining the gender gap in U.S. presidential elections, 1980–1992." *Political Research Quarterly* 51 (2): 311–39.

Clark, John A., John M. Bruce, John H. Kessel, and William G. Jacoby. 1991. "I'd rather switch than fight: Lifelong Democrats and converts to Republicanism among campaign activists." *American Journal of Political Science* 35 (3): 577–97.

Clinton, William Jefferson. 1992. "Our New Covenant." Acceptance speech at Democratic National Convention. New York. Available at www.presidency .ucsb.edu.

Cohen, Claudia E. 1981. "Goals and schemata in person perception: Making sense from the stream of behavior." In *Personality, Cognition, and Social Interaction,* edited by N. Cantor and J. K. Kihlstrom, 45–68. Hillsdale, N.J.: Erlbaum.

Conover, Pamela Johnston, and Stanley Feldman. 1989. "Candidate perception in an ambiguous world: Campaigns, cues, and inference processes." *American Journal of Political Science* 33 (4): 912–40.

Conover, Pamela Johnston, and Virginia Sapiro. 1993. "Gender, gender consciousness, and war." *American Journal of Political Science* 37 (4): 1079–99.

Converse, Philip E. 1964. "The nature of belief systems in mass publics." In *Ideology and Discontent,* edited by D. E. Apter, 206–61. London,: Free Press of Glencoe.

Converse, Philip E., and Gregory B. Markus. 1979. "Plus ca change . . . : The new CPS election study panel." *American Political Science Review* 73 (1): 32–49.

Cowden, Jonathan A., and Rose M. McDermott. 2000. "Short-term forces and partisanship." *Political Behavior* 22 (3): 197–222.

Dalton, Russell J., Paul A. Beck, and Robert Huckfeldt. 1998. "Partisan cues and the media: Information flows in the 1992 presidential election." *American Political Science Review* 92 (1): 111–26.

Danziger, Sheldon, and Peter Gottschalk. 1995. *America Unequal.* Cambridge: Harvard University Press.

Dawson, Michael C. 1994. *Behind the Mule: Race and Class in African-American Politics.* Princeton: Princeton University Press.

de la Garza, Rodolfo O., Louis DeSipio, F. Chris Garcia, John A. Garcia, and Angelo Falcon. 1992. *Latino Voices: Mexican, Puerto Rican, and Cuban Perspectives on American Politics.* Boulder, Colo.: Westview.

Democratic National Convention. 1992. "Democratic platform 1992: A new covenant with the American people." New York. Available at www.cnn.com/ ELECTION/2000/conventions/democratic/features/platform.92 (accessed May 2006).

Denton, Robert E., Jr. 2002. "Five pivotal elements of the 2000 presidential campaign." In *The 2000 Presidential Campaign: A Communication Perspective,* edited by R. E. Denton Jr., 1–16. Westport, Conn.: Praeger.

DeSipio, Louis. 1996. *Counting on the Latino Vote: Latinos as a New Electorate.* Charlottesville: University Press of Virginia.

Dionne, E. J. 2000. "Where did the meanness go?" *Denver Post,* August 2, B9.

Downs, Anthony. 1957. *An Economic Theory of Democracy*. New York: Harper.

Duverger, Maurice. 1963. *Political Parties: Their Organization and Activity in the Modern State*. New York: Wiley.

Edsall, Thomas Byrne, and Mary D. Edsall. 1991. *Chain Reaction: The Impact of Race, Rights, and Taxes on American Politics*. New York: Norton.

Elder, Charles D., and Roger W. Cobb. 1983. *The Political Uses of Symbols*. New York: Longman.

Eldersveld, Samuel J. 1964. *Political Parties: A Behavioral Analysis*. Chicago: Rand McNally.

Eldersveld, Samuel J., and Hanes Walton, Jr. 2000. *Political Parties in American Society*. 2nd ed. Boston: Bedford/St. Martin's.

Erwin, Carolyn K. 2000. "Black Republicans head to convention: A round table with Maryland's black GOP delegates." *Baltimore Afro-American*, August 4, A1.

Fiorina, Morris P. 1981. *Retrospective Voting in American National Elections*. New Haven: Yale University Press.

Fiske, Susan T., and Shelley E. Taylor. 1984. *Social Cognition*. Reading, Mass.: Addison-Wesley.

Franklin, Charles H., and John E. Jackson. 1983. "The dynamics of party identification." *American Political Science Review* 77 (4): 957–73.

Frankovic, Kathleen A. 1982. "Sex and politics: New alignment, old issues." *PS* 15 (3): 439–48.

Friedman, Thomas L. 2000. "Foreign Affairs; Jekyll and Hyde." *New York Times*, November 30, A29.

Frymer, Paul. 1999. *Uneasy Alliances: Race and Party Competition in America*. Princeton: Princeton University Press.

Gamson, William A. 1992. *Talking Politics*. Cambridge: Cambridge University Press.

Gans, Herbert J. 1979. *Deciding What's News: A Study of CBS Evening News, NBC Nightly News, Newsweek, and Time*. 1st ed. New York: Pantheon.

Germond, Jack W., and Jules Witcover. 1993. *Mad as Hell: Revolt at the Ballot Box, 1992*. New York: Warner.

Gilens, Martin. 1988. "Gender and support for Reagan: A comprehensive model of presidential approval." *American Journal of Political Science* 32 (1): 19–49.

Gilens, Martin. 1999. *Why Americans Hate Welfare: Race, Media, and the Politics of Antipoverty Policy*. Chicago: University of Chicago Press.

Goldman, Peter, Thomas M. DeFrank, Mark Miller, Andrew Murr, and Tom Mathews. 1994. *Quest for the Presidency 1992*. College Station: Texas A & M Press.

"GOP Stresses Inclusion: Republican National Convention hears from Powell and Rice," *Sacramento Observer*, August 8, 2000, A4.

Graber, Doris A. 1989. *Mass Media and American Politics*. 3rd ed. Washington, D.C.: CQ Press.

Green, Donald, Bradley Palmquist, and Eric Schickler. 2002. *Partisan Hearts and Minds: Political Parties and the Social Identities of Voters*. New Haven: Yale University Press.

Gurin, Patricia. 1985. "Women's gender consciousness." *Public Opinion Quarterly* 49 (2): 143–63.

Gurin, Patricia, Shirley Hatchett, and James S. Jackson. 1989. *Hope and Indepen-dence: Blacks' Response to Electoral and Party Politics.* New York: Sage Founda-tion.

Hamilton, David L., and Jeffrey W. Sherman. 1994. "Stereotypes." In *Handbook of Social Cognition,* edited by R. S. Wyer Jr. and T. K. Srull, 1–68. Hillsdale, N.J.: Erlbaum.

Hero, Rodney E. 1992. *Latinos and the U.S. Political System: Two-Tiered Plural-ism.* Philadelphia: Temple University Press.

Holsti, Ole R. 1969. *Content Analysis for the Social Science and Humanities.* Read-ing, Mass.: Addison-Wesley.

"How the GOP plans to divide the black vote." 2001–2. *Journal of Blacks in Higher Education* 34: 63–66.

Huckfeldt, R. Robert, and Carol Weitzel Kohfeld. 1989. *Race and the Decline of Class in American Politics.* Urbana: University of Illinois Press.

Hutchings, Vincent L., Nicholas A. Valentino, Tasha S. Philpot, and Ismail K. White. 2004. "The compassion strategy: Race and the gender gap in campaign 2000." *Public Opinion Quarterly* 68 (4): 512–41.

Iyengar, Shanto. 1997. "Media based political campaigns—Overview." In *Do the Media Govern? Politicians, Voters, and Reporters in America,* edited by S. Iyen-gar and R. Reeves, 143–48. Thousand Oaks, Calif.: Sage.

Iyengar, Shanto, and Donald R. Kinder. 1987. *News That Matters: Television and American Opinion.* Chicago: University of Chicago Press.

Jackson, John E. 1975. "Issues, party choices, and presidential votes." *American Journal of Political Science* 19 (2): 161–85.

Jamieson, Kathleen Hall, and Paul Waldman, eds. 2001. *Electing the President, 2000: The Insiders' View.* Philadelphia: University of Pennsylvania Press.

Just, Marion R., Ann N. Crigler, Dean E. Alger, Timothy E. Cook, Montague Kern, and Darrell M. West. 1996. *Crosstalk: Citizens, Candidates, and the Media in a Presidential Campaign.* Chicago: University of Chicago Press.

Kalk, Bruce H. 2001. *The Origins of the Southern Strategy: Two-Party Competition in South Carolina, 1950–1972.* Lanham, Md.: Lexington Books.

Karabell, Zachary. 1998. *The Rise and Fall of the Televised Political Convention.* Cambridge: Harvard University, John F. Kennedy School of Government.

Kaufmann, Karen M., and John R. Petrocik. 1999. "The changing politics of American men: Understanding the sources of the gender gap." *American Jour-nal of Political Science* 43 (3): 864–87.

Kellner, Douglas. 2001. *Grand Theft 2000: Media Spectacle and a Stolen Election.* Lanham, Md.: Rowman and Littlefield.

Key, V. O., Jr. 1942. *Politics, Parties, and Pressure Groups.* 4th ed. New York: Crowell.

Key, V. O., Jr. 1950. *Southern Politics in State and Nation.* 2nd ed. New York: Knopf.

Kinder, Donald R. 1998. "Opinion and action in the realm of politics." In *The Handbook of Social Psychology,* edited by D. T. Gilbert, S. T. Fiske, and G. Lindzey, 778–867. Boston: McGraw-Hill.

Kinder, Donald R. and Lynn M. Sanders. 1996. *Divided by Color: Racial Politics and Democratic Ideals.* Chicago: University of Chicago Press.

Kitschelt, Herbert. 1989. *The Logics of Party Formation.* Ithaca: Cornell University Press.

Kousser, J. Morgan. 1974. *The Shaping of Southern Politics: Suffrage Restriction and the Establishment of the One-Party South, 1880–1910.* New Haven: Yale University Press.

Krosnick, Jon A., and Laura A. Brannon. 1993. "The impact of the Gulf War on the ingredients of presidential evaluations: Multidimensional effects of political involvement." *American Political Science Review* 87 (4): 963–75.

Lamis, Alexander P. 1999. "Southern politics in the 1990s." In *Southern Politics in the 1990s,* edited by A. P. Lamis, 377–406. Baton Rouge: Louisiana State University Press.

Lin, Ann Chih. 1998. "Bridging positivist and interpretivist approaches to qualitative methods." *Policy Studies Journal* 26 (1): 162–80.

Lippmann, Walter. 1922. *Public Opinion.* New York: Harcourt Brace.

Lipset, Seymour Martin, and Stein Rokkan. 1967. "Cleavage structures, party systems, and voter alignments: An introduction." In *Party Systems and Voter Alignments: Cross-National Perspectives,* edited by S. M. Lipset and S. Rokkan, 1–64. New York: Free Press.

Lodge, Milton, Kathleen M. McGraw, Pamela Johnston Conover, Stanley Feldman, and Arthur H. Miller. 1991. "Where is the schema? Critiques." *American Political Science Review* 85 (4): 1357–80.

Lodge, Milton, Kathleen M. McGraw, and Patrick Stroh. 1989. "An impression-driven model of candidate evaluation." *American Political Science Review* 83 (2): 399–419.

Lopez, Steve, and Desa Philadelphia. 2000. "Wrong guy, good cause: Protesting the death penalty." *Time,* July 31, 24–25.

MacKuen, Michael B., Robert S. Erikson, and James A. Stimson. 1989. "Macropartisanship." *American Political Science Review* 83 (4): 1125–42.

Marable, Manning. 1995. *Beyond Black and White: Transforming African-American Politics.* London: Verso.

Matthews, Donald R., and James W. Prothro. 1964. "Southern images of political parties: An analysis of white and Negro attitudes." *Journal of Politics* 26 (1): 82–111.

McChesney, John. 2004. "Political advertising targets Hispanic voters." *All Things Considered,* July 19.

McClain, Paula D., and Joseph Stewart. 1999. *Can We All Get Along? Racial and Ethnic Minorities in American Politics.* 2nd ed. Boulder, Colo.: Westview.

McClerking, Harwood. 2001. *We're in This Together: The Origins and Maintenance of Black Common Fate Perception.* Ann Arbor: Department of Political Science, University of Michigan.

Mendelberg, Tali. 2001. *The Race Card: Campaign Strategy, Implicit Messages, and the Norm of Equality.* Princeton: Princeton University Press.

Milkis, Sidney M. 1999. *Political Parties and Constitutional Government: Remaking American Democracy.* Baltimore: Johns Hopkins University Press.

Miller, Joanne M., and Jon A. Krosnick. 1999. "New media impact on the ingredients of presidential evaluations: A program of research on the priming hypothesis." In *Political Persuasion and Attitude Change,* edited by D. C. Mutz, P. M. Sniderman, and R. A. Brody, 77–99. Ann Arbor: University of Michigan Press.

Miller, Joanne M., and Jon A. Krosnick. 2000. "News media impact on the ingredients of presidential evaluations: Politically knowledgeable citizens are guided by a trusted source." *American Journal of Political Science* 44 (2): 301–15.

Miller, Warren E., and J. Merrill Shanks. 1996. *The New American Voter.* Cambridge: Harvard University Press.

Milne, R. S., and H. C. MacKenzie. 1955. *Marginal Seat.* London: Hansard Society.

Mitchell, Alison. 2001. "Over some objections, Congress certifies electoral vote." *New York Times,* January 6.

Morrison, Toni. 1998. "The talk of the town." *New Yorker,* October 5, 32.

Murphy, Reg, and Hal Gulliver. 1971. *The Southern Strategy.* New York: Scribner's.

Myrdal, Gunnar. 1944. *An American Dilemma: The Negro Problem and Modern Democracy.* New Brunswick, N.J.: Transaction.

Nelson, Thomas E., Rosalee A. Clawson, and Zoe M. Oxley. 1997. "Media framing of a civil liberties conflict and its effect on tolerance." *American Political Science Review* 91 (3): 567–83.

Neuman, W. Russell, Marion R. Just, and Ann N. Crigler. 1992. *Common Knowledge: News and the Construction of Political Meaning.* Chicago: University of Chicago Press.

Newton, Lina Y. 2000. "Why some Latinos supported Proposition 187: Testing economic threat and cultural identity hypothesis." *Social Science Quarterly* 81 (1): 180–93.

Norrander, Barbara. 1999a. "The evolution of the gender gap." *Public Opinion Quarterly* 63 (4): 566–76.

Norrander, Barbara. 1999b. "Is the gender gap growing?" In *Reelection 1996: How Americans Voted,* edited by H. F. Weisberg and J. M. Box-Steffensmeier, 145–61. New York: Chatham House.

O'Reilly, Kenneth. 1995. *Nixon's Piano: Presidents and Racial Politics from Washington to Clinton.* New York: Free Press.

Patterson, Thomas. 1994. *Out of Order.* New York: Vintage.

Peffley, Mark, Jon Hurwitz, and Paul M. Sniderman. 1997. "Racial stereotypes and whites' political views of blacks in the context of welfare and crime." *American Journal of Political Science* 41 (1): 30–60.

Petrocik, John R. 1996. "Issue ownership in presidential elections, with a 1980 case study." *American Journal of Political Science* 40 (3): 825–50.

Philpot, Tasha S. 2004. "A party of a different color? Race, campaign communication, and party politics." *Political Behavior* 26 (3): 249–70.

Platt, Suzy, ed. 1989. *Respectfully Quoted: A Dictionary of Quotations Requested from the Congressional Research Service.* Washington, D.C.: Library of Congress.

Popkin, Samuel L. 1994. *The Reasoning Voter: Communication and Persuasion in Presidential Campaigns.* 2nd ed. Chicago: University of Chicago Press.

Powell, Colin. 2000. "Speech at Republican National Convention." Republican National Convention. Available at www.cnn.com/ELECTION/2000/conventions/republican/transcripts/u000731.html.

Price, Vincent, and Anca Romantan. 2004. "Confidence in institutions before, during, and after 'Indecision 2000.'" *Journal of Politics* 66 (3): 939–56.

Price, Vincent, and David Tewksbury. 1997. "News values and public opinion: A theoretical account of media priming and framing." In *Progress in Communication Sciences,* vol. 13, edited by G. A. Barnett and F. J. Boster, 173–212. Westport, Conn.: Greenwood.

Rahn, Wendy M. 1993. "The role of partisan stereotypes in information processing about political candidates." *American Journal of Political Science* 37 (2): 472–96.

Ranney, Austin. 1954. *The Doctrine of Responsible Party Government, Its Origin and Present State.* Urbana: University of Illinois Press.

Rapoport, Ronald B. 1997. "Partisanship change in a candidate-centered era." *Journal of Politics* 59 (1): 185–99.

Republican National Convention. 1998. "Republican platform 1988: An American vision: For our children and our future." New Orleans. Available at www.cnn.com/ELECTION/2000/conventions/republican/features/platform.88 (accessed May 2006).

Republican National Convention. 1996. "The 1996 Republican party platform: Restoring American world leadership." San Diego. Available at www.cnn.com/ELECTION/2000/conventions/republican/features/platform.96 (accessed May 2006).

Republican National Convention. 2000. "Republican Platform 2000. Renewing America's purpose. Together." Philadelphia: Available at www.cnn.com/ELECTION/2000/conventions/republican/features/platform.00 (accessed May 2006).

Republican National Convention. 2004. "2004 Republican party platform: A safer world and a more hopeful America." New York. Available at www.gop.com/media/2004platform.pdf (accessed May 2006).

Riffe, Daniel, Stephen Lacy, and Frederick G. Fico. 1998. *Analyzing Media Messages: Using Quantitative Content Analysis in Research.* Mahwah, N.J.: Erlbaum.

Robinson, Pearl T. 1982. "Whither the future of blacks in the Republican Party?" *Political Science Quarterly* 97 (2): 207–31.

Rosenstone, Steven J., and John Mark Hansen. 1993. *Mobilization, Participation, and Democracy in America: New Topics in Politics.* New York: Macmillan.

Sanders, Arthur. 1988. "The meaning of party images." *Western Political Quarterly* 41 (3): 583–99.

Schattschneider, Elmer Eric. 1942. *Party Government.* New York: Farrar and Rinehart.

Schattschneider, Elmer Eric. 1956. "United States: The functional approach to party government." In *Modern Political Parties: Approaches to Comparative Politics,* edited by S. Neumann, 194–215. Chicago: University of Chicago Press.

Scher, Richard K. 1997. *Politics in the New South: Republicanism, Race, and Leadership in the Twentieth Century.* 2nd ed. Armonk, N.Y.: Sharpe.

Schuman, Howard, Charlotte Steeh, Lawrence Bobo, and Maria Krysan. 1997. *Racial Attitudes in America: Trends and Interpretations.* Rev. ed. Cambridge: Harvard University Press.

Sears, David O. 1993. "Symbolic politics: A socio-psychological theory." In *Explorations in Political Psychology,* edited by S. Iyengar and W. J. McGuire, 113–49. Durham, N.C.: Duke University Press.

Sears, David O. 2001. "The role of affect in symbolic politics." In *Citizens and Politics: Perspectives from Political Psychology,* edited by J. K. Kuklinski, 14–40. Cambridge: Cambridge University Press.

Shapiro, Robert Y., and Harpreet Mahajan. 1986. "Gender differences in policy preferences: A summary of trends from the 1960s to the 1980s." *Public Opinion Quarterly* 50 (1): 42–61.

Shaw, Daron R. 2006. *A Simple Game: Uncovering Campaign Strategies and Effects in the 2000 and 2004 Presidential Elections.* Chicago: University of Chicago Press.

Sherman, Richard B. 1973. *The Republican Party and Black America from McKinley to Hoover, 1896–1933.* Charlottesville: University Press of Virginia.

Speel, Robert W. 1998. *Changing Patterns of Voting in the Northern United States: Electoral Realignment, 1952–1996.* University Park: Pennsylvania State University Press.

Spence, Lester K., and Hanes Walton Jr. 1999. "African-American politics in constancy and change: African-American presidential convention and nomination politics: Alan Keyes in the 1996 Republican presidential primaries and convention." *National Political Science Review* 7:188–209.

Steeper, Frederick T. 1978. "Public response to Gerald R. Ford's statements on Eastern Europe in the second debate." In *The Presidential Debates: Media, Electoral, and Policy Perspectives,* edited by G. F. Bishop, R. G. Meadow, and M. Jackson-Beeck, 81–101. New York: Praeger.

Stokes, Atiya Kai. 2003. "Latino group consciousness and political participation." *American Politics Research* 31 (4): 361–78.

Strickland, Bill. 2000. "Election 2000: Has duplicity overcome democracy?" *Crisis* 107 (6): 10–14.

Sundquist, James L. 1983. *Dynamics of the Party System: Alignment and Realignment of Political Parties in the United States.* Washington, D.C.: Brookings Institution.

Tate, Katherine. 1993. *From Protest to Politics: The New Black Voters in American Elections.* Cambridge: Harvard University Press.

Tatum, Wilbert A. 2000a. "Am News celebrates 90 years." *New York Amsterdam News,* December 7, AS1.

Tatum, Wilbert A. 2000b. "Libby and her fools." *New York Amsterdam News,* November 9, 1.

Tocqueville, Alexis de. 1835. *Democracy in America*. New York: Bantam.

Trilling, Richard J. 1976. *Party Image and Electoral Behavior*. New York: Wiley.

Tucker, Lauren R. 1998. "The framing of Calvin Klein: A frame analysis of media discourse about the August 1995 Calvin Klein Jeans advertising campaign." *Critical Studies in Mass Communication* 15 (2): 141–57.

Valentino, Nicholas A. 1999. "Crime news and the priming of racial attitudes during evaluations of the president." *Public Opinion Quarterly* 63 (3): 293–320.

Valentino, Nicholas A., Vincent L. Hutchings, and Ismail K. White. 2002. "Cues that matter: How political ads prime racial attitudes during campaigns." *American Political Science Review* 96 (1): 75–90.

Valentino, Nicholas A., and David O. Sears. 2005. "Old times there are not forgotten: Race and partisan realignment in the contemporary South." *American Journal of Political Science* 49 (3): 672–88.

Von Drehle, David. 2000. "Reality check on decidedly positive day." *Washington Post*, August 1, A1.

Walsh, Edward. 2000. "Delegates are accentuating the positive; Conservatives latch on to Bush's message as key to November victory." *Washington Post*, August 1, A11.

Walters, Ronald. 2000. "The Republican convention: How to dance with an elephant." *Baltimore Afro-American*, August 4, A5.

Walton, Hanes, Jr. 1972. *Black Politics: A Theoretical and Structural Analysis*. Philadelphia: Lippincott.

Walton, Hanes, Jr. 1975. *Black Republicans: The Politics of the Black and Tans*. Metuchen, N.J.: Scarecrow.

Walton, Hanes, Jr., and Robert C. Smith. 2000. *American Politics and the African American Quest for Universal Freedom*. New York: Addison-Wesley Longman.

Walton, Hanes, Jr., and Robert C. Smith. 2003. *American Politics and the African American Quest for Universal Freedom*. 2nd ed. New York: Addison-Wesley Longman.

Ware, Alan. 1995. *Political Parties and Party Systems*. New York: Oxford University Press.

Weiss, Nancy J. 1983. *Farewell to the Party of Lincoln: Black Politics in the Age of FDR*. Princeton: Princeton University Press.

White, Ismail K. 2005. *Alternative Spheres of Influence: The Impact of Divergent Political Elites on the Racial Divide in American Public Opinion*. Ann Arbor: Department of Political Science, University of Michigan.

Williams, Lloyd. 2000. "'New' GOP unveiled at convention . . . Grand Oreo party." *New Pittsburgh Courier*, August 16, A7.

Wirls, Daniel. 1986. "Reinterpreting the gender gap." *Public Opinion Quarterly* 50 (3): 316–30.

Wolseley, Roland Edgar. 1990. *The Black Press, U.S.A.* 2nd ed. Ames: Iowa State University Press.

Woodward, C. Vann. 1951. *Origins of the New South, 1877–1913*. Baton Rouge: Louisiana State University Press.

Zaller, John. 1992. *The Nature and Origins of Mass Opinion*. Cambridge: Cambridge University Press.

Index